EMERGENT WARFARE IN OUR EVOLUTIONARY PAST

Why do we fight? Have we always been fighting one another? This book examines the origins and development of human forms of organized violence from an anthropological and archaeological perspective. Kim and Kissel argue that human warfare is qualitatively different from forms of lethal, intergroup violence seen elsewhere in the natural world, and that its emergence is intimately connected to how humans evolved and to the emergence of human nature itself.

Nam C. Kim is Associate Professor in the Department of Anthropology at the University of Wisconsin-Madison, USA.

Marc Kissel is a Lecturer in the Department of Anthropology at Appalachian State University in Boone, North Carolina, USA.

New Biological Anthropology

Series Editor: Agustín Fuentes

Titles in series

Emergent Warfare in Our Evolutionary Past
Nam C. Kim and Marc Kissel

www.routledge.com/anthropology/series/NBA

EMERGENT WARFARE IN OUR EVOLUTIONARY PAST

Nam C. Kim and Marc Kissel

Routledge
Taylor & Francis Group

NEW YORK AND LONDON

First published 2018
by Routledge
711 Third Avenue, New York, NY 10017

and by Routledge
2 Park Square, Milton Park, Abingdon, Oxon, OX14 4RN

Routledge is an imprint of the Taylor & Francis Group, an informa business

© 2018 Taylor & Francis

The right of Nam C. Kim and Marc Kissel to be identified as authors
of this work has been asserted by them in accordance with sections
77 and 78 of the Copyright, Designs and Patents Act 1988.

Trademark notice: Product or corporate names may be trademarks or
registered trademarks, and are used only for identification and
explanation without intent to infringe.

Library of Congress Cataloging-in-Publication Data
A catalog record for this book has been requested

ISBN: 978-1-62958-266-5 (hbk)
ISBN: 978-1-62958-267-2 (pbk)
ISBN: 978-1-315-15102-1 (ebk)

Typeset in Bembo
by Keystroke, Neville Lodge, Tettenhall, Wolverhampton

Nam C. Kim dedicates this book to his parents, Chong and Hien, who experienced and survived war in two different countries and gave their children a better life in a third.

Marc Kissel dedicates this to his parents, Marcelle and Steve. While they might never have considered he'd go into academia, their support was critical at every step along the way.

Both authors also dedicate the book to the memory of Larry Keeley, who has been, and continues to be, an inspiration to so many people worldwide.

CONTENTS

LIST OF FIGURES AND TABLES

Figures

Tables

ACKNOWLEDGMENTS

The genesis of this book is somewhat unusual. Several years ago, we were sitting in a weekly brownbag lunch at the University of Wisconsin-Madison, whose conversational topic for the week was a paper suggesting warfare dated to over 800,000 years ago. Kim, as the resident warfare scholar, and Kissel, the paleoanthropologist in the room, were asked by a new graduate student what we thought of the paper and its claims. It was at that point that we experienced two significant (for us and this book) realizations – that we strongly shared an interest in the earliest origins of warfare, and that we both wanted to learn more in order to better evaluate the claims of the aforementioned article. Over a series of subsequent emails and discussions, we came to further realize that there is simply a plethora of unanswered questions as to the antiquity and origins of war and the avoidance of it. We also came to appreciate what we had already suspected – that research from various subfields of anthropology can provide very important insights into the question of origins. The amount of relevant research available today is simultaneously rich and staggering. This book is in essence our answer to our colleague's question all those years ago. In some sense, it is the book we wish we had when we first became interested in the topic. We hope this book will give our readers new ways to think about the origins of warfare, and offer a roadmap of sorts in their own journeys of intellectual discovery.

As scholars studying the past, we find it important to know where ideas, concepts, thoughts, and advice came from. As with all projects of this scope, so many people provided considerable help. We'd first like to thank Agustin Fuentes for his unending support and encouragement. He was the first to suggest we write a manuscript and has been a constant source of advice and critical analysis. His own research has been an important source of knowledge and inspiration for us, and it has left an indelible mark on our work. Beyond that, Agustin was instrumental for bringing this book into the light of day, shepherding it through a long journey to its final destination at Routledge.

We are also thankful to have received professional support from the editorial staff members of both Left Coast Press and Routledge. This includes Jack Meinhardt of LCP, and the fine folks at Routledge, especially Katherine Ong, Louisa Vahtrick, Marc Stratton, and Jashnie Jabson, all of whom offered useful editorial guidance and production assistance.

We have also been very fortunate to have had extensive conversations with other colleagues that have either directly or indirectly shaped our thinking and the arguments presented in this book. Various colleagues over the years helped by providing their expertise, whether through informal conversations or reviews of drafts, including Mark Allen, Susan Blum, Mary Davis, Mark Golitko, John Hawks, Rahul Oka, Travis Pickering, Sue Sheridan, Sissel Schroeder, Henry Bunn, Sarah Clayton, Michaela Howells, Mark Kenoyer, James Loudon, Chris Lynn, Carolyn Robinson, Katie Smith, and the late Neil Whitehead, Celia Deane-Drummond, Becky Artinian-Kaiser, Julia Feder, and Adam Willows. Karen Strier, in particular, provided valuable feedback and advice related to primate research literature. In addition, we have also benefitted from years of very productive classroom discussions with our students, to whom we are grateful, as these conversations have contributed to the research contained in this book.

Kim would also like to acknowledge and thank a few key individuals, starting with Jack Levy, whose course on war provided an early glimpse into anthropological theories on war. Next, Kim is indebted to Bob Carneiro, who first encouraged Kim to pursue research on war through an anthropological lens. Finally, Kim is indebted to Larry Keeley, who convinced him that archaeology was necessary to understand the evolution of war. Larry also provided invaluable insights on a draft of the book, along with its foreword, for which both Kim and Kissel are extremely grateful. Sadly, Larry passed away just months before the official publication of this book. His ideas and comments, however, still left an indelible mark.

Kissel would like to acknowledge Pam Crabtree, whose introductory class on archaeology taught him not only about prehistory but that some people are lucky enough to get to study it. John Hawks taught Kissel not just how to think about human evolution but how to be a well-rounded anthropologist. As we were writing this book, he joined the Notre Dame Anthropology Department as a postdoc. All of the faculty, grad students, and academic staff provided both insight and support. The staff and colleagues at the Centre for Theology, Science and Human Flourishing were also incredibly supportive.

And finally, we must acknowledge family members whose tremendous sacrifices enabled us to pursue our research passions. Kim thanks his partner Jane Koh and daughters, Amelia and Ramona, for their unfailing support and understanding, especially for the times when he has had to travel far from home to perform research. Kissel thanks his wife Jenna and daughters, Harper and Sutton, for putting up with a husband and father whose job is perhaps a bit different than most.

FOREWORD

Lawrence H. Keeley

In 1996, I published a book, *War Before Civilization*, that claimed that prehistoric and recent 'uncivilized' peoples (those without writing, cities and state-level socio-political organizations) had conducted warfare as frequent, destructive and deadly as any historical state. The archaeological and ethnographic evidence demonstrating this point was already manifold and clear. A number of other scholars at that time, while disagreeing with me regarding several issues regarding the causes, contexts and chronology of non-state warfare, also found such warfare common and effective (see the references here to the works of Milner, Haas, LeBlanc and Lambert). Despite our differences, we all argued that archaeologists and other social scientists should abandon the mythologies of 'the pacified past' and revive the study of this important, common and ancient form of human social behavior.

With remarkable rapidity, anthropologists have removed the blinders that sophistry and willful ignorance had created regarding non-state warfare. Of course, there are some die-hards, mostly those who were embarrassed by their palpably false claims; for example, that there was no warfare among the native tribes of the Americas until the cruel Europeans brought it, along with many other ills, to the New World Eden. Instead, archaeologists and other scholars have produced a plethora of new instances and analyses of ancient and prehistoric warfare. These new studies have been concerned with not *whether* warfare existed in the deeper human past but when, where, how and in what circumstances it occurred or was absent.

The authors here address an important question—when does warfare appear during the long evolutionary history, both biological and social, of human kind? The answers to this question have implications for issues regarding how inherent or genetically determined violent interactions between social groups are, and/or if certain forms of subsistence economies or social organization are more prone to warfare. During the past 25 years, several hypotheses have been advanced regarding this question and the time is ripe for a comprehensive review. The authors have compiled these hypotheses and evaluated them against the data now available. They fairly state these various claims, including some I regard as so divorced from physical fact and elementary logic as to be absurd. One example of the latter is the claim that the now commonly observed violent combat between the common chimp (*Pan paniscus*) is only a consequence of their being observed or being in contact with humans. This sophistry reminds me of my father's facetious claim that the flesh of watermelons is white until their skin is broken and it turns instantly red. These sophists cannot be disproved by archaeology, as are those were who have made analogous claims regarding pre-civilized warfare, because chimps have left no fossil remains or other evidence of their behavior. As the authors here demonstrate there are far more logical and realistic reasons for regarding such field studies as irrelevant to this question.

I found the authors' critique of relevant studies of chimp behavior and human genetics to be very useful. Observations of group homicides by chimp 'gangs' has been supposed to indicate a genetic cause for human warfare because chimps are the most closely related animals to humans and thus the 'war gene' has been inherited from our common ancestor. But, as the authors point out, such war-like behavior has not been observed among Pygmy chimps (Bonobos) who also shared this ancestor. Logically then, chimp fighting and homicide must have been independently developed. Regarding the supposed 'violence gene,' the authors demonstrate how ambiguous is the linkage of this gene to behavior. Also, as is usually the case with human genes that are related to behavior, at most this gene creates a capacity, not a necessity. Humans can be violent with each other but usually are not, sometimes even never, and are only so in certain circumstances.

I have two personal, experiential reasons for finding the authors' final conclusions agreeable. The most general reasons come from my half-century of research and teaching about the evolution of human behavior over the 2.5 million years that recognizable humans have existed. During this long span, humans have been selected for greater and greater capacities for changing their behavior by learning, whether by their individual observation and decision-making or following that of other humans. The great theme of human evolution is increasing behavioral plasticity, such that humans need not wait to adopt favorable behavior or body equipment through the slow and harsh process of the natural selection of gene frequencies. Humans can make remarkable changes in their behavior or substitute technology for needed body features very quickly, sometimes in mere moments. Changes can be made even more rapidly than learning alone would allow. Thus, as I observed two decades ago (see *War Before Civilization* 1996: 157–159), human biology, except in the sense noted above, is irrelevant for the explanation of warfare.

My specialty in anthropology is the prehistory of Europe. As the authors note several times, one issue that affects all studies of human prehistory is 'visibility'. Before the appearance or development of the Neandertals and their Mousterian culture, in Europe the archaeological visibility of homicide and warfare is poor because human remains are rare, usually consist of only a few bones, wooden-tipped spears or lances were used, and paleo-pathological studies are few. Neandertals, on the other hand, buried their dead so we have a couple of hundred nearly complete specimens that have been subject to paleo-pathological analyses. As well they used stone tipped spears (evidenced by the common Mousterian and Levallois points in their stone tool assemblages) that the broken-off tips of which could be permanently embedded in bone. Despite many skeletal injuries on Neandertals, far more common than among Anatomically-Modern Humans (AMHs), none can be clearly attributed to intra-species violence. The Neandertals are replaced and superseded by early Upper Palaeolithic AMHs migrating in from the Near East, ultimately from east Central Africa. Compared to the Archaic hominins that proceeded them, these AMHs evidence many novel behaviors: taking fish and waterfowl, killing healthy adults of their larger prey, mass kills of mammalian prey, spearthrowers, the production of standardized stone blades, musical instruments, arithmetic and counting, drilled beads, multi-household 'villages,' treating bone/antler/ivory as a kind of wood to be carved than a kind of stone to be flaked or ground, thus a variety of bone/antler tools and, of course, the spectacular representational art in figurines and on cave walls. From elsewhere or a bit later, there is evidence that AMHs were the first hominins to use water craft, permanently occupy high Arctic latitudes and closed-canopy tropical forests, and create sewn, tailored clothing. All of the novelties indicate a great increase in human intelligence and capacity for modifying their behavior to match circumstances. While the remains of these earliest European AMHs are less frequent than those of Neandertals, by 1995, archaeologists had already found a child with a bone point embedded in its neck, an adult male skull with scalping cut marks and a mass grave of victims with head injuries. Thus, it seemed, in Europe at least, there was neither war nor even homicide before the advent of hominins like ourselves.

The authors here argue cogently and comprehensively that warfare is one of many consequences of the development of the modern human brain. The same brain that directs us in countless peaceful endeavors does the same for warfare. As I would put it, the good news and bad news about modern humans is the same—we are terribly cooperative and damnably smart.

Chicago, Illinois
June 2017

Works Cited

Lawrence Keeley. 1996. *War Before Civilization*. Oxford University Press, Oxford.

1

PEERING INTO THE ABYSS

Why do we fight? Have we always been fighting one another? Warfare is a topic that generates much thought, opining, scholarship, and debate. And it is easy to see why. Take a look at any major newspaper's front page and you are likely to see at least a headline or two about conflict or violence happening somewhere on the globe. Such conflicts are occurring at various scales and involve disparate collections of people. Chances are that you know someone that has been affected either

FIGURE 1.1   German troops in a trench during World War I

directly or indirectly by warfare. In academia, researchers from various disciplinary backgrounds continue to investigate, and theorize about, the ubiquity of violence and warfare in the recent and contemporary world. For this book, any actions related to collective violence between politically distinct groups of people can be considered part of warfare, whether they involve nation-states, tribes, village communities, nomadic bands, or even terrorist organizations. By warfare, we are referring to myriad forms of organized violence, whether they are massed armies on a battlefield, revenge killings between smaller-scale societies, or intervillage raiding related to feuding communities. With this sort of inclusive definition, one not biased toward modern forms of war, we believe researchers are much better equipped to give the topic fuller scrutiny.

Increasingly, our collective knowledge has shown that forms of war have been part of humanity for a very long time. Signs of these behaviors appear as soon as our ancestors began recording ideas and messages on various media. Indisputable evidence comes to us from our earliest written records created several thousand years ago. But what can we see beyond that literary horizon? Material clues have been recovered hinting at violence occurring tens of thousands of years ago, maybe even hundreds of thousands of years ago. But, of course, violence is not warfare, especially if it is not part of some wider struggle, conflict, or clash between communities of people. Violence might be part of some interpersonal relationships

FIGURE 1.2   Bas-relief of Angkorian warfare from the temple wall of Ankor Thom (Cambodia). *Photograph by Nam C. Kim*

FIGURE 1.3   Ancient Macedonian warfare during the campaign of Alexander the Great *(1893 reconstruction of an original mosaic housed in National Archaeological Museum, Naples, Italy)*

and interactions within a community or society. Nonetheless, seeing so much violence around us today, along with hints of it in the past, begs the twin questions of how far back can we trace warfare, and how might the phenomenon have been connected to our earliest ancestral lineages in some evolutionary sense.

And so, this is a book about warfare and its beginnings. More specifically, it is about the origins of human forms of organized violence, or what we propose to call *emergent warfare*. As we will show, there are many divergent views about both the antiquity of warfare and its role in our evolution as a species. Our perspective overlaps with those of many others, but it is also a bit different, as it is by design informed by an anthropological perspective. For the category of human warfare, we see something qualitatively different from forms of lethal, intergroup violence seen elsewhere in the natural world. And so our concern here is to explore the onset of emergent warfare within our species, to see how various building blocks related to human biology and culture combined to set the stage for the earliest manifestations of warfare. Actually, that was the original intent of this book, but somewhere along the way, as we delved deeper into the research, we realized the story of emergent warfare was really a story within a story. It is one that needs to be told within a bigger purview. As we lost ourselves within the vast universe of evidence, case studies, and data from all over the world, we began to realize our perspective had to be broader, especially if we hope to answer some fundamental questions about "human" warfare. In the end, this is not simply a story about how, when, and why human warfare emerged, but is also a larger narrative about us, about humanity. *In other words, the emergence of warfare is intimately connected to the emergence of human nature.* And once we realized that the bigger story was our journey to becoming human, we then began to see the other half of the coin – namely that emergent warfare happened concurrently with what we might call emergent peacemaking abilities, or what we might call *emergent peacefare*. Hence, the real story is intimately linked to how we evolved ways to interact, how we pursue social strategies tied to both engaging in organized violence and ways to avoid and minimize its occurrences and consequences. As we will highlight, many scholars, philosophers, and other writers have emphasized either violent or peaceful behaviors in the story of human evolution, arguing how one or the other was a key driver, thus resulting in highly contentious debate. And oftentimes, some of these views were based on select categories or pieces of evidence and data. Our motivation with this book was to approach this set of questions by reviewing as much anthropological evidence as possible. Our resulting perspective is that it was a propensity for human sociality and cooperative behaviors that permitted warfare and peacefare to emerge, making them more outcomes than drivers of human evolution.

This book will provide the reader with both a starting point for answering basic questions about organized violence along with its relationship to our evolution as a species. We see this volume as a primer of sorts for all interested readers, from the uninitiated to the specialist. The amount of publications, research studies, and new datasets is growing at dizzying speeds, resulting in far more knowledge than we will be able to cover in this volume. However, we make an attempt here to capture a snapshot of the current state of research about the evolution of war, and to cover some of the main ideas researchers have published about this topic. As you will see, we firmly believe that the best way to approach this topic is to rely on an integrative, anthropological lens. It's the best way to fully and robustly consider the wealth of data available that are relevant to reconstructing behaviors of our distant ancestors. Think of this book as a roadmap to understanding the evolution of war, sociality, cooperation, and conflict avoidance in humans, and what that tells us about human evolution more generally. On our journey through theories, ideas, and evidence, we will be taking the reader on a guided tour of the distant and recent pasts. While we will offer our thoughts and interpretations of the currently available evidence, the larger mission of this book is to give our readers a small window into the general landscape of current research that connects the earliest forms of collective violence with our pathways of both biological and cultural evolution. We endeavor to equip our readers with a familiarity of traditional, current, and future research concerning early human warfare as well as how we may have evolved ways to thrive in co-existence, developing innovative ways to avoid or mitigate conflict and organized violence. We hope, especially, to give those readers fairly new to this topic the means to be critical consumers for all of the fascinating research that continues to surface about emergent warfare.

Outfitting Ourselves for the Journey

Situated within general debates about the nature of violence in humanity, the beginnings of warfare in our evolutionary past become all the more salient. The origins of war and violence have interested people from many academic disciplines (see Levy and Thompson 2010; Pinker 2011; Shackelford and Weekes-Shackelford 2014; Smith 2007), but we argue that anthropology, which studies all aspects of humanity and our societies both past and present, gives us the best tools to tackle the topic. For us, the anthropological discipline encompasses important sub-fields that offer insights into this topic, including ethnography, bioanthropology,

paleoanthropology, linguistics, and, of course, archaeology. While publications produced by non-anthropologists acknowledge and present anthropological data, many
do so without comprehensively engaging the evidence, methods of data collection,
and challenges in interpretation. As far as the deepest past is concerned, many non-
anthropological studies present depictions based on uneven considerations of all
available evidence. The material and fossil records have often been either under-
utilized or used in an unbalanced fashion by many researchers. Some read too much
from scant data, while others tend to overly downplay the evidence. Unfortunately,
there has been a tendency to oversimplify the past.

To truly understand human warfare, it is necessary to start with the earliest
perceivable instances of what might be considered emergent warfare, and to engage
all of the available data. What are the earliest expressions of what we would consider
human forms of collective violence? When did they occur? What were they like?
What became of them? How did they affect our cultural and biological evolution?
Because our principal research question is intimately tied to the origins of human
evolutionary behavior, the central research themes of this book must be addressed
primarily through a disciplinary lens of anthropology.

Anthropologists are concerned with all aspects of people, their societies, and their
cultures. This means looking carefully at all people through case studies of past and
present societies, and, in doing so, simultaneously looking at people separated by
space and time. We do this as a way to understand us, to gaze deeply at ourselves.
As noted by Patty Jo Watson (1995: 690), "Anthropology is still the only human
science all about humankind, from four million years ago to the present: Who are
we? Where did we come from? What happened to us between origin and now?"
The past and the present offer a mirror of sorts for us to confront and understand
ourselves, where we have come from, and what the future holds. The causes and
consequences of modern human variation have their roots in deep time. The
archaeological, ethnohistoric, and ethnographic records thus constitute an important
foundation for considering humanity's overall course of change, and anthropological
methods of data collection, interpretation, and theory building offer indispensable
tools for appreciating humanity. Consequently, our approach in this volume relies
on an integrative anthropological perspective, as we believe the discipline offers
an important voice in larger debates outside of academic arenas. Indeed, we see a
holistic anthropological approach as vital for giving us the most complete perspective
on early warfare. Without question, this sort of research enterprise is impossible
without fully marshaling the gamut of methodological approaches and frameworks
of the anthropological discipline.

Anthropology has a varied and long history of engagement with questions of
violence and warfare, and the origins and evolutionary arc of collective violence
have been the focus of increased archaeological investigation in recent decades
(Ferguson 2008, 2013a; Keegan 1993; Keeley 1996; Otterbein 2004). Of fundamental interest is whether or not forms of organized violence are universal for all
people, both past and present, and a comprehensive consideration of this research
focus necessitates a rich engagement with evidence from various anthropological

subfields. According to McCall and Shields (2008: 2), recognizing interpersonal violence in the fossil and archaeological records of our early hominin history "is extremely important to modern theoretical perspectives on the nature of interpersonal violence." We agree, and would say the same applies for studies of intergroup violence. As noted by many anthropologists, an "integrative" (Fuentes 2015) or "holistic" (see Harkin 2010) anthropology, one that pulls together information from across subfields, can offer powerfully informed perspectives on our species and the various ways in which our behaviors have taken expression in cultural patterning and forms. Anthropology is therefore well suited to contribute to questions about the evolutionary history of warfare in our species, allowing access into a variety of evidentiary sources. This diversity, in terms of research agendas, methodological approaches, and theoretical stances, has fostered a plurality in interpretations, and has already contributed to, and will continue to enrich, our understanding of warfare.

Beyond the Literary and Distant Horizons: Exploring Emergent Warfare and Emergent Peacefare

Warlike behaviors have been documented by humans for as long as writing has existed, and archaeological indications suggest an even deeper history for them. In our exploration of this deeper past, we are looking at emergent forms of warfare. To be clear, this book is not about why violence occurs in the natural world. Plenty of species fight their own (i.e., conspecific or intraspecific violence) and members of other species (interspecific violence). Aggression, competition, and violence are not rare in the animal kingdom. Depending on one's perspective, then, warfare and participation in organized violence are not necessarily unique to humans. But, as we will argue, many of the ways in which humans (and possibly our earliest ancestors) perform (and have performed) organized violence are unique. Hence for this book, we are interested in the roots of human warfare and how it, in variant forms, might be related to our evolutionary past and what it might reveal about our earliest capacities to work together and form group identities.

Our unique abilities as a species allow us to think, socialize, and cooperate in much more complex ways than seen with other species. And while we argue that this has resulted in distinctly human forms of warfare that require people to organize in order to fight other groups, this complexity in cognition and behavior also applies to the ways in which humans have evolved to get along and to avoid and resolve conflict – to cooperate, and to construct and perform peace. A recent volume edited by anthropologist Douglas Fry (2013a) explores the connections between human nature, peace, and war, and we see this convergence of research topics to be very important for understanding humanity's past and future with regards to war. Indeed, we propose that any examination of emergent warfare necessitates a consideration of emergent peacemaking. Furthermore, we submit that the emergence of all behaviors and cultural practices related to either phenomenon is intimately tied to "human nature" (see Barash 2013 and Sussman 2013). And when it comes to peace, we are not referring simply to an absence of war. Our view of peace is a bit more complicated than that. In a recent book, researcher Dane Smith (2010) uses the term "peacefare" when exploring US peace-building policies. Although we are dealing with peacemaking in far earlier contexts, we like Smith's notion of peacefare (and hence have adopted it for our purposes) as it suggests peace as something requiring collaboration. Indeed, as we will highlight in Chapter Seven, some formulations of peace are not only culturally constructed, but require complex forms of social interaction and institutions, and perhaps even political mechanisms, in order to develop and maintain over time. With peace, we are talking about actions, beliefs, cultural practices, and institutions that are deliberately created and performed in order to promote stability and cooperation among people. These social patterns consist of cooperative strategies, social networks, recognition of specific kinds of ties between individuals and groups of people. In that sense, peace is neither simply the absence of war nor some default state of nature. Forms of peace are socially constructed and actively maintained – so when we refer to peace, we are usually thinking of it in terms of peacemaking. From that perspective, we might also surmise that people have been living in sophisticated and complex sorts of social organizations for quite a long time, even well before the advent of so-called complex societies and civilizations that supposedly emerged only in the Holocene.

Our book builds on many studies and publications, offering a holistic anthropological perspective that marshals data from anthropology's subfields. We do so in an attempt to explain the connections between cultural evolution and human nature, as they relate to practices of violence, cooperation, competition, and conflict resolution. The capacities that make us human and that allow us to interact and socialize in very complex ways also give us creative ways to organize ourselves, whether in socially violent or nonviolent ways. The advent of a capacity for war-making behaviors (in complex human cultural forms) likely coincided with the advent of a capacity for peacemaking behaviors (also in complex human cultural forms). Indeed, the onset of complex human cognition and behavioral patterns probably opened the door for practices of both categories, in their broadest sense, to begin developing. As will be discussed throughout this book, emergent warfare could have included any forms of violence between distinct communities of people, regardless of specific tactics, equipment, outcomes, motivations, precipitating conditions, scale, or intensity. Such behaviors could thus include, for instance, raiding for resources or individuals.

Essentially, we do not see a natural state of either violence or nonviolence for humanity; rather, we see a potential for either depending on circumstances. And so, though this is a book about the emergence of warfare, our exploration cannot be completed in a context void of human culture and human capacities to practice both forms of war and peace. Becoming human meant we could engage in complex lifeways, contingently employing cooperative strategies related to both violence and the avoidance of violence. While much of this book is devoted to the origins of warfare, we will bring the discussion back to a larger consideration of warfare's relationship to the studies of human nature and cultural contexts of peace. We highlight some of the evidence that reflects developing human compassion and empathy. When it comes to peacefare, we will also highlight the ways in which humans have developed cultural institutions that help to construct and maintain social cohesion and stability.

With these goals of exploration in mind, the book is organized in a very straightforward way. Before presenting an overview of the evidence, we begin by discussing what researchers mean when writing about phenomena such as "warfare," "humanity," and "culture." We will then discuss the ways in which we can access the lifeways of our earliest ancestors. To be highlighted are various methodological approaches for interpreting archaeological signs of warfare, the skeletal evidence of interpersonal conflict, the relevance of primatological studies to the understanding of human warfare, indications of the genetic underpinnings of violence, and relevant ethnographic records. This will include the presentation of evidence gathered to date through these various methodologies. Where possible and appropriate, we will also bring in research insights from outside of anthropology. Finally, we will offer our thoughts and best guesses about the advent of warfare, peace, and their linkages with human evolution and human culture. We problematize theoretical notions of "peace" as merely the absence of war, instead pointing out the ways in which peaceful social conditions were just as likely a social outcome as warlike activities given ongoing evolutionary change in humanity.

A Few Words Before Going Down the Rabbit Hole

The current literature on the origins of violence and warfare is full of heated debate and controversy, sometimes with researchers coming to vastly different conclusions based on the same pieces of evidence. This somewhat chaotic but infinitely fascinating state of affairs can be a bit of the proverbial rabbit hole for those new to the research. Indeed, it can be mystifying even for the specialist. Before we embark on our journey down this rabbit hole, we offer a few preliminary thoughts about the major questions highlighted above.

As noted by anthropologist Mark Allen (2014: 19), there has been a persistent tendency in anthropology to take a default position promoting a short chronology of war. Some of this stems from a generalized anthropological perspective that equates hunter-gatherers with peaceful lifeways. But as Allen and many other researchers point out, this view ought to be continuously reappraised (Allen 2014; Allen and Jones 2014). In our book we take up this call to review and reappraise the evidence.

On the issue of warfare's origins, it should be fairly clear at this point in the book that we disagree with the notions that warfare is: 1) a relatively recent, modern, or historic phenomenon; 2) a product or byproduct of the political interactions associated with large-scale states or civilizations; and/or 3) a phenomenon largely created by shifts to sedentary or agriculturally lifeways. Such views restrict the range of cultural activities that might constitute categories of warfare, and would also confine warfare exclusively to the past 12,000 years. We adhere to a more inclusive definition of warfare, and we: 1) recognize the potential for it to have been a significant part of modern human behavior, whether within the past 12,000 years or even earlier; and 2) are open to the possibility that certain forms or facets of emergent warfare may have appeared at different points throughout the evolutionary history of hominin lineages. Ultimately, we do not believe it prudent to assume a natural state of either "peace" or "war" for our species and its evolutionary history. We argue that any assumption about human nature requires empirical evidence and support. By this logic, whereas research is needed to demonstrate the antiquity of warfare, we suggest that forms of peaceful behavior must also be placed within an empirical framework as well.

So, in asking about the onset of emergent warfare or peacemaking, we must also address the question of when humans first appeared in the world. Actually, the better question would be: when did we become human? Although there is still much debate about the concepts of physical and cultural modernity for humans, there is some growing consensus that significant behavioral changes did not occur abruptly but accumulated gradually, and that there are many ways to evaluate this developmental trajectory (or set of trajectories). We will discuss these throughout the book.

Our Argument

We take as our starting assumption that we became human gradually, and that what many folks would call "behavioral modernity" develops in piecemeal fashion, involving different physical and cultural developments in various places in the world. In other words, our ancestors became human through a long-term process rather than a singular event. The upshot here is that significant archaeological and bioanthropological evidence support the idea that humans, essentially like us, were living in various regions of the world by some 200,000 years ago, if not earlier (McBrearty and Brooks 2000). Their cognitive and physical abilities were like ours, and these traits enabled these ancestral populations to begin living in highly unprecedented and complex ways when it comes to cooperation and sociality. Building from this assumption, there are two interrelated hypotheses at the crux of our argument.

The first deals with what we are calling emergent warfare. We argue that once our ancestors began to be capable of very sophisticated forms of sociality and cooperation, they also became quite capable of what we refer to as *socially cooperative violence*. For us, activities involved in socially cooperative violence stand in contrast to forms of lethal intergroup violence we might see elsewhere in the natural world, as the former would involve human ideas, motivations, beliefs, morals, symbols, communications, and cultural logics. When such forms of socially cooperative violence became organized and directed at those deemed "outsiders" or "others," when violence takes on an inter-community dimension, then it may arguably be what we call emergent warfare.

The second hypothesis is that the very same human faculties that permitted the emergence of warfare also opened the door to complex forms of peacemaking.

We argue that such peacefare, as humans are capable of it, develops in tandem because it is enabled by the same predispositions for complex cooperation and sociality, and peacemaking practices and institutions would have been necessary not only to help promote stability and sociality, but also to prevent, justify, and regulate uses of violence, whether within groups or between groups. It is not simply conflict avoidance or post-conflict sociality (see Chapter Two for how non-human primates engage in conflict resolution) – by peacefare we are referencing various forms of social interaction and cultural production related to conflict resolution and the regulation of violence, affecting its practice or the norms and views associated with it.

Ultimately, we propose that when people began to behave in humanly complex ways, and when we became capable of the kinds of sophisticated cooperation and sociality that mark our species today, the door was thrown open for all kinds of group behaviors, whether involving violence or not. Hence, we hypothesize that the onset of socially cooperative violence and emergent warfare are tied to the origins of modern human behavior and human culture. Therefore, human complex cooperation was the foundation, and socially cooperative violence, emergent warfare, and emergent peacefare were outcomes. These hypotheses are admittedly speculative and require testing and the accumulation of evidence to support, refine, or refute. But, we hope that by presenting our case, others will join the debates and perhaps be open to new ways of looking at certain questions. In the end, these hypotheses, we feel, take into consideration various data and insights from across anthropological subfields, making the perspective anthropologically integrative. And since a capacity to wage either war or peace necessitates complex human thought and behavior, we will also deal with the debates and evidence for when such forms of human nature likely existed.

There are many perspectives on key behaviors that researchers consider to be hallmarks of *Homo sapiens*, activities and practices that reflect higher and more sophisticated cognition separating us from all other species. We have the ability to conceive of, express, and choose a much wider range of ideas, strategies, and belief systems than non-human primates do. These patterns have been variously labeled behavioral modernity, variability, flexibility, and other terms that emphasize our distinctively human lifeways. The common thread running through each of these schools of thought is a notion that something about our ways of thinking, planning, communicating, and interacting with others around us (human or non-human, tangible or intangible) is very peculiar to us and is generally absent in other members of the natural world.[1] When we consider the full range of what constitutes cultural expression and forms for those currently characterized as behaviorally modern (of say the past 200,000 years or so for which we have good supporting data), we ought to recognize that our ancestors would have been interacting in ways not all that dissimilar to our own. That is to say, humans are extremely social creatures, and our social relations run the gamut from peaceful and cooperative to conflictive and competitive. In this light, violence is but one option of many kinds of inter-action. In our social relationships, whether between family members, neighboring communities, or even nation-states, we can see that the relationships can and do undergo cycles of change. The US and Japan went from bitter enemies to close allies in the span of decades in the 20th century, and history is full of similar examples of cyclical patterns of positive and negative relations. Much of our decisions and actions are heavily influenced by social and environmental circumstances. What we are confident about is that those of our ancestors that exhibit cognitive qualities approximating what we may comfortably refer to as behavioral modernity or variability (see McBrearty and Brooks 2000; Shea 2011), meaning cognition, thought, and behaviors as equally complex as our own today, should have been just as capable of warfare given the right conditions. Regarding the likelihood of warfare's existence for behaviorally modern humans, we suggest that all were at least capable of related behaviors.

This last point brings us to the question of emergent warfare and its onset. In our humble opinion, arguing for either the presence or absence of it in our hominin lineages prior to the advent of behavioral modernity hinges on our collective knowledge around two key aspects. First, it is necessary to understand the nature of societies and social configurations that marked our hominin ancestors, and how variable these would have been throughout the 2 million years of our genus' history. This is because the scales and sizes of these groupings could have had effects on degrees of mobility, internal social ranking, and proximity to other groups and resources, perceptions of in- versus out-group identities, all of which would have had implications for the kinds of interactions that would have occurred between groups and communities. Second, we propose that sophisticated forms of communication would have been a crucial ingredient for emergent warfare.

A key for elucidating when emergent warfare started its developmental trajectory may be language. We suspect language, especially the capacity to communicate via speech and to transform ideas into more transferable forms, would have been a critical component for emergent warfare's inception for a number of reasons. For instance, it signals the ability to think symbolically and in abstract ways. "Many species communicate, but only humans have language, and only humans communicate through symbols" (Barnard 2012: 3). Importantly, and in contrast to forms of lethal intergroup aggression as seen in other species (such as chimpanzees), higher human cognition and communicative abilities would have permitted far more complex ways for violence to be organized, invoked, rationalized, and institutionalized. The ability to justify violence, to find reasons (sometimes mystical) and to share them, to convince, persuade and motivate others into dangerous and lethal actions through appeals to religion, belief systems, and kinship obligations, to coordinate and plan premeditated joint actions, to create enduring traditions, values, ideas, and cultural practices associated with violence – these abilities are what separate us from other species. That being said, we must explore our evolutionary pathways to becoming "human" and where violence, and the avoidance of it, may have fit within that puzzle.

Answering these types of questions may be beyond the reach of any definitive conclusions based on the available material record. Hence, as we submit some of these ideas, we recognize that we are venturing firmly into the realm of speculative interpretation, offering our best guesses. Nonetheless, we strongly suspect that cognitive capacities approximating our own would have been a key condition for emergent warfare for the reasons highlighted above. And once groups of people began to fight, finding ways to promote peace became all the more necessary. To go further down the rabbit hole of speculation, then, the question goes well beyond when we see the earliest concrete archaeological signals of emergent warfare. We must also consider when our ancestors begin to possess the capability to practice emergent warfare. As we will argue, this likely did not involve a flashpoint of biological and cultural evolutionary change. Rather, emergent warfare probably followed an evolutionary trajectory that mirrored our own development as a species, with a series of important fits and starts associated with a larger journey to the "us" of today. For instance, at the moment there should be no reason to doubt that our closest human cousins, such as Neandertals, were at least capable of organized violence. Recent research has indicated the possibility that Neandertals were exploiting marine shell material for personal ornamentation at approximately 45,000 years ago in parts of present-day northern Italy (see Peresani et al. 2013). With our current paleogenomic knowledge about interbreeding between the human populations, including Neandertal groups, a new area to consider would be how interactions between groups may have spanned a cooperative-competitive spectrum.

"People can cooperate, peacefully compete, or use violence in order to achieve their objectives, depending on what they believe will serve them best in any given circumstance" (Gat 2015: 123). Anthropologist Agustin Fuentes (2004; 2013: 84) notes the significance of a capacity for cooperation in the evolution of our species, stressing that conflict and competition were not the only drivers of our evolutionary systems. Instead, researchers like Fuentes stress the need to recognize behavioral flexibility that enhanced cooperation and information transfer (see Fuentes et al. 2010: 442). "Human behavior is plastic, open equally to both altruistic cooperation and deadly conflict" (Ferguson 2013b: 192). In the end, when we consider full range of plasticity associated with human thought and cultural patterning, with the myriad ways in which we perceive and under-stand our surroundings, and with how we choose to behave and achieve certain objectives, it should become apparent that we have probably always been at least capable of organized aggression. That said, we can and should explore how far back definitive evidence of violence (whether interpersonal or intergroup) is discernible, and how associated behavioral patterns could have played a role in both our biological and cultural evolution as a species. We return to these questions at the end of the book.

On a final note, we are not arguing that the Pleistocene world was filled with rampant violence in some Hobbesian sense. Far from it – we are instead arguing that the evidence is currently far too equivocal to make any definitive conclusions about the presence of "warfare" in the period between a few hundred thousand years ago and the terminal Pleistocene. Indeed, the archaeological study of warfare in the Holocene has revealed not only the occurrence of warfare in different times and places, but also stretches of time with virtually no signs of violent conflict in various world regions (Keeley 2014: 30). This reinforces the importance of considering the varied cultural mechanisms by which past human communities attempted to mitigate conflict and prevent warfare, to create and maintain "peace" and perceptions of equity through restraint, social mechanisms, and institutions (see Dye 2013; Ferguson 2013a; Fry 2006, 2013b; Milner et al. 2013). What we advocate is keeping an open mind as one considers the full range of evidence, research, and plausible scenarios. This becomes all the more necessary as researchers continue to bring exciting new information to us. Essentially, this is a book we wish we had when we first began asking questions about the evolutionary roots of human violence and warfare. We hope that you will find in our work a balanced presentation of current data and studies, one that can prepare all of us to engage in larger, public, and academic discourses about warfare, peacemaking, and humanity. And with that, we now dive down the rabbit hole.

Note

1 This ability is often referred to a symbolic thought, which is the capacity to link a sign to its object via convention rather than similarity or causal connection. Many scholars have suggested that only modern humans have the ability to do this, and see this behavior as the prerequisite for human language. See Chapter Six.

Works Cited

Allen, Mark. 2014. Hunter-Gatherer Conflict: The Last Bastion of the Pacified Past? In *Violence and Warfare Among Hunter-Gatherers*, edited by Mark Allen and Terry Jones, pp. 15–25. Left Coast Press, Walnut Creek, CA.

Allen, Mark, and Terry Jones (eds.). 2014. *Violence and Warfare Among Hunter-Gatherers*. Left Coast Press, Walnut Creek, CA.

Barash, David. 2013. Evolution and Peace. In *War, Peace, and Human Nature: The Convergence of Evolutionary and Cultural Views*, edited by Douglas P. Fry, pp. 25–37. Oxford University Press, New York.

Barnard, Alan. 2012. *Genesis of Symbolic Thought*. Cambridge University Press, Cambridge.

Dye, David. 2013. Trends in Cooperation and Conflict in Native Eastern North America. In *War, Peace, and Human Nature: The Convergence of Evolutionary and Cultural Views*, edited by Douglas P. Fry, pp. 132–150. Oxford University Press, New York.

Ferguson, R. Brian. 2008. Ten Points on War. *Social Analysis* 52(2), 32–49.

Ferguson, R. Brian. 2013a. Pinker's List. In *War, Peace, and Human Nature: The Convergence of Evolutionary and Cultural Views*, edited by Douglas P. Fry, pp. 112–131. Oxford University Press, New York.

Ferguson, R. Brian. 2013b. The Prehistory of War and Peace in Europe and the Near East. In *War, Peace, and Human Nature: The Convergence of Evolutionary and Cultural Views*, edited by Douglas P. Fry, pp. 191–240. Oxford University Press, New York.

Fry, Douglas. 2006. *The Human Potential for Peace: An Anthropological Challenge to Assumptions about War and Violence*. Oxford University Press, Oxford.

Fry, Douglas (ed.). 2013a. *War, Peace, and Human Nature: The Convergence of Evolutionary and Cultural Views.* Oxford University Press, New York.

Fry, Douglas. 2013b. Cooperation for Survival: Creating a Global Peace System. In *War, Peace, and Human Nature: The Convergence of Evolutionary and Cultural Views*, edited by Douglas P. Fry, pp. 543–558. Oxford University Press, New York.

Fuentes, Agustin. 2004. It's Not All Sex and Violence: Integrated Anthropology and the Role of Cooperation and Social Complexity in Human Evolution. *American Anthropologist* 106(4), 710–718.

Fuentes, Agustin. 2013. Cooperation, Conflict, and Niche Construction in the Genus *Homo.* In *War, Peace, and Human Nature: The Convergence of Evolutionary and Cultural Views*, edited by Douglas P. Fry, pp. 78–94. Oxford University Press, New York.

Fuentes, Agustin. 2015. Integrative Anthropology and the Human Niche: Toward a Contemporary Approach to Human Evolution. *American Anthropologist* 117(2), 302–315.

Fuentes, Agustin, Matthew Wyczalkowski, and Katherine MacKinnon. 2010. Niche Construction Through Cooperation: A Nonlinear Dynamics Contribution to Modeling Facets of the Evolutionary History in the Genus Homo. *Current Anthropology* 51(3), 435–444.

Gat, Azar. 2015. Proving Communal Warfare Among Hunter-Gatherers: The Quasi-Rousseauan Error. *Evolutionary Anthropology* 24(3), 111–126.

Harkin, Michael. 2010. Uncommon Ground: Holism and the Future of Anthropology. *Reviews in Anthropology* 39(1), 25–45.

Keegan, John. 1993. *A History of Warfare.* Vintage Books, New York.

Keeley, Lawrence. 1996. *War Before Civilization.* Oxford University Press, Oxford.

Keeley, Lawrence. 2014. War Before Civilization – 15 Years On. In *The Evolution of Violence*, edited by Todd Shackelford and Ranald Hansen, pp. 23–31. Springer, New York.

Levy, Jack, and William Thompson. 2010. *Causes of War.* Wiley-Blackwell, Malden, UK.

McBrearty, Sally, and Alison Brooks. 2000. The Revolution That Wasn't: A New Interpretation of the Origin of Modern Human Behavior. *Journal of Human Evolution* 39(5), 453–563.

McCall, Grant, and Nancy Shields. 2008. Examining the Evidence from Small-scale Societies and Early Prehistory and Implications for Modern Theories of Aggression and Violence. *Aggression and Violent Behavior* 13(1), 1–9.

Milner, George, George Chaplin, and Emily Zavodny. 2013. Conflict and Societal Change in Late Prehistoric Eastern North America. *Evolutionary Anthropology* 22(3), 96–102.

Otterbein, Keith. 2004. *How War Began.* Texas A & M University Press, College Station.

Peresani, Marc, Marian Vanhaeren, Ermanno Quaggiotto, Alain Queffelec, Francesco d'Errico. 2013. An Ochered Fossil Marine Shell From the Mousterian of Fumane Cave, Italy. *PLoS One* 8(7), 1–15.

Pinker, Steven. 2011. *The Better Angels of Our Nature: Why Violence Has Declined.* Viking, New York.

Shackelford, Todd, and Viviana Weekes-Shackelford (eds.). 2012. *The Oxford Handbook of Evolutionary Perspectives on Violence, Homicide, and War.* Oxford University Press, New York.

Shea, John. 2011. *Homo sapiens* Is as *Homo sapiens* Was. 2011. *Current Anthropology* 52(1), 1–35.

Smith, Dane. 2010. *U.S. Peacefare.* Praeger, Santa Barbara, CA.

Smith, David Livingston. 2007. *The Most Dangerous Animal.* St. Martin's Press, New York.

Sussman, Robert. 2013. Why the Legend of the Killer Ape Never Dies. In *War, Peace, and Human Nature: The Convergence of Evolutionary and Cultural Views*, edited by Douglas P. Fry, pp. 97–111. Oxford University Press, New York.

Watson, Patty Jo. 1995. Archaeology, Anthropology, and the Culture Concept. *American Anthropologist* 97(4), 683–694.

2

DROPPING INTO THE RABBIT HOLE

Tucked away in a mountainous corner of the world on the border between China and Myanmar (also known as Burma) are various communities of the Wa people. They live in rugged terrain in between the Mekong and Salween Rivers. Numbering one million people today, the Wa were traditionally warrior-farmers practicing rice agriculture and were, until recently, regarded by many as the most fearsome warriors and headhunters of the northernmost part of Southeast Asia (Fiskesjo 2001). During the late 19th and early 20th centuries, Wa communities were documented to have engaged in forms of warfare and headhunting, the latter of which figured very significantly within a complex system of religious beliefs and practices. Headhunting involved the ambush of people from an enemy settlement and the transport of victims' heads back to the home village. These heads then entered a series of ritual activities including public display. Why would people attack neighboring communities, then take their heads as trophies for display? And why would this practice become a cultural institution?

Researcher Ian Armit (2010: 14) describes the act of headhunting, as manifested in contemporary and ancient groups, as being linked to an objectification of others – of identifying them as something else. This is simultaneously objectification and dehumanization of others. Their bodies are transformed into something less than human. Moreover, research on headhunting contexts from the world over shows the taking of heads to be associated with disparate purposes. According to anthropologist Magnus Fiskesjo (2001: 127), the Wa headhunting practice likely had to do with the capture and deployment of the force of the enemy "Other" – using that force to help promote agricultural production at home. Interestingly, raids were provoked by different reasons, but also occurred during times of scarcity and dwindling resources. In this manner, we can see a connection between religious and practical, economic motives (Fiskesjo 2001: 128). A key takeaway from the Wa headhunting case is the recognition that violent actions are not all irrational or senseless. In fact, they may make perfect sense for those involved in violent events, for perpetrators, observers, and potentially even for victims. In a way, all of the activities related to headhunting are not enacted for just for religious and economic purposes (i.e., rice growing), but probably possessed a performative quality meant to transmit messages between people. These could be internal messages within a community, but also between communities.

Not far away in Cambodia, some 1.7 million of the country's 8 million inhabitants died from starvation, disease, overwork, and execution under the Khmer Rouge regime during the period of Democratic Kampuchea (1975–1977) (Hinton 2004: 157). Aside from the practices of genocide, one striking activity associated with this period was the practice of extracting and consuming the livers of enemies or prisoners. There were many cultural reasons for this action, and these ranged from the performance of symbolic acts to the augmentation of one's vitality or courage (Hinton 2004). Whatever the case, it is clear that for the societies involved in this type of violence, a cultural web of deeply embedded beliefs and ideas was involved. To cultural outsiders, these ideas and resulting practices may not make sense, but there are rationales behind them for participants on the inside.

What the two preceding cases show us is that violence can come in many forms, sometimes overt and obvious, and sometimes subtle and nuanced. The kinds of violence that are socially acceptable, politically or religiously sanctioned, or even deemed necessary can be highly variable from one society to the next. Even within a cohesive and culturally homogenous community, attitudes about violence can be extremely varied. Hence, violence can be viewed as legitimate, necessary, extreme, or mundane, and one's attitudes and perceptions depend on one's own cultural worldviews, social status, occupation, and many other factors. The most significant takeaway for this book and our exploration of the origins of warfare is the idea that violence is marked by high cultural variability, whether in the contemporary or ancient world.

There is little question that people living within or adjacent to ancient states of the world, existing within the last 5000 years, were familiar with various practices of violence. The case of the Wa people suggests to us that many smaller-scale, non-state societies of prehistory the world over may have also been engaging in forms of organized violence, and probably for all kinds of reasons that are not immediately apparent to us. Some of their practices and beliefs may seem foreign to many of us living firmly in a modern, industrialized, urbanized, nation-state society. But if we were to imagine a world filled with smaller-scale, pre-modern, non-industrial societies, which essentially encompasses the vast majority of human history on this planet, how much cultural variability might there have been throughout the past several hundred thousand years?

The possibility for an ancient and prehistoric world filled with either constant or periodic dangers related to outsiders, threats, and violence has been raised by many philosophers and scholars. Indeed, debates about the antiquity of violence, and its connection to human nature, are not confined to professional anthropologists or other social scientists of the past century. Charles Darwin's ideas about natural selection and struggles for survival stemmed from earlier writers, such as English philosopher Thomas Hobbes, who saw people as naturally selfish, competitive, and aggressive (Sussman 2013: 99). However, until the advent of an anthropological discipline, evaluation of humanity's lifeways of the deepest past was subject to little more than speculation based on observations of contemporary human societies. The outermost reaches of our proverbial rabbit hole could not provide much evidence for systematic consideration. In order to answer our questions about emergent warfare, researchers turn to a suite of methods for gathering empirical evidence about the deeper past. Generally speaking, these interpretive frameworks rely on analogical reasoning, using contemporary human societies and even primate populations, along with direct reconstruction based on the material traces of past lifeways. We discuss these methods in this chapter and the next, but must first attend to some other business.

Conceptualizing Human Culture, Violence, and Warfare

Before we journey further down the rabbit hole, there is the small matter of definitions. After all, how can we all agree (or politely agree to disagree) about the answers to our big questions without first drawing some definitional boundaries around our subject matter? One of our principal concerns is the earliest manifestations of behavioral patterns and cultural complexes associated with organized violence in our species, what we are dubbing emergent warfare. For various reasons, we suspect emergent warfare to be tied to the earliest expressions of modern human behavior and culture.

But what does it mean to be human? Did all members of our hominin lineages possess human "culture"? Should we distinguish between different kinds of culture? If so, at what point did our ancestors become more like us? Was there even a flashpoint or threshold to speak of, when our earliest ancestors became "human," or should we be thinking about a very gradual process replete with pivotal evolutionary changes? These questions are not easily answered, and there are ongoing (and quite contested) debates regarding these major lines of inquiry. Despite all the scholarly contention, however, most of us do agree on one thing: our species is distinct in terms of abilities, behavior, and thought, from all other species in our world. Regarding human cultures throughout evolutionary history, Political scientist Azar Gat (2006: 3) writes that we "have been carried to an almost incredible distance from our origins." Most of us would also concede that to know how and why our species is so different requires an appreciation of the evolutionary changes inherent in our lineages, developments that occurred through the course of millions of years. As illustration, recent research on ancient genomes and brain development has indicated that brain functions associated with language likely resulted from "a long cascade of small genetic changes to brain development" (Hawks 2013). In the end, we favor the view that the full articulation of modern human behavior did not occur in an evolutionary instant (Caspari and Wolpoff 2013). We agree with many of our colleagues that a series of important changes (in our physical makeup) occurring in our various ancestral lineages fostered cultural evolution, giving us significant and novel abilities and choices. These changes would have a role to play in emergent forms of both warfare and peace.

"Unworkable Monstrosities" and Human Culture

As succinctly observed by anthropologist Travis Pickering (2013: 59):

> It is not surprising that many evolutionary researchers consider the remarkable behavioral flexibility of humans as the ultimate (if somewhat intangible) characteristic that sets us apart from other animals, including even our closest ape relatives: behavioral lability as the essence of humanness.

For the sake of consistency, we will generally refer to this idea about remarkable behavioral lability as behavioral modernity or flexibility. To be sure, certain aspects of our behavior can be seen in other species, albeit in variegated forms. However, few would argue that there is any other extant species that exhibits the full range of human cognition and behavior.

Decades ago, the preeminent anthropologist Clifford Geertz (1973: 49) wrote that human nature is not independent of culture, that, without culture, we may be appropriately viewed as "unworkable monstrosities." In this view, because our central nervous system and our neocortex developed mainly while interacting with culture, our behaviors and organized experiences required guidance by culture and "systems of significant symbols." Although some may take issue with the observation that any human devoid of a cultural upbringing would be an unworkable monstrosity, Geertz's larger point is important to consider – that human biological evolution has been heavily intertwined with human cultural evolution. Research in the ensuing decades since Geertz's assertion has increasingly supported this notion, demonstrating vital links between our physical changes and our complex behavioral patterns throughout human evolutionary history. Indeed, anthropologist Agustin Fuentes (2012) notes that human behavior is almost always "naturenurtural." "When we think about humans it is a mistake to think that our biology exists without our cultural experience and that our cultural selves are not constantly entangled with our biology" (Fuentes 2012: 16). "We are simultaneously biological and cultural beings with complex schemata and social lives that shape and populate our perceptions and philosophies: we are naturenurtural" (Fuentes 2012: 65).

As expressed by researchers Francesco d'Errico and colleagues (2003: 2), humans "are the only species capable of communicating with an articulated oral language and creating symbolic ideational cultures." We see this characterization of "human" as a valid starting point when considering what it means to possess human culture and the ability to create, express, and store symbolic meanings. To be sure, other members of species engage in the transmission of behavioral patterns and what might be considered forms (or rudimentary reflections) of culture. Primates do learn, and that learning can be influenced by social opportunities (Strier 2010: 258).

For instance, there is interesting research demonstrating forms of learning and "culture" in various primates, such as baboons (Sapolsky 2013) and rhesus monkeys (Kempes et al. 2013). Distinct vocalizations among vervet monkeys, for instance, indicate different alarm calls that may refer specifically to different kinds of predators (Seyfarth et al. 1980), though the evidence does not indicate the ability to communicate about events beyond the present. Additionally, research has shown that great apes do possess some capacity for symbolic thought (Savage-Rumbaugh and Lewin 1994). As further illustration, researchers performing fieldwork at the Fongoli site in Senegal observed chimpanzees engaged in "tool-assisted hunting" (Pruetz et al. 2015). The chimpanzees created and used sharpened stick tools in efforts to hunt bushbabies hiding in tree hollows, and presumably these techniques and associated knowledge were passed from individual to individual. This is a highly significant case, and though it does not show fully human cognition among non-human primates, it does strengthen the notion that many of our earliest hominin ancestors may have possessed more of the cognitive abilities than we have traditionally reserved for ourselves.

Despite these glimpses of cognitive complexity among primates, there is no question that our species sits within a class of its own when it comes to higher cognitive capacities. No other species is capable of using language in the way that we do. Such cognition and abilities to express and share ideas with one another allows for highly complex sociality, organizations, and practices. Though there are likenesses of human culture elsewhere in the animal kingdom, some fainter or stronger than others, the kinds of complexity inherent to human behaviors, intentionality, sociality, and communication, are arguably unmatched.

We would agree with Pickering's (2013: 8) characterization of humanity when he writes about the difference between "humanness" and "human uniqueness." Captured in this view is the notion that "uniquely human capabilities" are "overlays on a now very, very deeply contained human essence" (Pickering 2013: 8). Hence, understanding what it means to be uniquely human and possess uniquely human culture requires a full grasp of the many aspects of human-like activities that helped to shape our evolutionary development, activities whose signals emerge at different times throughout the past few million years. Our complex nature did not develop overnight, and is quite the product of a very long timeframe of evolutionary change. The issue becomes how to model human cognitive development, and to determine when traits such as articulated oral language and symbolic thinking emerged, and how they were associated with specific hominin groups (d'Errico et al. 2003: 2). Which of our hominin ancestors could have hypothetically been dropped into a more recent human society as an infant and been raised in a contemporary society?

A full discussion of various hominin lineages and suspected behavioral suites lies beyond the scope of this story. But, the larger message coming through from biological anthropologists is that different behaviors that potentially display humanness appear at various points in time throughout the past 2 to 3 million years, from producing stone tools, to hunting, to the controlled use of fire. At the crux of humanity is our status as the makers and bearers of forms of culture that distinguish our species from the behavior of our counterparts in the natural world. Our abilities to make and bear "human culture" stem from the ways in which we understand, conceptualize, and adapt to the world around us, how we communicate with and relate to one another, how we create and pass on ideas, how we perform rituals and ceremonies, and, perhaps most importantly, *why* we perform such rituals. In this fashion, culture consists of our shared systems of belief, customs, traditions, technologies, innovations, and social organizations and institutions, all of which we transmit across time and space in different and wide-ranging ways. Human culture, then, comprises the full and highly variable range of our learned behaviors and ideas. And without doubt, human culture is tied to human nature, for it is our developed physical attributes and capacities that have enabled our creativities, which in turn have served to affect and shape our ongoing physical evolution. It is a cyclical process.

Research throughout the past century has resulted in numerous theories about human nature, and how we define humanity and human culture has been quite fluid and malleable. Our ideas and attitudes about humanity have changed dramatically even in just the past few decades, and with exciting new data emerging from the field of paleogenomics, our concepts continue to change. For the archaeologist, cultural practices are reflected in the material remains left behind by past peoples. Aside from the fossils of our earliest hominin ancestors, we can point to the artifacts directly manipulated and used by these ancestors, those materials sufficiently durable to survive relatively intact for us to find today. That we find evidence of stone tools in parts of Africa made by hominins as early as 2.5 million years ago (Semaw et al. 2003) is cause enough for us to explore the idea of emergent or proto-human behavior. Intriguingly, recent evidence suggests the presence of tools in parts of Kenya even earlier, dating to about 3.3 million years ago, predating the other finds by 700,000 years (see Harmand et al. 2015). Moreover, recent discoveries in South Africa of a possible new species, designated as *Homo naledi*, continue to complicate the picture of behavioral modernity or complexity, given the possibility of "deliberate disposal of bodies" dating to some 230,000–330,000 years ago in this remarkable case (see Dirks et al. 2015 and Dirks et al. 2017). While these cases are not wholly indicative of the kinds of cognition associated with anatomically modern humans, they do indicate the early developmental milestones of a long evolutionary march toward human uniqueness, complete with periodic appearances of humanness and "humanesque" behaviors.

But how far back can we see behaviorally modern culture? Decades ago, many researchers argued that the earliest signs of symbolic thought could only be seen in the material record in parts of Europe at around 40,000 years ago. They pointed to the magnificent paintings on rock walls inside cave complexes as evidence of higher cognition. Combined with revolutionary changes in lithic technologies, greater evidence of personal adornment and identity expression, and other clues, the entire suite of archaeological evidence suggested an "explosion" of new complex lifeways, dubbed the "Upper Paleolithic Revolution" or the "human revolution." Within this view, sophisticated cognition, the manipulation of symbols, and perhaps even the beginnings of language, were all thought to have arisen in Europe at this time. Essentially, this argument promoted the idea that modern behavior appeared in a virtual instant, when juxtaposed against millions of years of cultural evolution, in one place and time. But, a seminal paper published by archaeologists Sally McBrearty and Alison Brooks (2000) effectively argued that arguments about a "human revolution" were flawed. In recent years, as archaeological research has begun to pick up in more places outside of Europe, accumulations of evidence suggest that modern behavior did not appear so abruptly at 40,000 years ago in just one region. To illustrate, we now have evidence of rock art just as old in parts of Southeast Asia, specifically from caves on the Indonesian island of Sulawesi (Aubert et al. 2014). We also have evidence for the use of adornment and other behaviors expressive of personal identity far earlier in parts of Africa. This lends support to ideas about behavioral modernity having an earlier starting point, being marked by a more gradual unfolding process rather than a punctuated explosion (Kissel and Fuentes 2016; McBrearty and Brooks 2000).

So, the search for behavioral origins must begin further back in evolutionary time. Many anthropologists see a shared basis for complex social constructs between humans and other primate species. For instance, anthropologist Bernard Chapais (2014: 753) argues that many of our complex social traits, such as the recognition of highly intricate kinship patterns, are "phylogenetically composite traits whose origin coincided with the conjunction, in the course of human evolution, of more elementary components, many of which are observable in other primates." This type of thinking is at the basis for many research projects aimed at using primate analogy to propose and test hypotheses about our earliest ancestors, and, as we will discuss below, such frameworks have been important for considering the origins of warfare.

Aside from primate comparisons, researchers have explored the material remains of past hominin populations. Our distinct humanity did not appear in an instant within the archaeological and paleoanthropological records. Instead, the key ingredients emerged in different phenotypic and genotypic expressions throughout the past few million years of history in related hominin lineages. For instance, work by researchers like Henry Bunn (2006) has shown that early interest by hominins in meat consumption, some 2 million years ago, was a vital factor in our pathway to becoming human. Moreover, this dietary preference over time contributed to innovative strategies for procuring meat, such as forms of hunting (see Pickering 2013). The use of spears for hunting is hypothesized by some researchers to have occurred among early Pleistocene hominins, whether through stabbing, thrusting, or casting (see Pickering and Bunn 2012; see also Pickering and Dominguez-Rodrigo 2012). Interestingly, such researchers propose that the use of these technologies had the effect of providing both some degree of distance from potentially dangerous prey, as well as a control over emotional reactivity (see Pickering 2013 for an extended discussion). Though such implements may have existed earlier, we have solid evidence within the archaeological record of hunting spear technologies and related hunting practices dating to nearly half a million years ago, such as the wooden spears recovered from the Schoningen site in Germany.

There is also evidence for hafting stone points onto spears at roughly 500,000 BP at the site of Kathu Pan in southern Africa (Wilkins et al. 2012). In addition, there are indirect clues hinting at even earlier production and uses of spears, such as microwear analysis on some stone artifacts from sites at Koobi Fora in Kenya dating to 1.6 million years ago, which showed polishes consistent with wood-working (Keeley and Toth 1981). Even without the use of a tip for spears, fire-treating wooden spear ends could have strengthened their effectiveness, and there is evidence to suggest hominin-controlled fire in parts of eastern and southern Africa up to a million years ago if not earlier (Pickering and Bunn 2012: 163).

The currently available bodies of archaeological evidence suggest that the first signals for highly sophisticated, modern human behavior, cultural complexity, or what we might call "uniquely human capabilities" (Pickering 2013), appear in the archaeological record within the past 300,000 years (see Bouzouggar et al. 2007; d'Errico et al. 2003; Henshilwood et al. 2004; Kissel and Fuentes 2017; McBrearty and Brooks 2000; Shea 2011). According to some, the first appearances of such modern behavior may not necessarily be linked to increased cognitive capacity, but might actually be tied to demography and population size (see Powell et al. 2009). Likewise, it could be that rather than a change in demography there was a change in connectivity between human populations, which allowed for ideas and genes to move between groups. The scarcity in finds is also likely attributable in part to the patchiness of field investigations, artifact sampling, biases in preservation, and chance finds.

When it comes to larger packages of material evidence suggesting higher cognition and symbolic thought, the evidence becomes much more pronounced in association with anatomically modern humans and their close relatives. The earliest fossil specimens with physical features approximating our own bodies come to us from Africa. The fossil record for early *Homo sapiens*, or what researchers refer to as anatomically modern humans (AMH), only falls within a timespan of the past 200,000 years (McDougall et al. 2005; White et al. 2003). Currently, there are tantalizing clues about the antiquity of certain behaviors potentially correlated with AMH throughout the past 100,000 to 200,000 years, such as the uses of red ochre to decorate materials and the manipulation and uses of shells across the African continent during the Middle Stone Age. Our use of personal adornment is considered by many to be a tangible sign of symbolic material cultures (Bouzouggar et al. 2007: 9964). For example, at Blombos Cave in present-day South Africa, perforated tick shell materials, suspected to have been used as beads for personal adornment, have been recovered dating to approximately 75,000 years ago (Henshilwood et al. 2004). Similar artifacts dating to 82,000 years ago have been recovered from northern Africa, which were likewise covered in red ochre (Bouzouggar et al. 2007). There are two important implications to note here about these artifacts. First, they hint at the existence of "interlinking exchange systems or of long-distance social networks" (Bouzouggar et al. 2007: 9969). Second, they also reflect a potential capacity for language. The notion of social networks sharing ideas about the symbolic importance or meanings of specific materials not only reinforces ideas about complex cognition, but also raises the possibility of early kinds of competition, where interactions between members or communities of social networks can range from peaceful to conflictive actions. Situations that can sometimes lead to conflict are thus made plausible. As argued by Keeley (2014: 27) for more recent societies, relationships between trading or exchange partners can periodically cycle into disputes and conflict, as has been demonstrated through numerous historical and ethnographic cases. Could such scenarios have existed in the Late Pleistocene with human populations within the past 100,000 years?

Current evidence suggests that groups of AMH began to migrate out of the continent and into parts of the Eurasian landmass at around 100,000 years ago, encountering the descendants of populations of even earlier migrant groups that left Africa some 1–2 million years ago. A combination of physical traits and material culture of populations across Africa and Eurasia indicate that these peoples possessed most, if not all, of the behavioral and cognitive characteristics that we do today. This is especially the case for societies of the Late Pleistocene (Klein 2009). In addition to *Homo sapiens*, this would also include members of Neandertal and Denisovan populations, with whom the genetic evidence now shows important overlap (Green et al. 2010; Reich et al. 2011). It has become clear in recent years that populations of humans, Neandertals, and Denisovans exchanged both genes and culture in parts of Eurasia some 50,000 years ago. All of these populations could have been bearers of fully human or behaviorally modern culture, and future research will clarify and further test these ideas.

Evidence points to Neandertal manipulation of mineral pigments for symbolic and decorative purposes in sites in Iberia as early as 50,000 years ago (see Zilhao 2012). Arguably, as we are now beginning to recognize that Neandertals may have been engaging in highly complex social behaviors associated with higher cognition, symbolism, music, and aesthetics (see d'Errico 2003), we ought to simultaneously acknowledge the possibility that Neandertals had the option to organize and fight, as conferred upon them by their biological makeup. This is the case even if the social and environmental circumstances for Neandertal populations seldom fostered situations of conflict, thereby obviating any decisions to engage in intergroup violence. Indeed, some researchers have explored the idea of competition between *Homo sapiens* and Neandertals in parts of the Levant (see Shea 2003). As we will highlight in Chapter Four, the fossil record for Neandertals and AMH of the Late Pleistocene exhibit skeletal trauma that some have interpreted as signs of interpersonal violence.

There are other hints that our journey to becoming human was a very complex process. For instance, we know that *Homo erectus* groups in Asia were engraving on objects at over 430,000 years ago (Joordens et al. 2015). The Schoningen spears, referenced above, are often associated with *Homo heidelbergensis*. Scientists have also recovered ochre from Neandertal sites in Belgium (Roebroeks et al. 2012). These data suggest to some that the process of human origins may be better seen as the interplay between different groups of early humans rather than as only associated with modern humans.

The upshot of all this is that, over a mind-numbingly large expanse of time, key cognitive building blocks would come to be combined and recombined in ways that led to our species as constituted today, ultimately resulting in distinctly human capabilities and behavioral complexes. Being human thus means having the biological tools necessary to be bearers of complex cultural practices, and the story is very complex. But whether that resulted in the onset of warfare hundreds of thousands of years ago, or even earlier, is very unclear and highly debatable. Even if the cognitive and cultural capacities to engage in organized violence were present, the contexts conducive for those behaviors (e.g. environmental or social conditions) may not have been present or prevalent. After all, researchers estimate that the global population of humans throughout the Pleistocene was exponentially lower than corresponding numbers of today or even of the past 10,000 years with the advent of agricultural production (French 2015). With less people, there would have been fewer opportunities for competition to arise over resources, and it would have been far easier for groups to move away from threatening groups. We explore these questions further in Chapter Six, when we connect our discussion of modern behavior with cultural practices of warfare. For now, we need to continue drawing our definitional dotted lines around our subjects of study. Our next stop in this journey of exploration is the land of aggression and violence in the natural world.

Aggression and Violence in the Natural World

Aggression and violence are natural parts of a range of behaviors for many species in the world, and they can fall within both conspecific (within species) and interspecific (between species) categories. Because we seek to answer questions about humans fighting humans, we will deal almost exclusively with the research of conspecific aggression and violence. To be sure, an important facet of human violence extends beyond conspecific violence (see Linzey 2009 and Lockwood and Ascione 1997 for fuller discussions of human violence against other species). But the most salient kind of interspecific violence for our discussion is hunting in Pleistocene contexts, a topic we explore in greater detail later. Suffice to say that once our hominin ancestors began to see members of another species as potential targets for violence, and developed ways to capture and kill them, it may have led us down an important and slippery slope. Viewing other humans as less than human and placing them in the same category of other non-human life forms (i.e., the dehumanization of others), may have been one of the most significant features of emergent warfare. As will be discussed in Chapter Six, there is interesting paleoanthropological research around the origins of hunting practices among our hominin ancestors, and how these may be somehow correlated to other forms of aggression. For the time being, however, we focus our attention on conspecific violence in the natural world.

In a general sense, we favor a simple definition of aggression as actions directed against others, which can be perceived as threatening and potentially violent.

Aggression can be tied to a state of arousal associated with various emotional communicative strategies such as shouting or gesturing (McCall and Shields 2008: 2). With violence, such aggressive behavior results in actual harm of some kind. Accordingly, violence is physical attack or assault that occurs in a context of aggressive behavior (McCall and Shields 2008: 2). We would note, though, that there are certainly other sorts of attack and injury that are neither direct nor physical (more about this is discussed in Chapter Three). Harmful effects can be indirectly felt by a victim, for instance, if violent acts are perpetrated against property or family of the victim. They can also include actions that deprive a victim of some basic needs, which can lead to either psychological or physical harm.

Violence and aggression are clearly not restricted to our species, or even to just primates for that matter. In his well-known and comprehensive treatment of aggression, Konrad Lorenz (1963) wrote about observed animal aggression across a spectrum of vertebrates. Essentially, he described a "fighting instinct" or propensity to act aggressively under certain conditions, perpetrated by both "beast and man" and directed against the same species. There are, of course, different cases and contexts that can highlight these kinds of conspecific aggression and violence, along with extent of such violence. Given this assertion, one natural question to ask concerns the contexts within which we see (or would predict) the occurrence of conspecific or intraspecific violence.

For many researchers, the reasons that conspecific violence happens can usually be linked to selective pressures and evolutionary benefits, such as fitness. Many views within a sociobiological school of thought generally see various behavioral patterns happening in order to increase genetic fitness over time. These might include variations in behavior according to sex, competition related to reproduction and resources, dominance, as well as territoriality. In sociobiological perspectives, researchers would predict relatively low incidences of violence between related individuals and higher rates of violence between unrelated males in the context of male/male competition (McCall and Shields 2008: 2). This evolutionary perspective also predicts lower frequencies of violent behavior between females and their offspring as opposed to males and their offspring, given the certainty of offspring belonging to females.

Of particular relevance for our central questions around warfare are the instances of both conspecific killing, generally, and coalitionary killing, specifically. In the world of nonprimates, there is clear evidence of aggression and violence, sometimes with indications of high-level thought and understanding of consequences. Anthropologist Richard Wrangham has produced numerous illuminating and insightful publications on these topics (Wrangham and Peterson 1996, Wrangham 1999, and Wrangham et al. 2006). As Wrangham notes (1999: 4), research has shown that intraspecific killing occurs in a variety of species, commonly following patterns expected by natural selection theory. Adult spiders kill each other when competing over high-value resources (see Austad 1983). Colonies of ants will engage in inter-colony aggression and raiding if certain advantages are perceived, such as overwhelming numerical superiority (Adams 1990; Wrangham and

Peterson 1996: 162). Hence, to a certain degree, patterns of human killing appear to follow ordinary patterns of lethal aggression found in other species (Wrangham 1999: 4).

However, much human killing occurs in contexts of warfare, which is dominated by a coalitionary style of violence. In contrast, among many animals where aggression occurs in high rates, lethal violence is usually dyadic and not coalitionary (Wrangham 1999: 4). In the category of organized or coalitionary killing, the only nonprimate mammal for which coalitionary killing is known to be commonly responsible for adult deaths is wolves, and such killing tends to occur in buffer zones thus suggesting territoriality (see Mech et al. 1998). Though uncommon, occasional coalitional killing of adults from neighboring groups has also been observed among other social carnivores, such as spotted hyenas, cheetahs, and lions (Wrangham 1999: 4; Wrangham and Peterson 1996: 160). Male lions engage in lethal aggression against females from neighboring groups in order to gain a numerical advantage over other groups as larger groups may access better territories (Mosser and Packer 2009). Similarly, female lions calculate their odds of winning a fight against intruders based upon the number of roaring opponents they hear and are more likely to engage in a fight if they outnumber the intruders (McComb et al. 1994). However, in regions where population density is high they are more willing to attack even when outnumbered (Heinsohn 1997). For Wrangham (1999: 4), these data suggest that animals can be divided into three main categories: 1) species where conspecific killing is rare; 2) species where killing occurs more frequently, but only in dyadic interactions; and 3) species where killing is also frequent, but is polyadic or coalitionary. Most species would fall into the second category, while the third category is dominated by ants and "probably less than 10 mammalian species and perhaps no other vertebrates" (Wrangham 1999: 5). Ultimately, Wrangham points out that, among primates, it is only within chimpanzees and humans that we see frequent coalitionary killing to occur. This, of course, leads to the hypothesis that for our two lineages, coalitional killing may have had a long history in the evolutionary development of both species. Unsurprisingly, many researchers have analyzed chimpanzee behavior in efforts to model hominin behavior.

Regarding violence, we must also consider the killing of nonadults. For evolutionary biologists, the issue of infanticide is relevant to understanding conspecific violence. In both behavioral patterns, the promotion of one's own genetic interests is seen as a significant factor. Infanticide has been observed in many species, and many animals will kill infants of their own species more commonly than adults. For some researchers, the reason for this is that infants are easier targets, whereas adults present a greater threat to potential killers (Wrangham and Peterson 1996: 160). According to Wrangham and Peterson (1996: 160), spotted hyenas, lions, and wolves, like chimpanzees and humans, are examples of species where adults will kill other adults of their own species, thus breaking a general rule observed in nature. They argue that these species are marked by coalitionary bonds and variable party size, which they categorize as "party-gang species." In this argument, when these species are presented with an opportunity of significant numerical advantage, parties will form that tend to engage in aggression and attack. "But as with infanticide, the underlying formula that links the deliberate killers of the world looks clear, simple, and ignominious. Killing is possible in party-gang species because it is cheap" (Wrangham and Peterson 1996: 165).

As a general pattern in the natural world, we can point to a number of non-human and nonprimate examples of not only infanticide, but of cannibalism as well. Several non-human populations are believed to regulate their population through the killing of the young, a behavior seen in brown bears for instance (Young and Ruff 1982). A similar behavior may occur in polar bears (Taylor et al. 1985). More generally, cannibalism occurs in animals during times of resource stress or population pressure (Polis et al. 1984). However, the reasons for infanticide occurring in nature are not totally understood, and may be linked to reproductive strategies rather than population regulation.

Jane Goodall, one of the most influential anthropological voices on the subject of apes, has noted (1977) the practice of cannibalism among chimpanzees in the wild. It should be noted, however, that there have been relatively few attempts to quantify the frequency of chimpanzee cannibalism, and it is often described in the context of infanticide for which cannibalism may or may not be the primary goal. Recent research suggests cannibalism is a rare event among most primates, observed in only a few species (Dellatore et al. 2009). Among the great apes, it has been best documented in chimpanzees, though even here it seems to be an aberrant behavior. In one published report, cases are highlighted where patrolling adult male chimps attacked females, killing and eating their infants (Watts and Mitani 2000). Whatever the impetus, researchers cite infanticide correlated with cannibalism as an important force in chimpanzee social evolution. Intergroup violence also functions to reduce resource competition, though the reasons for this are debatable (Hrdy 1974; Wilson et al. 2004). Most cases of infanticide may simply be a genetically inconsequential epiphenomenon of tense, aggressive episodes (Bartlett et al. 1993: 984–985). Aside from chimpanzees, data suggest cannibalism occurs in gorilla populations, and orangutan filial cannibalism has been observed in a specific case between two reintroduced females as well (Dellatore et al. 2009). Both individuals consumed their own infant after its death, though they waited a few days before consuming the body. It is unclear why these individuals engaged in cannibalism, though it is most likely an aberrant behavior rather than an attempt at nutritional gain (Dellatore et al. 2009). In general, with regards to instances of cannibalism among great apes, in the rare instances in which the practice has been observed in chimpanzees, the behavior can involve young chimpanzees from neighboring populations. Given these observations, it is not surprising that primate behaviors are scrutinized in attempts to reconstruct hominin behavior.

Here, we would like to introduce the phrase *socially cooperative violence* as a way to distinguish human violence from that seen in other species. We suggest this term to distinguish it from other forms of violence seen in non-human animals. By doing so we are being explicit in suggesting that there is something inherently different about the way humans use violence, especially when it involves groups of people, and included within this category are forms of symbolic violence, structural violence, psychological violence, and economic violence, among others.

The World Health Organization defines violence as:

> The intentional use of physical force or power, threatened or actual, against oneself, another person, or against a group or community, that either results in or has a high likelihood of resulting in injury, death, psychological harm, maldevelopment or deprivation.
>
> *Krug et al. 2002*

It is notable that this definition includes both physical force and power, the latter of which may or may not require physicality. As we discuss later in this book, there are types of violence which do not require actual *physical* force but can still cause physiological harm. Indeed, some forms of violence, such as psychological abuse or forcing people to live without certain resources or freedoms, can be latent and manifest injury or harm years later. Violence does not have to leave physical marks. Of course, from an archaeological perspective the majority of the violence we see will be physical, though there are exceptions (Klaus 2012). One of the most striking parts of this definition is the intentionality. The WHO definition thus parses out accidents and unintentional incidents in their datasets. However, they also note that an aggressor's intention might not be to cause long-term harm, though that may indeed be an outcome.

Under the WHO perspective, collective violence is seen as:

> the instrumental use of violence by people who identify themselves as members of a group – whether this group is transitory or has a more permanent identity – against another group or set of individuals, in order to achieve political, economic or social objectives.
>
> *Krug et al. 2002: 215*

It can involve states, political groups, militias, and terrorist organizations and takes the form of wars, mass genocide, torture, disappearances, and other types of human rights violations.

The WHO has the goal of preventing violence, seeing it as a major public health problem. Thus, there is a need to have a good working definition that allows for data collection and analysis. In this book, we take a slightly nuanced approach, as we wish to emphasize the evolutionary aspects of both organized violence and peace-making. In our view, human socially cooperative violence stems from our hyper-sociality. Socially cooperative violence takes the interpersonal and intergroup violence seen in other species and adds a human veneer, specifically two aspects of human nature that are found in other behaviors and that may have their roots in the evolutionary origins of our species: our intense social and cooperative abilities.

By noting its social dimensions, we are stressing that violence is not simply a dyadic relationship between aggressor and victim, but rather that it takes place within a social web that allows for the various types of violence to exist. Aggression and conflict resolution are found throughout the animal kingdom (see the next section in this chapter) and the methods which non-human animals use for both these tasks are complex. Yet, we suggest there is a significant difference between the social nature of non-humans, such as chimpanzees, and that of humans.

By emphasizing "cooperative," we are stressing that socially cooperative violence often, though not always, involves multiple people cooperating toward some future goal. Sometimes this goal is to increase land ownership, sometimes to gain access to sacred ground, sometimes to appease gods, and sometimes to further political and economic interests. The fact that humans can come together in this way strikes us as fundamentally different from similar types of behaviors seen in ants and chimpanzees. Moreover, however abhorrent warfare is, we must admit that there is an immense level of cooperation that occurs in order for war to occur. As discussed in Chapter Eight, convincing soldiers to kill is not always an easy task. But, human behavior is highly influenced not just by our biological composition but also by our cultural systems and socialization. If you grow up in a culture that tells you the neighboring city is full of harmful people who want to kill you, then it may be easy to convince you to fight them, especially if doing so means you are a productive or respected member of your own society. But other cultures may be different. By examining group violence as socially cooperative, we can emphasize the variation in human behavior that is at the heart of anthropology. We will offer more on our views about early forms of socially cooperative violence and emergent warfare in Chapter Six.

Using Primates to Model Hominin Aggression

The order Primates consists of an array of animals (experts place the total number of species at ~250, though this number changes often) from the tiny mouse lemur to the large gorilla. While taxonomists debate the correct placement of each of these species, we often categorize primates into two main groups: the anthropoids and the prosimians. The latter consists of lemurs, lorisis, aye-ayes, and tarsiers, while monkeys and apes are placed in the anthropoid category. Monkeys are divided into New (capuchins, marmosets, tamarins, etc.) or Old World Monkeys (baboons, vervets, patas monkeys, etc.) based on where they live and their evolutionary relationships. The living apes (the hominoids) are our closest living cousins, made up of gibbons, gorillas, orangutans, and chimpanzees. Genetic and fossil studies show that the chimpanzees (made up of two species, the common chimpanzee and the bonobo) and humans share a last common ancestor 7 to 11 million years ago, though this number is constantly up for debate.

Because humans are primates, anthropologists often use data from primatological studies to understand what life was like for the earliest hominins (primates more closely related to us than to any other living primate). While in the past such work was dominated by studies of chimpanzees, recent research has suggested that we need to use the wide range of primate studies to fully understand how primates live and act. While chimpanzees are our closest living relative, it is important to remember that they too have evolved over the last ~10 million years. So while chimpanzees might receive the most attention, we need to be cognizant of how violence, aggression, conflict, and reconciliation occur in all primates in order to best understand what life was like for our ancestors.

So, since researchers look to living primate populations as a source for information and analogy for reconstructing hominin and early human behavior, many ideas about organized violence would fall within this category. There is ample primatological research indicating collective violence among select species of living primates, thus providing clues about the possible nature and patterns of violent behavior among early hominins and archaic humans (van der Dennen 1995). The premise that aggressive competition is a central component of primate social relationships owes its origins to the visible drama of displays of aggression as well as a preoccupation with the origins of human warfare and aggression during the years following World War II (Silverberg and Gray 1992).

Research studies indicate that great apes, including humans, bonobos, chimpanzees, gorillas, and orangutans, possess cognitive abilities that separate them from monkeys. According to conventional research, including DNA data, most researchers suspect that the last common ancestor of apes and monkeys lived some 25 million years ago, with our hominin ancestral lineages splitting from the other great apes at some point later. The most recent split for our ancestors occurred between 10 and 6 million years ago, where they diverged from the lineages leading to bonobos and chimpanzees (Klein 2009).

In recent decades, researchers have built up information regarding gorillas, orangutans, chimpanzees, and bonobos. In particular, chimpanzees, and to some lesser extent bonobos, have consistently been held up as robust extant models for reconstructing hominin behaviors, and this comparative framework has generated tremendous research insight, discussion, and debate. On the surface, it is easy to see why. Genetically, we are very closely related to both chimpanzees and bonobos. Using observations of their behaviors as a starting point, researchers have drawn implications about a hypothetical last common ancestor (LCA) and tested inferences about subsequent hominin patterns of behavior. Chimpanzees and bonobos are seen as productive sources for analogy, as these species defend their territories and fight with conspecifics, suggesting that the ancestor of hominins and *Pan* may have had similar tendencies (Boehm 2012; Ghiglieri 1987; Wilson 2013).

Chimpanzees and Bonobos

Chimpanzees (*Pan troglodytes*), which are today distributed across several study sites in geographically distinct locations in Africa, can be an excellent referent for proposing models of early hominin behavior. For instance, Pickering and Dominguez-Rodrigo (2012: 174) argue that extant chimpanzees can be carefully employed to model hunting by the earliest hominins before 2.6 millions of years ago (mya), "who presumably lacked the modified lithic cutting technology that characterized more derived species" after 2.6 mya. As noted by Pickering and

FIGURE 2.1 Common chimpanzee adult. © *Frans de Waal, Emory University. Licensed under Creative Commons 2.5*

Dominguez-Rodrigo (2010), it is possible to create chimpanzee analogies that can be used to model human evolution and, in turn, to test hypotheses using complementary paleoanthropological data.

Wrangham and Peterson (1996: 24) remark that when it comes to patrilineal, male-bonded communities, only two animal species are marked by intense systems of male-initiated, territorial aggression that feature lethal raiding: humans and chimpanzees. Documented by field research, it is clear male chimpanzees engage in various kinds of violence, and females without babies will sometimes engage in hunting and territorial patrolling (Goodall 1986). Generally, the observations that chimpanzees participate in intercommunity aggression offer a glimpse into how our earliest ancestors may have engaged in similar kinds of group aggression. Much of this thinking has been enhanced by Goodall's (1986, 1990) research, wherein she observed numerous examples of organized violence, such as patrolling and aggression, in Tanzania's Gombe National Park over several years of field study. Her research documented aggressive interactions between two communities, namely the Kasakela and Kahama, which involved violent attacks that eventually led to the disappearance of the Kahama community (see Sousa and Casanova 2005–2006 and Wrangham and Peterson 1996: 12–18). Similar patterns have also been observed in other locations, such as the Mahale Mountains National Park (Nishida and Hosaka 1996). Additionally, data have been collected suggesting that chimpanzees are able to coerce others into participation in lethal aggression (Arcadi and Wrangham 1999).

Based on these kinds of data, Wrangham (1999) has proposed a principal adaptive hypothesis for explaining the species distribution of intergroup coalitional killing,

FIGURE 2.2 Adult bonobo. © *Trisha Shears. Licensed under Creative Commons 3.0*

namely the imbalance-of-power hypothesis, which sees such killing as an expression of a drive for dominance over neighbors. According to Wrangham, there are two necessary and sufficient conditions, a state of intergroup hostility and sufficient imbalances of power that allow for attacks occur with minimal risk or cost. In such scenarios, selection favors these tendencies, though he acknowledges that further studies are needed to determine proximate factors. The upshot, however, is that both chimpanzees and humans strongly exhibit this propensity, suggesting a long history in their respective evolutionary histories.

In contrast to perspectives that tend to see a biological basis for aggression and violence in both hominins and humans, other researchers suggest that a potential reason for the aggression observed in those specific chimpanzee cases is attributable to human impact. In such critiques, one example offered for human impact as precipitating chimpanzee competition is food provisioning, which may have led to increased frustration among rival chimpanzee groups (see Ferguson 2011 and Sussman 2013). However, recent counter-arguments have been published citing additional field investigations that have furnished new data. In one study, collating data from five years of fieldwork within 18 chimpanzee communities and four bonobo communities, researchers documented 152 killings by chimpanzees and one killing by bonobos (Wilson et al. 2014). The data show that males were the most frequent attackers (92% of participants) and victims (73%), and that most killings (66%) involved intercommunity attacks. Finally, the results suggest an adaptive explanation for lethal aggression as opposed to one rooted in human impact, with the former viewing these killings as part of "an evolved tactic by which killers tend to increase their fitness through increased access to territory, food, mates or other benefits" (Wilson et al. 2014: 414).

In a very recent study on intragroup lethal aggression among West African chimpanzees, Jill Pruetz and colleagues (2017) report on an inferred lethal attack by resident males on a former alpha male at Fongoli in Senegal. The male was overthrown and socially peripheralized for several years before attempting to rejoin the community. The researchers suspect he was attacked and killed by members of the group. Moreover, the deceased body was repeatedly beaten and bitten by both males and females. This case is interesting in that lethal coalitionary aggression in West African chimpanzees usually involves adult males in different communities, rather than within communities. The case is also interesting in that there are few recorded instances of lethal coalitionary aggression in West African chimpanzees as compared to East African populations (Pruetz et al. 2017). One key takeaway offered by the authors is that compared to East African chimpanzees, their West African counterparts, along with bonobos, appear to have faced less selective pressures over evolutionary time under which such aggression was likely to provide fitness benefits for attackers. Hence, this may have resulted in a decreased propensity toward such behavior.

Given these sorts of data, some researchers have proposed that early hominins may have engaged in similar behaviors. Otterbein (2004), for instance, argues that these data would suggest the presence of fraternal interest groups for chimpanzee communities, somewhat akin to those observed with raiding patterns among human hunter-gatherer communities. In writing about raiding, Otterbein proposes that bands of related males within a hunter-gatherer community will form such fraternal interest groups (2004: 60–62). For Otterbein (2004, 2009), the "fraternal interest groups" may have existed among early hominin populations, and if so, could have been a pivotal component for organized aggression.

When it comes to the possibility that both humans and chimpanzees have evolved or become "hard-wired" for these kinds of propensities, Paul Roscoe

(2007) offers a contrasting argument regarding coalitional killing. Citing research suggesting that humans and chimpanzees may actually have an aversion to conspecific killing, Roscoe proposes that their lethal violence is more readily explained by other factors, chief of which is the development of intelligence that affords "envisioning of the future" and the disabling of such aversions to effectuate desired outcomes. Roscoe (2007: 489) writes: "The ability to suppress the perceptions or interpretations that trigger an aversion to killing has been greatly assisted in recent times by developments in military technology, tactics, and organization." He argues that "intelligence is responsible both for the origins of conspecific killing among chimpanzees and humans as well as for its intensification and elaboration among the latter" (Roscoe 2007: 492). This brings up a larger point about the importance of both cognition and culture, and not just biological propensities.

For now, it seems the debates about the significance of biological "hard-wiring" for violent propensities are ongoing, and there are data to support viewpoints that vary both dramatically and in more nuanced ways. But, one pressing question to also consider is: are chimpanzees the only or optimal referent for modeling patterns of hominin behavior? Although mounting reports of chimpanzee lethal aggression have drawn the most attention in the anthropological literature, there are also many reported instances of chimpanzee sociality and conflict resolution that need to be considered (see Verbeek 2013 for examples). In that sense, chimpanzee data used to support a depiction of a warlike and aggressive extant species or of evolutionary ancestors may be a somewhat biased and fragmentary sample. As shown in a recent meta-analysis, by the year 2004, and with more than two hundred years of observation time, there were only 17 suspected and 12 observed examples of adult chimpanzees killing other adults (Sussman 2013). Sussman notes that it is also telling that much of these reports come from regions that may have been disturbed by human presence (Sussman 2013).

Subscribing to a "chimpocentric" (Pickering and Dominguez-Rodrigo 2010: 109) view runs the risk of overlooking or downplaying behavioral aspects of other appropriate referents. Moreover, chimpanzee behavior extends far beyond aggression and includes various forms of sociality. Chimpanzee interactions span a wide social expanse, from peaceful and cooperative to competitive and aggressive (Wilson 2013). In addition, chimpanzee evolutionary change surely has not been stagnant. Extant chimpanzees are the product of millions of years of evolutionary change, and it is possible the kinds of aggressive behavior displayed today were not as prevalent in the deeper past. Different ecological conditions, leading to variations in habitats, predatory pressures, and food availability, have not remained constant throughout geologic history, and chimpanzees have evolved as much as people. As such, how closely do chimpanzees approximate the behavioral patterns of a last common ancestor and/or later hominin populations? As argued by Haslam (2012: 301), the current lack of comparative *Pan* fossils might erroneously promote a sense of stagnancy for the phenotype of all chimpanzees, past and present. However, different ancestral panins, members of the bonobo-chimpanzee lineage, must have existed during their trajectories of evolution during the last 5 to 7 million years

(Haslam 2012: 301; Kumar et al. 2005). And finally, humans are simply behaviorally and cognitively different, implying that many of our hominin ancestors would have been as well. We return to this last point later in this chapter when we discuss "human warfare." In sum, we agree with Carvalho and McGrew (2012: 202) when they argue: "Chimpanzees are insufficient models, if they are presented as the only useful species for reconstructing the hominin fossil record, nor are they time machines, whereby chimpanzee behavior precisely mimics LCA or hominin behavior."

Verbeek (2013: 56–57) points out that chimpanzee sociality is complex and characterized by close relationships among kin and nonkin, somewhat approximating human sociality. But he also argues that they are "sophisticated social actors for whom the interplay between aggression and peace is a fact of life." Related to this point, the intricate interplay of aggression and peace in the lives of chimpanzees does not draw the most attention in comparative investigations of war and peace (Verbeek 2013: 57). Instead, it is predominantly one single aspect of their behavior that garners the most consideration, namely their lethal intergroup aggression. Essentially, the larger message here is that we ought to acknowledge and consider different categories of chimpanzee behaviors, such as both aggressive ones and non-aggressive, peace-promoting ones.

Chimpanzees are not the only referents for modeling human evolutionary behavior, nor are they necessarily the best. A close relative of chimpanzees, the bonobo, has received much research scrutiny in recent years, particularly because of marked contrast in behaviors related to aggression. Bonobos (*Pan paniscus*) are restricted in distribution to the Democratic Republic of the Congo and are less well studied than chimpanzees, with fewer long-term study sites (Doran et al. 2002: 14–15). In many ways, they are similar to chimpanzees. For instance, they are highly frugivorous and marked by a fission-fusion society with female dispersal (Doran et al. 2002: 15). But, as summarized by Wrangham and Peterson (1996: 204–219), bonobo and chimpanzee societies differ in key ways when it comes to violence. "They have reduced the level of violence in relations between the sexes, in relations among males, and in relations between communities" (Wrangham and Peterson 1996: 204–205).

Based on years of observation, researchers have noted a general absence of males forcing copulations, battering females, or practicing infanticide. Tellingly, females cooperate with one another in important ways, and it is possible that female cooperation helps to maintain peace and deter male aggression. An example from wild bonobos helps to illustrate this point. Bonobos are male-philopatric, which means the males stay in their natal group and the females migrate out to new groups. This proves to be an interesting test case for cooperation between females, since the adults in the group are not necessarily genetically related. In other words, they do not gain a fitness boost by helping each other. In a study by Nahoko Tokuyama and Takeshi Furuichi (2016), older females were observed supporting younger females by helping attack males who were aggressive toward them. The researchers argue that such coalitions form to mitigate male harassment, and may also lead to more tolerance among females. Thus, female bonds between nonkin may help to prevent male aggression toward female bonobos.

Additionally, there is comparatively less intercommunity violence, and in some cases, intercommunity interactions can be friendly and cordial. In field observations, such friendliness has always been instigated by females, through various acts ranging from grooming to sexual activities. While violence is not entirely foreign, researchers have not documented the sorts of border patrols, raiding, and lethal aggression seen with chimpanzees. Overall, it is clear that male bonobos do not exhibit the same kinds of violent behavioral patterns sometimes seen with male chimpanzees. For some researchers, this key contrast may be correlated to the hunting and killing of mammals by male chimpanzees (Wrangham and Peterson 1996: 216).

Whether both species of ape lived in their current environmental region for the past 7 million years is, of course, currently unknown. However, the most significant question is to what degree the behavior of chimpanzees and bonobos would be similar to forms of behaviorally modern human culture, especially in light of recent discoveries which suggest that chimpanzees should not be considered the sole referential model for elucidating early human behavior (Sayers et al. 2012).

Overall, the accumulated data on chimpanzees suggest "that we probably share with them the potential for severe aggression between groups and male coercion of females" (Fuentes 2012: 129). But, as Fuentes goes on to write, even chimpanzees vary in how aggression and violence play out across species, subspecies, and communities. Ultimately, these data give us interesting starting points to consider the presence and role of organized violence among our earliest ancestors, but as Fuentes (2012: 129) states, they alone are not sufficient to reflect "an evolved system of lethal aggression and violence in the shared chimpanzee and human history."

Other Primates

Among the other great apes, it is instructive to also note observations of aggression and violence for gorillas and orangutans (see Sousa and Casanova 2005–2006 for a comprehensive summary of great ape agonistic behavior). Generally speaking, orangutans are marked by variable community sizes and social organizations. Violence has been documented between males, and while there are no examples of territoriality analogous to that seen with chimpanzees, resource competition has been seen. Moreover, researchers have documented instances of sexual coercion (Wrangham and Peterson 1996: 132).

With gorillas, forms of sociality and agonistic behavior appear to be variable, with differences existing between populations depending on their habitat and associated food resources (Sousa and Casanova 2005–2006: 81). Though generally peaceful, gorilla interactions can sometimes result in violence. One particularly insightful pattern of behavior is the practice of infanticide by adult males. Though not common, bachelor silverback males have been seen engaging in the killing of infants of other males in attempts to draw the mother away from her current mate (Wrangham and Peterson 1996: 150–151).

As observed by Sapolsky (2013: 421), there is no archetypal "nonhuman primate," and there is enormous variability when it comes to sociality and social groupings among primate species. Recent scholarship seeing *Ardipithecus*, one of the earliest known hominins at 4.4 mya, as being substantially different from chimpanzees has suggested that scientists need to broaden the uses of evolutionary contexts within which they model early human behavior (Sayers et al. 2012). Interesting research on other primates can offer additional insights about human evolution and behaviors related to aggression and violence. Male spider monkeys have been reported to conduct raids similar in behavior to that of chimpanzees (Aureli et al. 2006). The extant *Papionini* are useful analogues for understanding human evolution and behavior, not only due to their complex phylogeny but also because of a wide array of exhibited adaptive behaviors (Jolly 2001). As illustration, a high degree of social malleability was recently observed between two different troops of baboons in Kenya, resulting in contrasting levels of aggression and sociality (Sapolsky 2013). Indeed, as anthropological knowledge of primate behavior has grown, it has become clear significant diversity marks primate adaptation, and concepts such as aggression are less uniform among primates than often believed (Strier 1994). This suggests chimpanzee intergroup violence is not necessarily representative as an analogy for early forms of hominin intergroup violence, and perhaps we ought to augment our consideration of analogies by looking at other primate populations (Fuentes 2013: 84–85; see Brosnan 2013, Kempes et al. 2013, and Sapolsky 2013), or even nonprimate populations (Kokko 2013; Verbeek 2013).

FIGURE 2.3   Olive baboon. © *Sharp Photography. Licensed under Creative Commons 4.0*

Moreover, there is plenty of research to suggest that focusing solely on instances of violent or aggressive behaviors among primates would give us skewed perspectives not only about their behaviors, but about the possible behaviors of our earliest ancestors as well. As noted by Fuentes (2012: 124), a broad overview of the primatological research literature, which would encompass the studies of hundreds of species and tens of thousands of observation hours, demonstrates that intraspecies violence resulting in death is extremely rare and not wide scale. This does not mean that primate life is devoid of conflict or aggression, but it does mean that putting more emphasis on aggression runs the risk of downplaying the overwhelming majority of interactions that are prosocial and cooperative.

Aside from these questions about primates as appropriate referents for modeling hominin behaviors related to violence, we might also ask if there are qualitative differences between human forms of organized violence and those of other species, including great apes. This line of inquiry is especially pertinent for considerations of when we might expect emergent warfare to have made its earliest appearances. To address this question, we must first identify human practices of violence and warfare.

Human Patterns of Organized Violence and Warfare

> Military action is important to the nation – it is the ground of death and life, the path of survival and destruction, so it is imperative to examine it.
>
> *reputedly by Sun Tzu,* The Art of War,
> *5th or 4th century* BC *[1988: 41]*

> May the conscience and the common sense of the peoples be awakened, so that we may reach a new stage in the life of nations, where people look back on war as an incomprehensible aberration of their forefathers.
>
> *Albert Einstein 1934 [1994: 122]*

Captured in the two remarks recorded above by Sun Tzu and Albert Einstein are revealing attitudes about war. Though they were recorded in two very different times and places, they are germane to our discussion about war's place in humanity. Sun Tzu was a warrior-philosopher living over 2000 years ago in ancient China, at a time when the foundations of Chinese civilization were being laid for the birth of an unprecedented imperial phase. Clearly, the quote attributed to him relays the absolute necessity in studying and understanding war, not simply for intellectual reasons, but as a matter of what might be called national security. Telling is the emphasis on the survival of a nation and its people. In regards to the sociopolitical environment of the time and place, warfare was intimately tied to power and society. Textual records exist documenting the significance of war during the first millennium BC of China's Yellow River Valley region, and it is within that era that the earliest parts of what would eventually become the Great Wall of China were being constructed as defensive works. Indeed, both textual and archaeological evidence clearly indicate the cultural importance of violence during the preceding millennium in that region, within what is known as Shang Civilization.

Regarding Einstein's quote, there are two aspects worth noting. First, he references the interactions of nations when it comes to warfare. Second, he appears to espouse the notion that war is an aberration. Hence, it appears that he views war as very much an unfortunate and potentially aberrant phenomenon of our modern nation-state world, and, as such, something that can be avoided through choices. This perspective is not dissimilar to ideas offered by anthropologists and social scientists writing in the 1930s and 1940s, during a time when the horrors of World Wars I and II undoubtedly shaped attitudes about humanity and violence. Indeed, renowned anthropologist Margaret Mead published a paper in 1940 arguing that warfare is a social invention, implying that we can learn to practice new behaviors that make it obsolete.

There are varying perspectives on who engages in warfare, and on true or complex versus simple or inconsequential forms of war (see Keegan 1993; Keeley 1996). Some researchers from certain disciplines such as political science would place war strictly within a context of the historically recent and modern interstate world (see Levy and Thompson 2010 for a discussion). Anthropologists, however, would generally subscribe to a more inclusive conceptualization of warfare, seeing it as a phenomenon that can mark the interactions of various kinds of social groups and societies. Doing so is imperative if we are to understand its long-term history of evolutionary change. This fact is not lost on political scientists Jack Levy and William Thompson (2010: 19) when they write: "The conduct of war has certainly evolved over the millennia – in terms of the nature and size of the political units, the number of combatants, and the nature and lethality of weaponry." For many ethnographers and archaeologists studying warfare, one simultaneously astonishing and sobering observation pertains to the cultural variability associated with practices of organized violence, and how communities of all kinds have been seen to participate in warfare. Given such variability, how should we define warfare?

Some researchers argue that only large-scale societies engage in "true" and what might be called "civilized" war (Keegan 1993). In this view, there is a "military horizon" (Turney-High 1949) that distinguishes the real and "civilized" warfare conducted by states from "primitive" forms of warfare conducted by smaller-scale societies (see Keeley 1996: 10–11). Essentially, this perspective emphasizes that with smaller-scale societies, there is an absence of punitive sanctions for non-participation, as well as clear and institutionalized military leadership (Glowacki and Wrangham 2013: 444). But, we would argue that these are differences more along dimensions of scale rather than kind. Warfare is warfare, especially when you ask people that are involved in all aspects of it. Even with modern warfare today, there are all manner of differences in terms of cultural preferences, motivations, and logistical scale, but also in regards to social organizations and other factors. By that logic, we advocate for an open mind when defining it.

Humans have lived in a world full of large-scale, complex societies for only a small fraction of our entire history on earth. For the vast majority of our species' history, our communities were far smaller, more mobile, and involved hunting and gathering patterns of subsistence (see Chapter Four for more details about various kinds of societies and social organizations). Hence, a consideration of how warfare may have looked in prehistoric manifestations requires both an inclusive definition of warfare as well as an understanding of violence within these smaller-scale societies. The notion that warfare is not a phenomenon restricted to large-scale, highly complex societies allows us to consider a range of social configurations. It also, consequently, permits a consideration for many kinds of behavioral patterns and cultural practices related to various strategies and tactics. These would include murders, raiding, feuding, ambushes, sieges, as well as armed groups engaging on a battlefield. Indeed, much ethnohistoric and ethnographic research shows that the most common form of "combat" among non-state, smaller-scale societies has been raiding or ambushing (Keeley 1996: 65). Hence an inclusive conceptualization of warfare is most useful for anthropological studies. For instance, one of the most influential anthropologists of the 20th century, Bronislaw Malinowski (1968: 247) defined war as "armed contest between two independent political units, by means of organized military force, in pursuit of a tribal or national policy." Along these lines, David Webster (1998: 313) defines warfare as "organized and sanctioned group violence that involves armed conflict, including confrontations that combatants recognize may result in deliberate killing." In his study on the origins of war, Keith Otterbein (2004: 10) offers as his definition "armed combat between political communities." In addition, a productive perspective comes from Brian Ferguson (1984: 5) when he writes that "the basic underlying phenomena characteristic of war can be described as follows: organized, purposeful group action, directed against another group that may or may not be organized for similar action, involving the actual or potential application of lethal force." As should be evident from these characterizations, how one interprets the participants and actions of the phenomenon of warfare will affect how one defines it. What should also be evident is the social nature of warfare. It involves social interactions and coordination among and between groups.

For the purposes of our present study, we would advocate a fairly general definition of warfare, such as the one offered by Slavomil Vencl (1984: 121): warfare as intercommunity armed violence. Of course, researchers can and do specify different kinds of warfare, such as non-state, civil, gang, germ, guerilla, revolutionary, and so forth. But Vencl's definition offers an excellent starting point for evaluating how far back we might see evidence for warfare. It should be noted, however, that this definition and others like it do not specify motivations, agendas, or objectives. Warfare can happen over resources, slights of honor, ideological beliefs, political power, and a myriad of other factors and reasons. While the question of causes is an important one, we are primarily interested in the questions of earliest discernible manifestations for this book.

Warfare: A Human Phenomenon?

"Because war and peace are the staging ground of human actions from dedicated altruism to absolute atrocity, these assumptions about war and peace contain a deeper set of cultural codes concerning fundamental views of humanity and the inhumane" (Nordstrom 1998: 149). In agreement with anthropologist Carolyn Nordstrom, we would see the question of "what is war?" as fundamentally linked to a larger question of "what does it mean to be human?" There is no doubt, of course, that competition, aggression, and violence mark the behavior of many life forms on our planet. Such behaviors connected to non-humans are certainly germane to our understanding of human violence and warfare. But how are human forms of warfare different from lethal intergroup violence seen with other members of the natural world? As discussed earlier, when it comes to coalitionary (and not dyadic) lethal violence, there are notable non-human examples to consider, such as wolves, hyenas, cheetahs, lions, and even certain species of ants. Most intriguing, of course, is evidence of such coalitionary violence among chimpanzees. But, how much similarity is there between human behaviors and practices related to warfare with lethal intergroup violence seen in these other cases?

At their most basic level, the similarities can be striking. Such behaviors involve a degree of cooperation, and, at least for non-human examples, often appear to be precipitated by competition over resources and status. This is particularly the case when considering the chimpanzee referent. But there are important differences to note as well. According to anthropologist Karen Strier (1998: 253), if comparisons between humans and chimpanzees lead to connections about male violence and aggression, then we must also consider the ways in which human patterns could be different. Although chimpanzees use tools and exhibit a form of culture, their behaviors are much less sophisticated and complex in comparison with humans. They lack what some have referred to as a cooperative-communicative ability that humans possess (see Pickering 2013: 59). As noted by Pickering (2013: 59), possession of a "theory of mind" is not unique to humans, as demonstrated by various experiments with chimpanzees. But chimpanzees, in contrast to humans, appear unable to use theory of mind to see and react to cooperative social cues in sophisticated ways, being only able to use it when they are in competitive situations (see Hare 2007 and Karg et al. 2015). Such experimental findings have a very important implication for human warfare, which we see as a highly cooperative-competitive behavioral pattern. By definition, warfare requires cooperation within groups in order for those groups to compete in violent and complex ways with other groups. Although chimpanzees participate in lethal intergroup organized violence, absent is evidence of a capacity for complex communication and sophisticated organization on par with humans engaging in similar kinds of organized violence.

Aside from obvious physical differences, we have evolved to create and bear human culture, which in turn fosters far more complexity in the ways in which we interact and communicate with one another. For instance, humans differ from chimpanzees and other primates in an ability to construct social relationships on a wider scale far beyond the local band, and human warfare occurs within a "social environment" (Layton 2005: 47). The manipulative potential of leaders can play a key role in fomenting organized forms of violence or war (Layton 2005: 47). Though seeing clear parallels in the evolutionary history of both chimpanzees and humans in terms of coalitional killing, Wrangham (1999: 24) does acknowledge a chief difference between the two species when he points out a human use of ideas and "cultural exaggeration of motivating forces" to foster decisions to attack even without any perceived, overwhelming advantage or imbalance of power. When lethal intergroup violence occurs in non-human contexts, it is unclear whether perpetrators of such violence are operating beyond instinctual motivations. As observed by Wrangham (1999), a necessary condition for coalitional violence among chimpanzees involves possession of a preponderance of physical power. In other words, without the numbers, chimpanzees will not attack or participate in organized violence. Humans, on the other hand, operate beyond such proximate determinants. In the end, human culture is a key building block for emergent warfare.

Cultural Practices

The inescapable observation we have come to in our journey is that organized violence for humans is intertwined with our cultural systems. "War is a social practice adopted to achieve specific purposes, but those practices vary with changing political, economic, and social environments and with the goals and constraints induced by those environments" (Levy and Thompson 2010: 1). Indeed, our cultural ideas and practices are such a potent facet of our lifeways that we can create harm in very complex ways, and we can also codify or institutionalize the practices of violence and warmaking. We can devise highly creative ways to harm others without even resorting to the application of violent force. As one of us has written elsewhere, "social inequalities related to power, status, wealth, and access to health can all be considered forms of tacit or latent violence, wherein harm is being caused in some way and over time" (Kim 2012: 249). A host of researchers have provided very interesting insights into various kinds of structural, cultural, and symbolic violence in contemporary societies (Bourdieu 2002; Farmer et al. 2006; Galtung 1969, 1990; Morgan and Bjokert 2006; Scheper-Hughes and Bourgois 2004). While these latent forms of violence might not qualify as overt kinds that result in directly observable physical harm and injury, they can impact quality of life and produce permissible or conducive conditions for violent behavior. Anthropologists Nancy Scheper-Hughes and Philippe Bourgois (2004: 1) note that the violence of poverty, hunger, social exclusion, and humiliation inevitably translates into intimate and domestic violence, and violence can never be understood solely in terms of its physicality alone. In that sense, the social and cultural dimensions of violence provide it with power and meaning (Scheper-Hughes and Bourgois 2004: 1). "A concomitant observation is that violence is culturally patterned behavior, and that rather than being seen as the absence of order, both harmful practices and their contested legitimacy have their roots in cultural logics and socially inculcated dispositions" (Campbell 2014: 5).

The late anthropologist Neil Whitehead produced numerous insightful treatments about human violence, and embedded in his theoretical contributions was a notion of the cultural logic behind acts of violence, which, consequently, leads to a tremendous range of cultural variability attached to attitudes, beliefs, and practices related to violence. As argued by Whitehead (2004: 57), a wide variety of violence "has no immediate material correlates, such as sorcery or verbal aggression." For humans, violence is also part of meaningful cultural expression and is subject to cultural logics (Whitehead 2007). "Violent acts embody complex aspects of symbolism that relate to both order and disorder in a given social context" (Whitehead 2007: 46). Building from this perspective on violence, we must be careful not to subscribe to the idea that warfare is abnormal or pathological (Carneiro 1994: 4). Similarly, in describing human violence, Nordstrom (1998: 154) emphasizes its embedded nature within "a culture-bound system of learned rules, ethics, and actions." In that sense, how, when, why, and where we choose to engage in, or refrain from, organized violence can depend heavily on culture. Our culture-bound systems also shape the ways in which we interpret certain social cues and actions which can lead to violence. As we will discuss in Chapter Six, our earliest forms of warfare may have stemmed precisely from our abilities to embed and perform violence collectively within social milieus.

Insights from the Ethnographic Record

Ethnographic study of contemporary and recent hunter-gatherer societies, of course, is of particular significance in exploring the advent of warfare. This is the case given how long humans have lived in various forms of a hunting, gathering, fishing lifestyle and subsistence pattern. Up until some 10,000 years ago, all people in the world lived in this way. The ethnographic study of violence and warfare, especially among and within hunter-gatherer societies, has produced numerous publications in recent decades (see Allen and Jones 2014; Ember and Ember 1997; Gat 2015; Keeley 1996; LeBlanc 2003, 2014; Otterbein 2004). Many researchers see significant parallels between smaller-scale societies of both the ethnographic present and the prehistoric past before the rise of large-scale, highly complex and agrarian societies. With the mounting evidence that warfare is not a phenomenon restricted to these large-scale societies, such as states, there are vital implications to be drawn from the ethnographic evidence of warfare. It should be noted, though, that many researchers caution against an over-reliance on ethnographic analogues and the extent to which our understanding of hunter-gatherer warfare of the contemporary world can be projected into the past, citing various methodological challenges (see Ferguson 2006 and Haas and Piscitelli 2013). While the uncritical projection of current cultural practices into the contexts of the remote past can be fraught with problems, the use of hunter-gatherer ethnographic data is an indispensable starting point to explore societies of the distant past, particularly because states and other kinds of highly populous and politically centralized societies typically hold a greater monopoly over the use of violence.

A review of the ethnographic record pertaining to violence and warfare makes clear the significance of symbolic thought and cultural ideas. Whether for ritual, political, ideological, or some other reason, humans engage in torture, sacrifice, overkill, and mutilation of other humans. We take captives, body parts as trophies. We enslave each other. Humans will perform rituals of magic or sorcery with the express intent of causing harm to others, and those perceiving magical "assault" might see a legitimate reason to retaliate with physical violence, or to incite their kin to participate in such actions. Research in the 1980s on the Gebusi communities of south-central Papua New Guinea by Bruce Knauft (2011) indicates that much social conflict resulted from perceptions of assault by sorcery causing people to fall ill. Suspected perpetrators of such magical assaults would be subject to execution by the victim's kinfolk, which can ultimately result in communal consumption of the butchered sorcerer (Kelly 2000: 8). Documented ethnographically by Neil Whitehead among contemporary Amerindians of the highlands in Guyana, Venezuela, and Brazil, practitioners of kanaima have participated in "assault sorcery" and "spiritual malignancy," acts involving the ritual stalking, mutilation, lingering death, and consumption of human victims (Whitehead 2002).

For researcher Johan Galtung (1990), the notion of "cultural violence" pertains to the uses of our symbolic sphere of interaction to justify or legitimize forms of harm and violence. The symbols can include anything from flags to speeches to posters. "Cultural violence makes direct or structural violence look, even feel right – or at least not wrong" (Galtung 1990: 291). From that standpoint, it is easy to see how culture is such a vital component in fostering (and inciting) group participation in aggressive and violent acts directed toward others. Ideas about what is acceptable or morally necessary can permeate decisions to use violence. In many nonstate societies, ethnographic research indicates that the stated motivation for feuding and warfare is often tied to revenge or a sense of justice (Keeley 1996). Besides a willingness or ability to engage in violence to rectify any wrongdoing, groups must also use violence or threats of it to protect themselves as deterrence against would-be aggressors (Armit 2010: 3). Whereas larger societies, such as states, have codified laws and ways to enforce justice, such social constructs might come in varied forms in smaller-scale societies, in personal, familial, or community-wide ideas about honor and morality.

In various kinds of post-mortem treatment of the dead, such as dissection, dismemberment, or mutilation, we must note that the acts may be highly cultural, emotionally charged, and symbolic (Nystrom 2014: 767). The mutilation of war dead, for instance, can be a powerful message to enemies, to instill fear, promote political agendas, or deter future retaliation.

One area of study that powerfully illustrates the connection between cultural beliefs, violence, and warfare examines the practice of anthrophagy, or human cannibalism. There are strong indications that our earliest and more recent ancestors participated in forms of cannibalism, as we will discuss in the coming chapters. This can involve the consumption of certain body parts for ritual or symbolic purposes, or it can involve consumption of human meat as food (known as culinary cannibalism) (Keeley 1996: 103). While there is evidence of cannibalism in the natural world, within most non-human contexts, especially for other primates, it appears that cannibalism is conducted mainly in contexts of infanticide. Moreover, the behavior is generally manifested during times of resource stress or in association with reproductive strategies. In contrast, human cannibalism occurs in a wide variety of social contexts, irrespective of environmental conditions or strategies for reproduction. Human cannibalism is far more complex than corresponding behaviors in other extant primates.

As will be discussed in the coming chapters, there is equivocal evidence for cannibalism in very early Pleistocene contexts. But, there are stronger indications of it in more recent Pleistocene timeframes, such as the case of Gough's Cave in present-day Great Britain. Dating to some 15,000 years ago, researchers have uncovered over 200 bones, representing a minimum of six individuals (an infant, two adolescents, and three adults), with good evidence that the bones were processed to extract nutrients. This includes not just cutmarks on the bones but human teeth marks as well (sometimes referred to as 'chew marks'). Perhaps most tellingly, taphonomic reconstruction shows that the heads were removed from the bodies, and then carefully processed to leave the skull cap intact. Researchers conclude that these skull caps were most likely curated. Based on these analyses, it is argued that we have evidence of endocannibalism, showing a ritual practice that may have been common for parts of the Magdalenian population (Bello et al. 2015). But, without more contextual clues, we do not know if such actions were related to violent death, much less a wider social context of intergroup violence.

Citing ethnographic research on cultural practices related to warfare in Fiji (in the South Pacific), anthropologist Robert Carneiro (1990: 202) notes cannibalism as "perhaps the most striking accompaniment of warfare." Observations were recorded in the late 19th century detailing the ways in which warfare between communities often resulted in the cannibalization of enemy victims, with revenge usually a main motive. The victims included more than just enemy warriors, as captive women and children of the enemy community would also be eaten. Surely, these actions were not only retaliatory or vengeful, but would have been important forms of messaging to people both within and outside their community. Carneiro (1990: 205) writes that the practice of cannibalism, while arising out of warfare, "had infiltrated into other aspects of culture." Essentially, the practice became institutionalized, and the capture of potential victims to eat was not only a consequence of war, but came to be a cause for it (Carneiro 1990: 207). War captives, and even members of one's own society, would be sacrificed and eaten for ritual and religious purposes, such as to mark the construction of a new building. The actions related to anthrophagy can thus serve highly complex and symbolic functions – they are culturally laden. This is true for both forms of endocannibalism (targeting members of one's own community) and exocannibalism (targeting members of an outside community). Consider, again, the accounts of cannibalism reported during the Cambodian genocide of the 1970s. These acts did not stem from nutritional need or starvation, but were instead part of symbolic actions meant to convey powerful meanings.

From a wealth of information provided by ethnographic studies and ethnohistoric texts, we can see that violence among human societies is extremely variable and highly embedded in social-cultural systems (Whitehead 2000). Violence writ large is manifested in war and killing, in behaviors such as headhunting, cannibalism, torture, rape, and mutilation (Whitehead 2000: 1). That violent practices and ideas about their moral acceptability may have been important parts of cultural lifeways in the past may be very difficult for many of us in our society to fathom today. But the research on contemporary, recent, and ancient societies makes clear that violence is, and has been, a significant tool of cultural beliefs and interactions.

Going back to the genocide of Cambodia in the 1970s, we can see that violent actions were made legitimate when groups were able to manufacture boundaries in identities (Hinton 2004: 162). This was clearly an artificial and cultural act – to label certain people as insiders versus outsiders, thus making them socially and morally acceptable targets for persecution. Mass killing in Rwanda in 1994 was also facilitated by an arbitrary delineation of one group versus another, pitting a Hutu identity against a Tutsi one. These cases demonstrate the importance of cultural notions of identity, and how people construct identities.

One of the most controversial researchers within anthropology, Napoleon Chagnon, conducted important ethnographic studies of the Yanomami people inhabiting relatively isolated highland areas of Brazil and Venezuela (1968). Perhaps the most contentious of his conclusions was that the Yanomami tribes lived in a state of chronic warfare, marked by constant intervillage raiding, thus holding them up as a contemporary example of humanity's ferocious nature. Many researchers have challenged this Hobbesian depiction of the Yanomami in subsequent years of research (see Ferguson 2004). Despite the critiques of Chagnon's conclusions, there is one aspect of his findings that is very relevant for notions of human warfare. Specifically, Chagnon's research (1988) clearly shows an association between "blood revenge" and motivations for warfare. In blood revenge, kinship obligations are a prime motivation for people to participate in intervillage violence.

For anthropological thought, kinship comprises the complex web of social relationships that are most important in the lives of people. These relationships are with family members, but can be with people related by means other than blood. A fundamentally important feature of kinship is that it can be constructed – someone can be identified as kin through cultural practice. How people affiliate with one another, how they recognize descent, ancestry, and lineage, and how they thus construct identities for themselves and those around them, can play a critical role in obligations they have for one another. A significant amount of research literature has demonstrated a correspondence between aspects of kinship systems, particularly post-marital residence, and patterns of warfare (Ferguson 1990: 36).

Anthropologist Raymond Kelly (2000: 5) outlines how feuds and warfare are grounded in cultural principles or logics of social substitutability. In this notion, people would perceive an injury to an individual member of a group as an injury to the entire group. By the same logic, retaliatory blood revenge can be appropriately taken against any member of the offender's group as well. Therefore, we can clearly analyze warfare as "meaningfully entailed social action" rather than "simply in behavioral terms" (Kelly 2000: 5). Along these lines, researchers recognize the potential that some of the earliest military organizations in human societies would have been made up of individuals that were related or self-identified as kin (Otterbein 2004, 2009). In regards to feuding, Otterbein (2009: 43) refers to a series of revenge-based killings that requires the involvement of kinship groups. In his argument, these are often fraternal interest groups, made up of localized groups of related males that can resort to aggressive measures when the interests of their communities are threatened (Otterbein 2004: 5). Based on these observations about the importance of group identity, it should be clear that emergent warfare may have been intricately linked to the earliest stages of kinship reckoning within social networks and systems. We will return to this notion later in the book.

For now, we reiterate that the ethnographic record of contemporary small-scale societies demonstrates that human violence and warfare are culturally laden. Their associated values, behaviors, rituals, and motivations are what make it distinct from forms of group-on-group violence found elsewhere in the natural world. Many of the cases mentioned above richly illustrate our cultural institutions of war-making, and how they are often intricately tied to many other aspects of societies, from religion to economics. It should also be clear, then, that people choose to adhere to certain ideas and practices related to war. Since that is the case, people can (and do) also choose to produce and follow norms and social rules that promote peace. In other words, the very same basic human capacities for thought and interaction, that serve as a fount for war-making, do so for peacemaking as well. The biological and cultural foundations for emergent warfare provide the same basis for emergent peace. The same sorts of kinship recognition that can be so important in triggering organized violence have the opposite effect as well – they can keep peace. We return to these notions in a later chapter.

Coming Full Circle – Human and Non-human Violence

Recent books about warfare written for general audiences have importantly generated much insight and debate about the evolutionary underpinnings of organized violence (see, for instance, Gat 2006, Pinker 2011, and Smith 2007). Such publications plainly demonstrate the strength of multi-disciplinary and popular interest in topics of aggression and the antiquity of warfare (Cashdan and Downes 2012). Situated within these general debates is a larger one about the nature of violence in humanity.

At this point in our journey, we have by now (hopefully) persuaded you to give certain ideas strong consideration. To recap, uniquely human behaviors and culture separate us from other species, despite the fact that there is no complete consensus around when we become distinctively human. Moreover, today there is sufficient evidence for viewing the emergence of modern human behavior as a gradual process of change, with certain attributes developing at different points in evolutionary time, rather than in some revolutionary moment (circa 40,000 years ago) in just one region (i.e., Europe). We might say that the same kinds of argumentation, ambiguities, and debates that permeate questions of human nature also mark research around early group violence and the origins of warfare. Ultimately, though, we hope we have convinced you that human forms of organized violence are qualitatively different than those seen in other species, despite some similarities along certain dimensions.

As we have seen in this chapter, the work of many researchers has pointed out intriguing parallels between violence in non-human and human populations, whether we are talking about competition over resources and territory, cannibalism, or raiding and ambushing. However, there are clear differences given how humans perceive and interact with each other and the world around us. Humans live not only in a natural world, but very much in highly complex social worlds, ones that we manufacture literally and figuratively. And so much of our behaviors and attitudes is plugged into these latter realms. From that standpoint, the cultural dimensions of warfare of any human society, whether a nation-state of a billion people or a small band of twenty-five, arguably have more in common with each other than with aspects of organized violence within other species. Even those researchers that see parallels between the intergroup aggression of chimpanzee communities and that of human hunter-gatherer communities still acknowledge important differences. Primatologists Richard Wrangham and Luke Glowacki (2012), for instance, observe clear contrasts in regards to risk-taking and risk-aversion. Both chimpanzees and humans are equally risk-averse to fighting, due to the potential for injury and death. But, self-sacrificial war practices are found in humans (think kamikaze suicide attacks during World War II), and they result from cultural systems of group solidarity, prestige, obligation, reward, punishment, and coercion rather than evolved adaptations to greater risk-taking. Hence, cultural overlays are crucial for human forms of warfare. They dictate when people decide to fight and when they decide to avoid fighting. Further, they play a role in how people align themselves in order to develop complex relationships that can promote stability, justice, and peace. "As a broad generalization, war starts when those who start it believe that course is in their own, practical self-interest. Practicality is culturally and historically specific" (Ferguson 2013: 192).

Conflict, competition, and violence are integral parts of the natural world, past and present, and we accept the assumption that our earliest hominin ancestors would have been capable of engaging in analogous forms of conflict, aggression, and violence. However, the larger, fundamental question to be addressed revolves around the notion of human emergent warfare and emergent peacefare. And, for us, this coincides with a human ability to perceive, symbolize, and convey inter-community differences in complex ways. To us, that sort of cognition would be the key to elucidating the timing of emergent warfare and peacefare. In order to address these questions, we have to explore various strands of evidence from the Pleistocene, from fossils to artifacts to genes. But before we do that, we must first turn our attention to how archaeologists and paleoanthropologists actually see violence and warfare in the remote past, beyond the purview of written records. Next stop: the archaeology of violence and war.

Works Cited

Adams, Eldridge. 1990. Boundary Disputes in the Territorial Ant *Azteca trigona*: Effects of Asymmetries in Colony Size. *Animal Behaviour* 39(2), pp. 321–328.

Allen, Mark and Terry Jones. 2014. Hunter-Gatherer Conflict: The Last Bastion of the Pacific Past? In *Violence and Warfare Among Hunter-Gatherers*, edited by Mark Allen and Terry Jones, pp. 15–25. Left Coast Press, Walnut Creek, CA.

Arcadi, Adam, and Richard Wrangham. 1999. Infanticide in Chimpanzees: Review of Cases and a New Within-group Observation from the Kanyawara Study Group in Kibale National Park. *Primates* 40(2), 337–351.

Armit, Ian. 2010. Violence and Society in the Deep Human Past. *British Journal of Criminology* 51(3), 499–517.

Aubert, M., A. Brumm, M. Ramli, et al. 2014. Pleistocene Cave Art from Sulawesi, Indonesia. *Nature* 514(7521), 223–227.

Aureli, Filippo, Colleen Schaffner, Jan Verpooten, Kathryn Slater, and Gabriel Ramos-Fernandez. 2006. Raiding Parties of Male Spider Monkeys: Insights into Human Warfare? *American Journal of Physical Anthropology* 131(4), 486–497.

Austad, Steven. 1983. A Game Theoretical Interpretation of Male Combat in the Bowl and Doily Spider (*Frontinella pyramitela*). *Animal Behaviour* 31(1), 59–73.

Bartlett, Thad Q., Robert W. Sussman, and James M. Cheverud. 1993. Infant Killing in Primates: A Review of Observed Cases with Specific Reference to the Sexual Selection Hypothesis. *American Anthropologist* 95(4), 958–990.

Bello, Silvia M., Palmira Saladié, Isabel Cáceres, Antonio Rodríguez-Hidalgo, and Simon A. Parfitt. 2015. Upper Palaeolithic Ritualistic Cannibalism at Gough's Cave (Somerset, UK): The Human Remains from Head to Toe. *Journal of Human Evolution* 82, 170–189.

Boehm, Christopher. 2012. Ancestral Hierarchy and Conflict. *Science* 336(6083), 844–847.

Bourdieu, Pierre. 2002. *Language and Symbolic Power*. Polity Press, Cambridge, MA.

Bouzouggar, Abdeljalil, Nick Barton, Marian Vanhaeren, et al. 2007. 82,000-year-old Shell Beads from North Africa and Implications for the Origins of Modern Human Behavior. *Proceedings of the National Academy of Sciences* 104(24), 9964–9969.

Brosnan, Sarah. 2013. Conflicts in Cooperative Social Interactions in Nonhuman Primates. In *War, Peace, and Human Nature: The Convergence of Evolutionary and Cultural Views*, edited by Douglas P. Fry, pp. 406–420. Oxford University Press, New York.

Bunn, Henry. 2006. Meat Made Us Human. In *Evolution of the Human Diet: The Known, the Unknown, and the Unknowable*, edited by P. Ungar, pp. 191–211. Oxford University Press, Oxford.

Campbell, Roderick. 2014. Introduction: Toward a Deep History of Violence and Civilization. In *Violence and Civilization*, edited by Roderick Campbell, pp. 1–22. Oxbow Books, Oxford.

Carneiro, Robert. 1990. Chiefdom-level Warfare as Exemplified in Fiji and the Cauca Valley. In *The Anthropology of War*, edited by Jonathan Haas, pp. 190–211. Cambridge University Press, Cambridge.

Carneiro, Robert. 1994. War and Peace: Alternating Realities in Human History. In *Studying War: Anthropological Perspectives*, edited by S.P. Reyna and R.E. Downs, pp. 3–27. Routledge, New York.

Carvalho, Susana and William McGrew. 2012. The Origins of the Oldowan: Why Chimpanzees (*Pan troglodytes*) Still Are Good Models for Technological Evolution in Africa. In *Stone Tools and Fossil Bones: Debates in the Archaeology of Human Origins*, edited by Manuel Dominguez-Rodrigo, pp. 201–221. Cambridge University Press, Cambridge.

Cashdan, Elizabeth and Stephen Downes. 2012. Evolutionary Perspectives on Human Aggression: Introduction to the Special Issue. *Human Nature* 23(1), 1–4.

Caspari, Rachel, and Milford H. Wolpoff. 2013. The Process of Modern Human Origins: The Evolutionary and Demographic Changes Giving Rise to Modern Humans. In *Origins of Modern Humans: Biology Reconsidered*, pp. 355–390. John Wiley & Sons, Hoboken, NJ.

Chagnon, Napoleon. 1968. *Yanomamö: The Fierce People*. Case Studies in Cultural Anthropology. Holt, Rinehart and Winston, New York.

Chagnon, Napoleon. 1988. Life Histories, Blood Revenge, and Warfare in a Tribal Population. *Science* 239(4843), 985–992.

Chapais, Bernard. 2014. Complex Kinship Patterns as Evolutionary Constructions, and the Origins of Sociocultural Universals. *Current Anthropology* 55(6), 751–783.

d'Errico, Francesco. 2003. The Invisible Frontier. A Multiple Species Model for the Origin of Behavioral Modernity. *Evolutionary Anthropology* 12(4), 188–202.

d'Errico, Francesco, Christopher Henshilwood, Graeme Lawson, et al. 2003. Archaeological Evidence for the Emergence of Language, Symbolism, and Music – An Alternative Multidisciplinary Perspective. *Journal of World Prehistory* 17(1), 1–70.

Dellatore, David, Corri Waitt, and Ivona Foitova. 2009. Two Cases of Mother-infant Cannibalism in Orangutans. *Primates* 50(3), 277–281.

Dirks, Paul, Lee Berger, Eric Roberts, et al. 2015. Geological and Taphonomic Context for the New Hominin Species Homo *naledi* from the Dinaledi Chamber, South Africa. *eLife* 4, e09561. DOI: 10.7554/eLife.09561.

Dirks, Paul, Eric M. Roberts, Hannah Hilbert-Wolf, et al. 2017. The Age of Homo *naledi* and Associated Sediments in the Rising Star Cave, South Africa. *eLife* 6, e24231. DOI: 10.7554/eLife.24231.

Doran, Diane, William Jungers, Yukimaru Sugiyama, John Fleagle, and Christopher Heesy. 2002. Multivariate and Phylogenetic Approaches to Understanding Chimpanzee and Bonobo Behavioral Diversity. In *Behavioural Diversity in Chimpanzees and Bonobos*, edited by Christophe Boesch, Gottfried Hohmann, and Linda Marchant, pp. 14–34. Cambridge University Press, Cambridge.

Einstein, Albert. 1994. *Ideas and Opinions*. The Modern Library, New York.

Ember, Carol and Melvin Ember. 1997. Violence in the Ethnographic Record: Results of Cross-Cultural Research on War and Aggression. In *Troubled Times: Violence and Warfare in the Past*. War and Society Volume 3, edited by D. Martin and D. Frayer, pp. 1–20. Gordon and Breach, Amsterdam.

Farmer, Paul E., Bruce Nizeye, Sara Stulac, and Salmaan Keshavjee. 2006. Structural Violence and Clinical Medicine. *PLoS Medicine* 3(10), 1686–1691.

Ferguson, R. Brian. 1984. Introduction: Studying War. In *Warfare, Culture, and Environment*, edited by R. Ferguson, pp. 1–81. Academic Press, Orlando, FL.

Ferguson, R. Brian. 1990. Explaining War. In *The Anthropology of War*, edited by Jonathan Haas, pp. 26–55. Cambridge University Press, Cambridge.

Ferguson, R. Brian. 2004. Tribal Warfare. In *Violence in War and Peace*, edited by N. Scheper-Hughes and P. Bourgois, pp. 69–73. Blackwell, Malden, MA.

Ferguson, R. Brian. 2006. Archaeology, Cultural Anthropology, and the Origins and Intensifications of War. In *The Archaeology of Warfare: Prehistories of Raiding and Conquest*, edited by E. Arkush and M. Allen, pp. 469–523. University Press of Florida, Gainesville.

Ferguson, R. Brian. 2011. Born to Live: Challenging Killer Myths. In *Origins of Altruism and Cooperation*, edited by Robert Sussman and C. Robert Cloninger, pp. 249–270. Springer, New York.

Ferguson, R. Brian. 2013. The Prehistory of War and Peace in Europe and the Near East. In *War, Peace, and Human Nature: The Convergence of Evolutionary and Cultural Views*, edited by Douglas P. Fry, pp. 191–240. Oxford University Press, New York.

Fiskesjo, Magnus. 2001. The Question of the Farmer Fortress: On the Ethnoarchaeology of Fortified Settlements in the Northern Part of Mainland Southeast Asia. *Indo-Pacific Prehistory Association Bulletin* 5(21), 124–131.

French, Jennifer C. 2015. Demography and the Palaeolithic Archaeological Record. *Journal of Archaeological Method and Theory*, 23(1), 1–50.

Fuentes, Agustin. 2012. *Race, Monogamy, and Other Lies They Told You*. University of California Press, Berkeley.

Fuentes, Agustin. 2013. Cooperation, Conflict, and Niche Construction in the Genus *Homo*. In *War, Peace, and Human Nature: The Convergence of Evolutionary and Cultural Views*, edited by Douglas P. Fry, pp. 78–94. Oxford University Press, New York.

Galtung, Johan. 1969. Violence, Peace, and Peace Research. *Journal of Peace Research* 6(3), 167–191.

Galtung, Johan. 1990. Cultural Violence. *Journal of Peace Research* 27(3), 291–305.

Gat, Azar. 2006. *War in Human Civilization*. Oxford University Press, Oxford.

Gat, Azar. 2015. Proving Communal Warfare Among Hunter-Gatherers: The Quasi-Rousseauan Error. *Evolutionary Anthropology* 24(3), 111–126.

Geertz, Clifford. 1973. *The Interpretation of Cultures: Selected Essays*. Basic Books, New York.

Ghiglieri, Michael. 1987. Sociobiology of the Great Apes and the Hominid Ancestor. *Journal of Human Evolution* 16(4), 319–357.

Glowacki, Luke and Richard Wrangham. 2013. The Role of Rewards in Motivating Participation in Simple Warfare: A Test of the Cultural Rewards War-risk Hypothesis. *Human Nature* 24(4), 444–460.

Goodall, Jane. 1977. Infant Killing and Cannibalism in Free-living Chimpanzees. *Folia Primatologica* 28(4), 259–289.

Goodall, Jane. 1986. *The Chimpanzees of Gombe*. The Belknap Press of Harvard University Press, Cambridge, MA.

Goodall, Jane. 1990. *Through a Window, My Thirty Years with the Chimpanzees of Gombe*. Houghton Mifflin Company, Boston.

Green, Richard E., Johannes Krause, Adrian W. Briggs, et al. 2010. A Draft Sequence of the Neandertal Genome. *Science* 328(5979), 710–722.

Haas, Jonathan and Matthew Piscitelli. 2013. The Prehistory of Warfare: Misled by Ethnography. In *War, Peace, and Human Nature: The Convergence of Evolutionary and Cultural Views*, edited by Douglas P. Fry, pp. 168–190. Oxford University Press, New York.

Hare, Brian. 2007. From Nonhuman to Human Mind: What Changed and Why? *Current Directions in Psychological Science* 16(2), 60–64.

Harmand, Sonia, Jason Lewis, Craig Feibel, et al. 2015. 3.3-million-year-old Stone Tools from Lomekwi 3, West Turkana, Kenya. *Nature* 521(7552), 310–315. DOI: 10.1038/nature14464.

Haslam, Michael. 2012. Towards a Prehistory of Primates. *Antiquity* 86(332), 299–315.

Hawks, John. 2013. Significance of Neandertal and Denisovan Genomes in Human Evolution. *Annual Review of Anthropology* 42, 433–449.

Heinsohn, Robert. 1997. Group Territoriality in Two Populations of African lions. *Animal Behaviour* 53(6), 1143–1147.

Henshilwood, Christopher, Francesco d'Errico, Marian Vanhaeren, Karen van Niekerk, and Zenobia Jacobs. 2004. Middle Stone Age Shell Beads from South Africa. *Science* 304(5669), 404.

Hinton, Alexander. 2004.The Poetics of Genocidal Practice. In *Violence*, edited by Neil Whitehead, pp. 157–183. School of American Research Press, Santa Fe, NM.

Hrdy, Sarah. 1974. Male-Male Competition and Infanticide among the Langurs (*Presbytis entellus*) of Abu, Rajasthan. *Folia Primatologica* 22(1), 19–58.

Jolly, Clifford. 2001. A Proper Study for Mankind: Analogies from the Papionin Monkeys and Their Implications for Human Evolution. *Yearbook of Physical Anthropology* 204, 177–204.

Joordens, Josephine C., Francesco d'Errico, Frank P. Wesselingh, et al. 2015. Homo Erectus at Trinil on Java Used Shells for Tool Production and Engraving. *Nature* 518(7538), 228–231.

Karg, Katja, Martin Schmelz, Josep Call, and Michael Tomasello. 2015. The Goggles Experiment: Can Chimpanzees Use Self-experience to Infer What a Competitor Can See? *Animal Behaviour* 105, 211–221.

Keegan, John. 1993. *A History of Warfare*. Vintage Books, New York.

Keeley, Lawrence. 1996. *War Before Civilization*. Oxford University Press, Oxford.

Keeley, Lawrence. 2014. War Before Civilization –15 Years On. In *The Evolution of Violence*, edited by T. K. Shackelford and R. D. Hansen, pp. 23–31. Springer, New York.

Keeley, Lawrence and Nicholas Toth. 1981. Microwear Polishes on Early Stone Tools from Koobi Fora, Kenya. *Nature* 293(5832), 464–465.

Kelly, Raymond. 2000. *Warless Societies and the Origin of War*. University of Michigan Press, Ann Arbor.

Kempes, Maaike, Liesbeth Sterck, and Bram Orobio de Castro. 2013. Conflict Resolution in Nonhuman Primates and Human Children. In *War, Peace, and Human Nature: The Convergence of Evolutionary and Cultural Views*, edited by Douglas P. Fry, pp. 439–447. Oxford University Press, New York.

Kim, Nam. 2012. Angels, Illusions, Hydras and Chimeras: Violence and Humanity. *Reviews in Anthropology* 41(4), 239–272.

Kissel, Marc, and Agustin Fuentes. 2016. From Hominid to Human: The Role of Human Wisdom and Distinctiveness in the Evolution of Modern Humans. *Philosophy, Theology and the Sciences* 3(2), 217–244.

Kissel, Marc, and Agustin Fuentes. 2017. Semiosis in the Pleistocene. *Cambridge Archaeological Journal*. In press.

Klaus, Haagen D. 2012. The Bioarchaeology of Structural Violence: A Theoretical Model and a Case Study. In *The Bioarchaeology of Violence*, edited by Debra L. Martin and Ryan P. Harrod, University Press of Florida, Gainesville.

Klein, Richard. 2009. *The Human Career: Human Biological and Cultural Origins, Third Edition*. University of Chicago Press, Chicago, IL.

Knauft, Bruce. 2011. Violence Reduction Among the Gebusi of Papua New Guinea – And Across Humanity. In *Origins of Altruism and Cooperation*, edited by Robert Sussman and C. Robert Cloninger, pp. 203–225. Springer, New York.

Kokko, Hanna. 2013. Dyadic Contests: Modelling Flights Between Two Individuals. In *Animal Contests*, edited by I. Hardy and M. Briffa, pp. 5–32. Cambridge University Press, Cambridge.

Krug, Erienne, Linda Dahlberg, James Mercy, Anthony Zwi, and Rafael Lozano (eds.). 2002. *World Report on Violence and Health*. World Health Organization, Geneva.

Kumar, Sudhir, Alan Filipski, Vinod Swarna, Alan Walker, and S. Blair Hedges. 2005. Placing Confidence Limits on the Molecular Age of the Human–Chimpanzee Divergence. *Proceedings of the National Academy of Sciences* 102(52), 18842–18847.

Layton, Robert. 2005. Sociobiology, Cultural Anthropology and the Causes of War. In *Warfare, Violence and Slavery in Prehistory*, edited by Mike Parker Pearson and I.J.N.

Thorpe, pp. 41–48. British Archaeological Reports International Series 1374. Archaeopress, London.

LeBlanc, Steven (with Katherine Register). 2003. *Constant Battles*. St. Martin's Press, New York.

LeBlanc, Steven. 2014. Forager Warfare and Our Evolutionary Past. In *Violence and Warfare Among Hunter-Gatherers*, edited by Mark Allen and Terry Jones, pp. 26–46. Left Coast Press, Walnut Creek, CA.

Levy, Jack, and William Thompson. 2010. *Causes of War*. Wiley-Blackwell, Malden, UK.

Linzey, Andrew (ed.). 2009. *The Link Between Animal Abuse and Human Violence*. Sussex Academic Press, Portland, OR.

Lockwood, Randall, and Frank Ascione (eds.). 1997. *Cruelty to Animals and Interpersonal Violence*. Purdue University Press, Lafayette, IN.

Lorenz, Konrad. 1963. *On Aggression*. Harcourt, Brace and World, New York.

Malinowksi, Bronislaw. 1968. An Anthropological Analysis of War. In *War*, edited by L. Bramson and G. W. Goethals, pp. 245–268. Basic Books, New York.

McBrearty, Sally, and Alison Brooks. 2000. The Revolution That Wasn't: A New Interpretation of the Origin of Modern Human Behavior. *Journal of Human Evolution* 39(5), 453–563.

McCall, Grant, and Nancy Shields. 2008. Examining the Evidence from Small-scale Societies and Early Prehistory and Implications for Modern Theories of Aggression and Violence. *Aggression and Violent Behavior* 13(1), 1–9.

McComb, Karen, Craig Packer, and Anne Pusey. 1994. Roaring and Numerical Assessment in Contests between Groups of Female Lions, Panthera leo. *Animal Behaviour* 47(2), 379–387.

McDougall, Ian, Francis Brown, and John Fleagle. 2005. Stratigraphic Placement and Age of Modern Humans from Kibish, Ethiopia. *Nature* 433(17), 733–736.

Mead, Margaret. 1940. Warfare Is Only an Invention, Not a Biological Necessity. *Asia* 15(8), 402–405.

Mech, L. David, Layne Adams, Thomas Meier, John Burch, and Bruce Dale. 1998. *The Wolves of Denali*. University of Minnesota Press, Minneapolis.

Morgan, Karen, and Suruchi Thapar Bjorkert. 2006. "I'd Rather You'd Lay Me on the Floor and Start Kicking Me": Understanding Symbolic Violence in Everyday Life. *Women's Studies International Forum* 29(5), 441–452.

Mosser, Anna, and Craig Packer. 2009. Group Territoriality and the Benefits of Sociality in the African Lion, Panthera leo. *Animal Behaviour* 78(2), 359–370.

Nishida, Toshisada, and Kazuhiko Hosaka. 1996. Coalition Strategies among Adult Male Chimpanzees of the Mahale Mountains, Tanzania. In *Great Ape Societies*, edited by William McGrew, Linda Marchant, and Toshisada Nishida, pp. 114–134. Cambridge University Press, Cambridge.

Nordstrom, Carolyn. 1998. Deadly myths of aggression. *Aggressive Behavior* 24(2), 147–159.

Nystrom, Kenneth. 2015. The Bioarchaeology of Structural Violence and Dissection in the 19th-Century United States. *American Anthropologist* 116(4), 765–779.

Otterbein, Keith. 2004. *How War Began*. Texas A & M University Press, College Station.

Otterbein, Keith. 2009. *The Anthropology of War*. Waveland Press, Long Grove, IL.

Pickering, Travis. 2013. *Rough and Tumble: Aggression, Hunting, and Human Evolution*. University of California Press, Berkeley.

Pickering, Travis, and Henry Bunn. 2012. Meat Foraging by Pleistocene African Hominins: Tracking Behavioral Evolution beyond Baseline Inferences of Early Access to Carcasses. In *Stone Tools and Fossil Bones: Debates in the Archaeology of Human Origins*, edited by Manuel Dominguez-Rodrigo, pp. 152–173. Cambridge University Press, Cambridge.

Pickering, Travis, and Manuel Dominguez-Rodrigo. 2010. Chimpanzee Referents and the Emergence of Human Hunting. *The Open Anthropology Journal* 3, 107–113.

Pickering, Travis, and Manuel Dominguez-Rodrigo. 2012. Can We Use Chimpanzee Behavior to Model Early Hominin Hunting? In *Stone Tools and Fossil Bones: Debates in the Archaeology of Human Origins*, edited by Manuel Dominguez-Rodrigo, pp. 174–197. Cambridge University Press, Cambridge.

Pinker, Steven. 2011. *The Better Angels of Our Nature: Why Violence Has Declined*. Viking, New York.

Polis, Gary, Christopher Myers, and William Hess. 1984. A Survey of Intraspecific Predation within the Class Mammalia. *Mammal Review* 14(4), 187–198.

Powell, Adam, Stephen Shennan, and Mark G. Thomas. 2009. Late Pleistocene Demography and the Appearance of Modern Human Behavior. *Science* 324(5932), 1298–301.

Pruetz, J.D., P. Bertolani, K. Boyer Ontl, S. Lindshield, M. Shelley, and E.G. Wessling. 2015. New Evidence on the Tool-assisted Hunting Exhibited by Chimpanzees (Pan troglodytes verus) in a Savannah Habitat at Fongoli, Sénégal. *Royal Society Open Science* 2(4), 140507.

Pruetz, Jill, Kelly Ontl, Elizabeth Cleaveland, Stacy Lindshield, Joshua Marshack, and Erin Wessling. 2017. Intragroup Lethal Aggression in West African Chimpanzees (Pan troglodytes verus): Inferred Killing of a Former Alpha Male at Fongoli, Senegal. *International Journal of Primatology* 38(1), 31–57. DOI: 10.1007/s10764-016-9942-9.

Reich, David, Nick Patterson, Martin Kircher, et al. 2011. Denisova Admixture and the First Modern Human Dispersals into Southeast Asia and Oceania. *The American Journal of Human Genetics* 89(4), 516–528.

Roebroeks, Wil, Mark J. Sier, Trine Kellberg Nielsen, et al. 2012. Use of Red Ochre by Early Neandertals. *Proceedings of the National Academy of Sciences* 109(6), 1889–1894.

Roscoe, Paul. 2007. Intelligence, Coalitional Killing, and the Antecedents of War. *American Anthropologist* 109(3), 485–495.

Sapolsky, Robert. 2013. Rousseau with a Tail: Maintaining a Tradition of Peace Among Baboons. In *War, Peace, and Human Nature: The Convergence of Evolutionary and Cultural Views*, edited by Douglas P. Fry, pp. 421–438. Oxford University Press, New York.

Savage-Rumbaugh, Sue and Roger Lewin. 1994. *Kanzi: The Ape at the Brink of the Human Mind*. John Wiley and Sons, Inc., New York.

Sayers, Ken, Mary Ann Raghanti, and C. Owen Lovejoy. 2012. Human Evolution and the Chimpanzee Referential Doctrine. *Annual Review of Anthropology*, 41, 119–138.

Scheper-Hughes, Nancy, and Philippe Bourgois. 2004. Introduction: Making Sense of Violence. In *Violence in War and Peace: An Anthology*, edited by Nancy Scheper-Hughes and Philippe Bourgois, pp. 1–27. Blackwell Publishing, Oxford.

Semaw, Sileshi, Michael Rogers, Jay Quade, et al. 2003. 2.6-million-year-old Stone Tools and Associated Bones from OGS-6 and OGS-7, Gona, Afar, Ethiopia. *Journal of Human Evolution* 45(2), 169–177.

Seyfarth, Robert, Dorothy Cheney, and Peter Marler. 1980. Vervet Monkey Alarm Calls: Semantic Communication in a Free-Ranging Primate. *Animal Behaviour* 28(4), 1070–1094.

Shea, John. 2003. Neandertals, Competition, and the Origin of Modern Human Behavior in the Levant. *Evolutionary Anthropology* 12(4), 173–187.

Shea, John. 2011. *Homo sapiens* Is as *Homo sapiens* Was. 2011. *Current Anthropology* 52(1), 1–35.

Silverberg, James, and J. Patrick Gray. 1992. Violence and Peacefulness as Behavioral Potentialities of Primates. In *Aggression and Peacefulness in Humans and Other Primates*, edited by James Silverberg and J. Patrick Gray, pp. 1–36. Oxford University Press, New York.

Smith, David Livingston. 2007. *The Most Dangerous Animal*. St. Martin's Press, New York.

Sousa, Claudia, and Catarina Casanova. 2005–2006. Are Great Apes Aggressive? A Cross-species Comparison. *Antropologia Portuguesa* 22–23, 71–118.

Strier, Karen. 1994. Myth of the Typical Primate. *Yearbook of Physical Anthropology* 37, 233–271

Strier, Karen. 1998. On Demonic Males: Apes and the Origins of Human Violence by R. Wrangham and D. Peterson. *American Journal of Physical Anthropology* 105(2), 252–253.

Strier, Karen. 2010. *Primate Behavioral Ecology*, 4th Edition. Routledge, New York.

Sun, Tzu. 1988. *The Art of War*. Translated by Thomas Cleary. Shambhala Publications, Boston.

Sussman, Robert. 2013. Why the Legend of the Killer Ape Never Dies. In *War, Peace, and Human Nature: The Convergence of Evolutionary and Cultural Views*, edited by Douglas P. Fry, pp. 97–111. Oxford University Press, New York.

Taylor, Tim. 2005. Ambushed by a Grotesque: Archaeology, Slavery and the Third Paradigm. In *Warfare, Violence and Slavery in Prehistory*, edited by Mike Parker Pearson and I.J.N. Thorpe, pp. 225–232. BAR, Oxford.

Taylor, Mitchell, Thor Larsen, and R.E. Schweinsburg. 1985. Observations of Intraspecific Aggression and Cannibalism in Polar Bears (Ursus Maritimus). *Arctic* 38(4), 303–309.

Tokuyama, Nahoko, and Takeshi Furuichi. 2016. Do Friends Help Each Other? Patterns of Female Coalition Formation in Wild Bonobos at Wamba. *Animal Behaviour* 119, 27–35.

Turney-High, Harry. 1949. *Primitive War: Its Practice and Concepts*. Reissue with new preface and afterword. University of South Carolina Press, Columbia, 1971.

van der Dennen, J.M.G. 1995. *The Origin of War: The Evolution of a Male-coalitional Reproductive Strategy*. Origin Press, Groningen, Netherlands.

Vencl, Slavomil. 1984. War and Warfare in Archaeology. *Journal of Anthropological Archaeology* 3(2), 116–132.

Verbeek, Peter. 2013. An Ethological Perspective on War and Peace. In *War, Peace, and Human Nature: The Convergence of Evolutionary and Cultural Views*, edited by Douglas P. Fry, pp. 54–77. Oxford University Press, New York.

Watts, David, and John Mitani. 2000. Infanticide and Cannibalism by Male Chimpanzees at Ngogo, Kibale National Park, Uganda. *Primates* 41(4), 357–365.

Webster, David. 1998. Warfare and Status Rivalry. In *Archaic States*, edited by Gary Feinman and Joyce Marcus, pp. 311–351. School of American Research Press, Santa Fe, NM.

White, Tim, Berhane Asfaw, David DeGusta, et al. 2003. Pleistocene Homo sapiens from Middle Awash, Ethiopia. *Nature* 423(6941), 742–747.

Whitehead, Neil. 2000. A History of Research on Warfare in Anthropology – Reply to Otterbein. *American Anthropologist* 102(4), 7–9.

Whitehead, Neil. 2002. *Dark Shamans: Kanaima and the Poetics of Violent Death*. Duke University Press, Durham, NC.

Whitehead, Neil. 2004. On the Poetics of Violence. In *Violence*, edited by Neil Whitehead, pp. 55–77. School of American Research Press, Santa Fe, NM.

Whitehead, Neil. 2007. Violence & the Cultural Order. *Daedalus* 136(1), 40–50.

Wilson, Michael. 2013. Chimpanzees, Warfare, and the Invention of Peace. In *War, Peace, and Human Nature: The Convergence of Evolutionary and Cultural Views*, edited by Douglas P. Fry, pp. 361–388. Oxford University Press, New York.

Wilson, Michael, William Wallauer, and Anne Pusey. 2004. New Cases of Intergroup Violence among Chimpanzees in Gombe National Park, Tanzania. *International Journal of Primatology* 25(3), 523–549.

Wilson, Michael, Christophe Boesch, Barbara Fruth, et al. 2014. Lethal Aggression in Pan is Better Explained by Adaptive Strategies than Human Impacts. *Nature* 513(7518), 414–417.

Wilkins, Jayne, Benjamin J. Schoville, Kyle S. Brown, and Michael Chazan. 2012. Evidence for Early Hafted Hunting Technology. *Science* 338(6109), 942–946.

Wrangham, Richard. 1999. Evolution of Coalitionary Killing. *Yearbook of Physical Anthropology* 42(S29), 1–30.

Wrangham, Richard, and Luke Glowacki. 2012. Intergroup Aggression in Chimpanzees and War in Nomadic Hunter-Gatherers: Evaluating the Chimpanzee Model. *Human Nature* 23(1), pp. 5–29.

Wrangham, Richard, and Dale Peterson. 1996. *Demonic Males: Apes and the Origins of Human Violence.* Houghton Mifflin, Boston.

Wrangham, Richard, Michael Wilson, and Martin Mueller. 2006. Comparative Rates of Violence in Chimpanzees and Humans. *Primates* 47(1), 14–26.

Young, Barry and Robert Ruff. 1982. Population Dynamics and Movements of Black Bears in East Central Alberta. *The Journal of Wildlife Management* 46(4), 845–860.

Zilhao, Joao 2012. Personal Ornaments and Symbolism among the Neandertals. *Developments in Quaternary Science* 16, 35–49.

3

THE RECENT, THE ANCIENT, AND THE VERY ANCIENT PAST

How far back can we see clear evidence of warfare in the world? Superficially, the answer is as far as historical horizons allow us to see. Far to the west of China's Yellow River Valley, which was the geographic locus of Sun Tzu's descriptions of ancient warfare, the importance of violence for powerful, large-scale civilizations throughout parts of Southwest Asia, the Near East, and Northern Africa have been recorded on various media, such as the Narmer Palette of ancient Egyptian Civilization and the Standard of Ur with its depiction of a Sumerian army, both created some 5 thousand years ago. This time period sees some of the earliest forms of writing and recorded history anywhere in the world. From those ancient, early historic eras through today, echoes of warfare have reverberated from the past, chronicled in textual accounts and oral traditions the world over. Globally, the majority of the earliest written records from various regions are filled with reports of fighting and wars (Vencl 1984: 117). Any review of humanity's recorded history of the past several thousand years reveals "a continuous stream of warfare and violence between nations, states, ethnic groups and religions" (Haas 2004: 11).

But, if we were to rely solely on textual records, we would leave blank the overwhelming majority of humanity's history. After all, our earliest ancestors in Africa were walking upright several million years ago, making crude stone tools as early as 3 million years ago, and may have been intentionally harnessing and controlling the power of fire around 1 million years ago. Historical documents can provide a rich source of information about our current, recent, and ancient practices of warfare and violence. But how do we explore the very ancient (and even recent) eras for which we have no literary sources? Lying beyond the boundaries of history, beyond domains of myth and legend, are hazy areas of the past that require recovery and analysis of material remains of past peoples. Archeological research allows us to reconstruct events, cultural patterns, and lifeways. To date, a host of innovative approaches and methods of archaeological research has yielded interesting ideas about the antiquity of warfare.

The Long and the Short of It

Various methodological tools have been developed within the discipline of archaeology to help us penetrate the prehistoric and deeper areas of our past. In recent decades, more and more archaeologists have turned their attention to aspects of violence and warfare in prehistory. A robust archaeology of violence and warfare has been developed since the 1990s, and has resulted in a plethora of case studies worldwide. One of the pivotal publications that helped to catalyze this surge of research was a book by Lawrence Keeley, entitled *War Before Civilization* (1996). Chief among his arguments was the idea that the prehistoric past was not as peaceful as many believed. Using a combination of ethnographic analogy, historical documents, and archaeological data, Keeley persuasively demonstrated that for many world regions, smaller-scale, nonstate societies were not unfamiliar with outbreaks of warfare, no matter how sporadic or infrequent these episodes may have been. Certain smaller-scale societies, observed in contemporary settings, provided glimpses into the past, yielding information that could then be used as a starting point to interpret the archaeological record. In sum, he argued that warfare was an activity that any kind of society, whether "civilized" or not, could have experienced given the right circumstances.

Though elements of his arguments have been challenged and critiqued (see Ferguson 2013a; Haas and Piscitelli 2013), the larger thrust of his message has proven to be quite influential – that archaeologists ought to start looking for signs that violence may have been just as deadly and consequential in a deeper past of "non-civilizations" as it has been in a more recent past dominated by "civilizations." His work, along with the research of many other anthropologists and archaeologists, led to a burgeoning archaeology of warfare (Gat 2006; Arkush and Allen 2006; Carman and Harding 2004; Chacon and Mendoza 2007; LeBlanc 2003; Kim 2012). "These works, particularly Keeley's, put forward a persuasive call for archaeologists to take a fresh look at the evidence for warfare in their respective regional records" (Allen 2014: 15). Prior to this new trend, most of the 20th-century anthropological attempts to explore prehistoric or nonstate warfare were based primarily on ethnographic information, with little input from archaeologists (Allen 2014: 16).

There have been two important outcomes of this recent surge in research. The first, as mentioned, has been the accumulation of archaeological data from countless studies and global areas. The second outcome, just as significant, has been an intensification of debates around the antiquity of warfare. Unquestioned is the existence of warfare in the recent past, but how do we now evaluate its variability, intensity, and frequency in ancient and very ancient contexts? How far back into the "very ancient" past might we see evidence of warfare? As noted by Mark Allen (2014: 17), there is a general polarity in views between a long versus short chronology of warfare, and there is even disagreement over what constitutes "long" and "short." Does warfare have deep or shallow roots? In a nutshell, contrasting views over a long versus short chronology hinge on how one appreciates the totality of evidence.

Otterbein (2004: 30) provides a comprehensive overview of the history of Western social scientific research on warfare. Depending on the school of thought, warfare is seen to have begun at different points in humanity's history, as early as 2 million years ago or as late as 6000 years ago. Sometime within the past 12,000 years or so (known geologically as the Holocene Epoch), many human societies began to change in their patterns of subsistence lifestyles. For many researchers, the roots of warfare are seen only in the (more recent) ancient past, coinciding either with the rise of agriculture or the emergence of civilizations (see Fry 2006 and Haas 2001). In this view, true, impactful, or significant warfare only occurred with larger-scale, populous, complex societies or civilizations, which did not exist prior to the Holocene. Whether tied to the political agendas of complex or highly populous polities or to the advent of agricultural production with fixed assets locked into landscapes, many argue that true warfare begins in the Holocene. Some even make a distinction between "primitive" or "ritual" warfare versus "true" or "civilized" warfare, separated by a "military horizon" (Keegan 1993). In contrast, others propose a longer history of consequential warfare, moving back into the Pleistocene Epoch (a geological time period lasting from about 2.6 million years ago to the start of the Holocene) (Gat 2006; Guilaine and Zammit 2001; Keeley 1996; Kelly 2000, 2005; LeBlanc 2003, 2014a, 2014b). Before discussing the methods by which the material record is explored and evaluated for warfare, we first outline the general state of debates around warfare's proposed antiquity.

The Antiquity of Organized Violence: The Last 12,000 Years

Although we may hold spectacular mental images and notions of wars occurring between large forces or massive armies on a battlefield, the archaeological record reveals that different kinds of organized fighting have occurred throughout the Holocene. We can today point to many different kinds of warfare, all connected to myriad tactics, ideologies, values, and cultural practices (Campbell 2014; Fry 2013; Gat 2006; Levy and Thompson 2010; Otto et al. 2006). Researchers have documented clear signs of violent practices in the material record of various world regions within the Holocene Epoch (Arkush and Allen 2006; Keeley 1996; Martin et al. 2012). The world entered the Holocene Epoch some 12,000 years ago, at which point the Ice Ages of the preceding Pleistocene Epoch came to an end. Warmer and wetter climates around the globe contributed to a very general shift toward more sedentary living and increased experimentations in the care of wild plants and animals. It is no accident that the earliest signs of domestication and farming begin at this time, with the earliest evidence coming from what is referred to as the Fertile Crescent (parts of modern-day Iraq, Syria, Lebanon, Jordan, Israel, and Egypt). A combination of environmental and social conditions set the stage for a gradual shift from predominantly hunting and gathering to mixed and agricultural lifeways. Within a few millennia, many societies around the world began to live in more settled and agricultural ways. With more people living in larger, more permanent settings with greater investments into the land, more surpluses were generated, more mouths could be fed, and civilizations began to grow. It is within this period that signs of organized violence ramp up, prompting many researchers to conclude that the origins of warlike behaviors are to be found within this time period (Ferguson 2013b; Fry 2006; Haas and Piscitelli 2013). Additionally, some researchers would also argue that warfare was largely absent or insignificant for humanity prior to the advent of sedentary, large-scale, and complex societies of the past 6,000 years, due to a lack of material clues about warfare in earlier eras.

Although it is possible that warfare began in the Holocene after general shifts to large-scale, sedentary, agricultural settlements, it is just as likely that we see more signs of warfare in this more recent time period simply because of access to material evidence – we have more evidence of all aspects of lifeways in general. This would be a matter of sampling bias, wherein absence of evidence of warfare does not necessarily mean that warfare was nonexistent or inconsequential. With larger, more permanent settlements, there is much more evidence of residential patterning, subsistence practices, trash, various products, burials, and so forth. This may be the reason why we see more evidence of warfare after the rise of civilizations – because we have far more cultural data to unearth and sift through. Consequently, finding any signs of violence in prehistoric smaller-scale communities, many of which were highly mobile, can be very telling.

To address the issue of sampling bias, we can look at ethnohistoric and ethnographic accounts of recent and contemporary societies that are smaller scale and mobile, seeing evidence of organized violence within these cases. Doing so suggests that warfare is not restricted to complex, sedentary, farming societies. Though social and political conditions in large-scale societies may be conducive for large-scale aggression, all peoples in any sociopolitical configuration are capable of performing organized violence. Believing otherwise runs the risk of trivializing the cultural practices of some populations, including their ways of warfare, thus downplaying their cultural agency.

Pleistocene Stones and Bones: Variations and Manifestations Before 12,000 Years Ago

Various lines of anthropological research strongly suggest that practices of violence and warfare have been present, to varying degrees, in humanity's history well into the Holocene past and likely earlier than the appearance of highly complex societies (Bowles 2009; Carman and Harding 2004; Estabrook 2014; Guilaine and Zammit 2001; Golitko and Keeley 2007; Gordon 2014; Haas 2004; Haas and Piscitelli 2013; Keeley 1996; Kelly 2005; LeBlanc 2003; Milner 2005; Otterbein 2004; Vencl 2004). Of course, the behaviors (and their resulting material correlates) that qualify as warfare can be subjective and highly debatable. But, if we were to broaden the activities to be explored into a category of emergent warfare and the earliest expressions of interpersonal and group violence in our species, what can we see in the material record?

Currently, there is an important debate regarding the presence and prevalence of organized violence within our deeper evolutionary past, and just how early such forms of behavior began to transpire. For some researchers, both within and outside of anthropology, humanity's distant past was probably marked by extreme violence, and it is only with the advent of complex civilizations and state societies that we began to see greater levels of peace, security, and stability as part of the human condition (Goldstein 2011; Pinker 2011). Much of this perspective is necessarily based on how one interprets certain anthropological, paleoanthropological, and archaeological datasets. For example, political scientist Bradley Thayer (2004) argues for a clear link between natural selection, fitness, and warlike behaviors within our evolutionary past, offering clues about the origins of war.

The Pleistocene commenced over 2.5 million years ago, coming to a close when the last Ice Age ended and the Holocene Epoch began. Archaic humans lived much more mobile lifeways, and usually did not leave their dead in contexts that would be easy for modern-day archaeologists to find. Though they may have used all kinds of materials to make tools, products, and clothing, the oldest evidence of human culture comes to us only in the form of stone. A very small sample size of stone tools and fossil remains has survived in the archaeological record for our earliest ancestors. For these very distant pasts, it becomes vital to use both material evidence and analogical comparison, since the material evidence is scarce and often equivocal, leading to sometimes wildly different opinions about the presence or absence of violence. We are today using a combination of complementary anthropological approaches, consisting of the fossil record, the archaeological record, primatological studies, ethnographic research on extant populations of small-scale human communities, and innovations in paleogenomic studies (which will be discussed in detail in Chapter Five).

At the moment, there are enough clues in the fossil record of the entire globe demonstrating various forms of trauma, suggesting the possibility of interpersonal violence and even of cannibalism. Indications warranting greater attention, as will be discussed in the next chapter, come from parts of Europe and Asia and date to the past 1 million years. According to some researchers, finds such as the Maba cranium and its indications of blunt force trauma to the head strongly indicate interhuman aggression. Dating to about 130,000 years ago, the cranium is part of a small but important sample of Middle or Late Pleistocene human remains with probable evidence of humanly induced trauma (Wu et al. 2011).

There are, of course, issues to consider when interpreting these sorts of finds. First, the signs of trauma and skeletal damage, including signs of butchering and possible cannibalism, may or may not be related to interpersonal violence and homicide. Second, even in cases of interpersonal violence and homicide, we may not necessarily be looking at organized violence (or some emergent form of warfare), though these cases may suggest the possibility for the latter's presence. Third, how one interprets these finds depends on one's own perspective. Does the presence of such indicators on scarce finds means that violent behaviors are common? Or does the absence of a plethora of such finds suggest violence was uncommon? Whatever the case may be for these kinds of questions, it is clear that there are enough clues to warrant ongoing research and much closer scrutiny. This is especially so for the later part of the Pleistocene, within the past 20,000 years or so, where the bodies of data for violence increase and become much more compelling (Guilaine and Zammit 2001). It is only toward the end of the Pleistocene that the evidence for interpersonal violence becomes stronger, with greater indications of intercommunity violence.

Evolutionary psychologist Steven Pinker, in his volume *The Better Angels of Our Nature* (2011), maintains that we are living in the most peaceable era of human history, and that our earliest and even recent ancestors were far more violent than we are today. While Pinker offers an intriguing assertion, there are some problems to note with this view (Kim 2012). To begin, this perspective about the prevalence of violence in prehistory is based on a fragmentary and incomplete view of available research, especially when considering our deeper evolutionary past. As will be discussed in the next chapter, the evidence suggesting possible trauma and violence in the Pleistocene tends to be both limited and ambiguous. Based solely on the material record, arguments can be made for either the presence and intensity, or general rarity, of organized violence. Moreover, not everyone would characterize our current era as the most peaceable. According to Grant McCall and Nancy Shields (2008: 8), there has been no time in human prehistory with a larger scale of violence than at the present. And, importantly, a perspective emphasizing the pervasiveness of violence deep in human ancestry tends to minimize or ignore the social and cooperative behaviors of hominins, to the detriment of a fuller understanding of humanity (Fuentes 2004, 2013; de Waal 1996). Surely, the reality of social worlds that our hominin ancestors lived in must have been much more complicated. In response to views held by researchers such as Pinker, we do not deny the possibility that forms of collective violence occurred within our deeper past, but we advocate a fuller engagement with all of the available evidence. We are in agreement with Armit (2010: 2) when he argues that we should not view violence in isolation, "but at one end of a spectrum that extends from empathy and friendship to antipathy and hate." In the end, the material record does provide strong signs of violence within the Pleistocene, mostly of an interpersonal variety, but with some indications of organized violence. We explore this world of Ice Ages (pre-12,000 BP) in the next chapter. But first we discuss the archaeological methods that researchers use in order to identify warlike practices.

Archaeological Methods for Identifying Violent and Warlike Behaviors

Documenting the existence of warfare in prehistoric contexts, much less its frequencies and impacts, is not an easy task. Depending on the time period, the nature of materials, preservation conditions, and a host of other factors (including pure chance for when things are found by archaeologists), certain activities leave traces in the material record while others leave absolutely nothing for us to find. To complicate the matter, war is complex. As noted by Ferguson (1990: 26), war is not simply action. "It is a condition of and between societies, with innumerable correlates in virtually every dimension of culture" (Ferguson 1990: 26). There may be pre-parations for war that do not lead to actual combat, for instance, or ceremonies performed before or after war that leave no material record. How does one archaeo-logically recognize a condition or situation of the ancient past, especially one that, as we have established in the last chapter, can be extremely variable in cultural practice, involving all manners of tools, activities, and rituals? This makes the archaeological study of very ancient warfare highly complex, and it may be part of the reason why people traditionally did not see much violence/warfare in prehistoric contexts. Faced with this vast universe of cultural facets linked to war, how can we hope to identify it in all its manifestations and related activities in the prehistoric past?

The simple answer is we cannot identify all facets, at least not for all cases and with a high degree of accuracy and comprehensiveness. We can catch glimpses here and there, at times with a more complete picture than others. That being said, researchers have come up with very good methods to collect clues, interpret them, and combine streams of evidence in piecing together the larger puzzle that is war. We are able to produce snapshots of bygone eras. Moreover, because archaeological evidence spans long stretches of time we are able to show how cultures and their practices emerge and transform. We now highlight these tools and methods, presenting the suite of material markers people use to identify the presence of (or concerns over) violent activities in the past.

There are several categories of material evidence that can help us recognize warfare in the past (Haas 2001; Keeley 1996; Keeley et al. 2007; Kim and Keeley 2008; Kim et al. 2015; Lambert 2002; LeBlanc 2003). Because warfare is an activity that involves the behavior and actions of many individuals and affects several aspects of social life, several independent lines of evidence are necessary (Keeley 2001: 339). "Warfare leaves many different kinds of traces in the archaeological record, so debates that hinge on a single question of interpretation – the use of a tool-weapon or the design of a wall – will best be resolved through the exploration of other lines of evidence" (Arkush and Stanish 2005: 20). A diversity in the forms of warfare means that we need a package of material signatures to document its existence and cultural importance. In the coming pages, we review the ways in which scientists have been able to archaeologically ascertain evidence for warfare. This is not an exhaustive treatment, but is meant to provide an overview. In particular, we pay more attention to those markers that are most relevant to studying the earliest possible instances of violence and warfare.

Site and Settlement Markers

Site and settlement data comprise a useful signal to indicate warfare, though these markers can often be hard to interpret. Warfare can be reflected by concerns over

TABLE 3.1 Material markers for warfare (adapted from Kim et al. 2015)

Direct	Indirect
Trauma on skeletal remains	Habitation in elevated or inaccessible areas
Defensive architecture and settlement features	Sites in strategic locations
Deliberate destruction of property	Refuges or temporary habitation sites
Specialized equipment, such as weapons and armor	Buffer zones and fortified frontiers
Iconographic depictions	Sudden disruption/intrusion of cultural patterns

threats, and archaeologists can determine such concerns through a number of ways, such as how communities choose locations for settlement. Examples can include living in inaccessible areas or elevated areas, such as hilltops or ridges, suggesting considerations of natural barriers, visibility, and protection. If such areas are sited far away from water sources or agricultural fields, they may indicate a very real concern over outside threats.

Related to settlement data would be evidence of destruction or sudden abandonment. Arson, burning episodes, and other deliberate acts of destruction of property and structures provide strong contextual evidence for warfare. The burning of structures is a common consequence of war, and burned structures and settlements can document actual attacks (Kim and Keeley 2008). Researchers must be careful, however, to separate instances of deliberate burning due to attack from accidental fires, or from intentional fires due to clearing, ritual, or ceremony. Again, a larger context of evidence is required to accompany this type of signal.

Another potential indicator comes in the form of buffer zones or "no-man's-lands," which are unpopulated or sparsely populated areas between two potentially adversarial communities. Although communities along frontier areas can experience peaceful interactions, episodic breakdowns in relationships and disputes can occur, promoting the avoidance of such areas (Keeley 2001: 338). Frontiers between different cultural and subsistence traditions can be particularly dangerous (Hill and Wileman 2002: 96–97). Buffer zones have been documented in various contexts from Africa, Asia, North America, South America, and Oceania (Keeley 1996: 111). It should be noted, though, that these areas can only be identified when population sizes are large and when there is sufficient settlement data (Theler and Boszhardt 2006), information we simply do not have for the Pleistocene.

Fortifications

Sitting in the Jordanian Desert, the archaeological site of Jericho has yielded evidence of habitation and settlement dating as far back as the beginning of the Holocene. Successive settlements at the location saw constructions of various architectural features, including, at some point, a large perimeter wall and tower made of stone. For some, these features may be defensive, while for others they served non-military functions (see Hill and Wileman 2002: 22; Otterbein 2004: 32). There is significant and ongoing debate about the functions, and this case aptly illustrates how interpretations of data can vary greatly, leading to very different theoretical implications. Many of those arguing for the defensiveness of Jericho's architecture would thus point to a healthy concern over security and possible war in the early Holocene. Many of those arguing for other functions, such as flood control, would see warfare as largely absent prior to the mid-Holocene, or without the existence of a complex polity such as an ancient state.

Not all walls or enclosures are fortifications, nor do all the features typically found at known fortifications have purely military functions (Keeley et al. 2007: 56). Curtain walls might simply operate as peaceable barriers with no military function. In present-day Pakistan, the ancient settlement of Harappa (c. 5000 years ago), for example, had very large walls, but they appear to have functioned in a symbolic or commercial way, regulating traffic and restricting access for exchange purposes (Kenoyer 2008: 56). In North American prehistory, Mississippian towns and settlements, including Cahokia, had walls, fences, and enclosures to socially divide space, protecting ritual space (and potentially elite private space) from the

FIGURE 3.1   Photograph of the archaeological site of Jericho, which was first settled some 11,000 years ago. Depicted in the photograph is the "tower", the function of which has been the source of much debate. *Photograph by Reinhard Dietrich*

outside world, while also excluding those on the outside from interior activities (Pauketat 2007: 100).

However, many enclosures of ancient settlements did possess defensive utility in addition to other functions. For instance, we know from a combination of archaeological and historical evidence that cities in ancient China during the first millennium BC were fortified with outer walls, and that Roman legions would typically build palisade walls and defensive ditches when on the move in foreign territories. When historical documentation attesting to a military purpose is unavailable, archaeologists rely on other clues about architectural designs and attributes to infer defensive function, such as V-shaped or deep ditches, defended or baffled gates, bastions, and a host of other indicators (Keeley et al. 2007: 57). We have become increasingly aware of many examples of prehistoric fortified sites the world over, associated with different kinds of culturally distinct societies. Cahokia, for instance, featured a palisade wall perimeter that was punctuated by bastions spaced evenly apart, showing us that functions can be mixed – walls can simultaneously demarcate space, provide privacy, and also defend.

During the Holocene and by the time people started living in a more settled, agricultural lifestyle with houses, villages, and fields, many societies began fortifying their homes and communities (Hill and Wileman 2002: 11). Fortifications had the potential to alter regional political landscapes dramatically. They constitute one of the most obvious indicators of warfare or the threat of war, and they are essentially omnipresent in the archaeological record of most cultural regions (Allen and Arkush 2006: 7). Defensive features have been built by all types of state and nonstate societies, and according to Keeley (1996: 55), fortifications are the costliest and

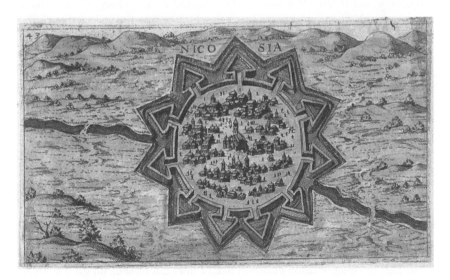

FIGURE 3.2 Historic map of Nicosia, circa 17th century. Note the presence of bastions which are still visible in present-day Nicosia. *From Viaggio da Venetia a Constantinopoli per Mare (1597)*

largest-scale pieces of pre-industrial technology and thus demonstrate that threats of attacks were strong enough to warrant such costly constructions.

Some of the earliest farming communities of Europe, the bearers of Linearbandkeramik (LBK for short) Culture, began moving from areas of Eastern Europe into points further west some 7,000 years ago. Hundreds of LBK sites have been documented, making the LBK one of the best-studied Neolithic cultures of Europe, and in recent decades researchers have been documenting much evidence that LBK communities were not only concerned about settlement defense but also participated in organized violence (Golitko 2015; Golitko and Keeley 2007; Keeley 1996). There is clear evidence that many of their villages were fortified against potential attack, either by neighboring hunter-gatherer communities or by other LBK village communities (Golitko and Keeley 2007). The evidence comes in the form of palisade walls with defensive ditches and human remains with evidence of violent trauma. Moreover, archaeologists have also analyzed the chemical composition of artifacts to see patterns of trade and exchange between groups of people, and have used those patterns to infer community ties and possible alliances against threats (see Golitko 2015). The data for the LBK culture underscore the need to use multiple lines of evidence, while also telling us that nonstate, smaller-scale communities are just as capable of using organized violence as an option when deemed necessary.

Related to fortifications is the use of refuges (see Webster 1998: 326). As seen in numerous archaeological and ethnographic cases, refuges have been used by many different kinds of societies, such as the refuge caves of Hawai'i (Kolb and Dixon 2002), refuge rock-island escapes or lookouts in Pacific Rim islands off Alaska (Maschner and Reedy-Maschner 1998: 32), and rock shelters of East African communities hiding from slave-raiders (Kusimba 2006). Refuges, even those found far from settlements, should be interpreted as evidence for warfare (Arkush and Stanish 2005: 9). The use of refuges as opposed to the fortification of settlements can provide some indication about the frequency or expectation of warfare within a region. Rather than maintaining an enclosure around an entire village, having a temporary refuge location nearby would have been a less costly option if the threat of attack was not constant.

Iconography

While artistic representations of warfare are common in historic times,[1] artistic expression of this type is fairly recent and does not show up until the Neolithic and Bronze Age (which dates to between approximately 3300–500 BC in various parts of the Old World), when we begin to see state-level societies. Some classic examples, like the Royal Standard of Ur, dated to around 2600 BC, suggest warfare at a grand scale. But, the interpretation of these kinds of finds can be difficult since it is hard to know what might be propaganda inherent in many of these artifacts. Nonetheless, the imagery of warfare, whether it depicts actual history or not, still indicates that warfare is known and has happened.

Iconographic depictions can come in the form of rock art, sculptures, figurines, and pottery decoration. Depictions of warfare-related activities, warriors, and associated paraphernalia can offer clues about past cultural practices. They can provide some functional context for the weapons and tactics of different societies, even if it is difficult to determine the frequency or intensity of warfare for a given society. Again, however, a problem with these representations is an uncertainty over whether they represent scenes of real life or mythological events (Lambert 2002: 211).

Nevertheless, over the past 20,000 years, rock art has been found in Western European contexts depicting forms of violence (Guilaine and Zammit 2001: 54). Examples depict scenes in which human or anthropomorphic figures have been struck by projectiles or are possibly being tortured (Guilaine and Zammit 2001: 54–60). While violence is shown in these cases, it is difficult to determine whether they represent actual cases of warfare. Less ambiguous examples are seen in a collection of Neolithic rock paintings, known generally as the art of the Levant, which have been discovered in parts of Mediterranean Spain (Guilaine and Zammit 2001: 102–111). In these cases, battle scenes are depicted in greater detail, where separate groups of people are shown fighting using bows and arrows. In South American prehistoric contexts, there is ample evidence of artistic depictions of

FIGURE 3.3   The "Decapitator" Plaque associated with the Moche Culture of the Andes in South America, dating to the first millennium AD. *Source: The Metropolitan Museum of Art*

headhunting, captive-taking, and sacrifice throughout the Andean mountain chain and highlands (Proulx 1999). Representations of head taking can be seen in the art of various cultures and societies, including the Chavin, Moche, Huari, Nasca, and the Inca.

Weapons and Specialized Equipment

Depending on context, weapons designed for use against humans can potentially indicate the presence of warfare. There are challenges in identifying implements as weapons (designed for warfare) versus tools for hunting, construction, or farming. In prehistoric North America weapons were mostly the same as, or virtually indistinguishable from, everyday tools (Milner 1999: 109). But, again, context is very important. For instance, implements found in warrior burials can usually be interpreted as having possible military functions (Junker 1999; Underhill 2006). Additionally, certain types of implements are more clearly specialized for warfare, such as close-range shock weapons like tomahawks, maces, lances, daggers, and swords (Keeley 1996: 50).

In discussing categories of weapons, John Chapman (1999) proposes a solution to the problem of overlapping function of objects equally useful for both warlike and peaceful aims: a continuum with four classes of artifact category – tools, tool-weapons, weapon-tools, and weapons. Similarly, Vencl (2004: 65) uses ethnographic analogues to offer a number of categories for human weapon technologies: occasional (any tool used in emergency, such as sickle or pebble); non-specialized (all artifacts combining both tool and weapon functions, such as bow, knife, or axe); and specialized, made primarily for the purpose of inter-human violence, such as swords. Ultimately, tools can be used as weapons and weapons may be used as tools, making it hard to ascertain function in many situations. One example, given by Brian Ferguson (Ferguson, 2013a), concerns mace-heads. While we tend to think of maces as weapons, many mace-heads are made of light material and are quite small, and thus inefficient as weapons. Instead, they may symbolize authority. However, that does not obviate the likelihood that the mace came to take on a powerful symbolic meaning after its uses as a physical instrument of power.

Bioarchaeological Markers

Bones, CSI, and other forensic-based TV shows have increased the public awareness of how scientists are able to ascertain cause of death in recent murder victims. Interestingly, some of these same principles can be applied to ancient skeletons as well. In 1991, hikers stumbled across the well-preserved body of a man who died in the Alps some 5,300 years ago. This man, who would come to be called Otzi, has been one of the most intensely studied ancient persons (Pernter et al. 2007). Otzi was so well preserved that we can see tattoos on his body, and much of his clothing and possessions were found intact. Researchers continue to study these remains, and as new technologies are brought to the table, astonishing information continues to emerge. For instance, based on the study of his stomach contents, scientists can figure out what he ate shortly before death, even determining the season of his death (spring or early summer). Using computed tomography (CT) analysis, researchers were also able to see evidence of massive bleeding after a flint arrowhead pierced his shoulder and lacerated an artery. An unhealed wound to the hand along with trauma to the back of the head combine to suggest he was probably involved in some kind of fight that resulted in his death. Blood residues recovered and analyzed from some of his associated artifacts even suggest that at least three other people may have been involved in events leading to his death. Now, whether this was part of warfare is anyone's guess. The only conclusion we can reach with this case is that Otzi was a victim of interpersonal violence or homicide.

Some of the best evidence we have for organized violence comes from the study of human remains. Biological anthropologists and bioarchaeologists study human remains in order to understand the culture and behavior of an individual's life. This can be done in many different ways. Bioarchaeologists study the human skeleton to search for signs of trauma and stress in the individual's life, providing a picture into not only that individual's history but also indicating something about the culture they lived in. These scholars often refer to a specialized science known as taphonomy, which studies everything that can happen to an individual (be it a human or animal) from the moment the organism dies to when it is studied by an archaeologist.

"Bioarchaeology offers empirical data that help unravel large and important questions about humans and their long relationship with violence" (Martin et al. 2012: 2). As many publications and studies show, the analysis of human remains is one of the most important ways to consider both interpersonal and organized violence, regardless of time period (Knusel and Smith 2014; Martin et al. 2012; Walker 2001). The archaeological study of human remains offers a unique source of data on both violent conflict and peaceful coexistence (Walker 2001). The remains of humans can thus operate as the best indicator of violence, and, as we discuss in the next chapter, this is especially the case for the earliest contexts of violence in the Pleistocene.

In many archaeological contexts, telltale signs for violence can include projectile points embedded in skeletal materials, fractures or cutmarks on bones, scalp or cut marks on crania, and dismemberment or other signs of trophy taking (Kim and Keeley 2008). The unceremonious treatment or mutilation of bodies is also a potential indicator of violence. Parry fractures on forearms, suggesting attempts to defend against blows, is also a very good indicator of violent actions. Sometimes such evidence comes from the recovery of a single individual, like Otzi, or from cemeteries, or even, very rarely, in battlefield or aftermath contexts. The kinds of contexts can be very revealing. Generally speaking, mass graves, or exposure and unceremonious burials without grave goods and signs of ceremony for the dead, can all be potential indicators, as well as a higher frequency of adult male deaths within a cemetery.

For many researchers, signs of violent deaths at the Jebel Sahaba cemetery site in northern Sudan along the Nile represent some of the earliest definitive evidence for collective violence. Dating to some 12–14,000 years ago, artifacts and trauma found in association with skeletal remains strongly imply high rates of violence occurring among different social communities. Here, men, women, and children exhibited either direct evidence of weapons trauma or projectile points associated with their remains (Wendorf 1968). Several adults had multiple wounds, and many of the children had execution style wounds on the head or neck. Somewhat akin to the Otzi case, whether these individuals were killed in warfare is up for debate, and more information would be needed.

In the previous chapter, we talked about headhunting and how this practice could be culturally variable in why it happens and its meanings. While decapitation can be related to any number of various motivations, some of which have nothing to do with warfare, the act can also be heavily tied to intergroup violence. The act of decapitation, when linked to acts of trophy-taking, can indicate the possible presence of intergroup violence or warfare. For many societies, a warrior's prestige or spiritual power could be increased depending on the reputation of a defeated adversary, and often the head served as a personal manifestation of that enemy (Carneiro 1990; Keeley 1996: 100). Such trophies could symbolize a warrior's prowess and courage. For North American prehistory, the removal of scalps and heads was often part of the mutilation of enemies (Milner et al. 1991: 584). In South American prehistory, trophy heads were often taken and carefully displayed in ritual in the Andean highlands of societies such as the Wari Culture of the first millennium AD (Arkush 2006). An important Wari ceremonial structure at Conchopata contained a cache of six burned trophy heads – skulls with post-mortem perforations on the forehead enabling them to be carried or displayed with cord (Arkush 2006: 291). Research by Tiffiny Tung and Kelly Knudson (2011) indicates that some of the victims whose heads were used as trophies were likely non-locals, captured during raids and warfare. Andean trophy heads were often carefully prepared and cached in locations associated with ritual, suggesting that they held ideological significance (Arkush 2006: 292). Decapitation and the subsequent ritual use of human heads was a common practice in ancient Peruvian cultures (Proulx 1999). In the end, we can point to the practice of trophy-taking not just of heads, but of all body parts, with the archaeological record of many regions showing these kinds of practices occurring for thousands of years (Andrushko et al. 2010; Keeley 1996; Lambert 2007; Walker 2001).

Another potential sign of violence directed against members of an outside community can be seen in cannibalism, as detailed in the last chapter. Archaeologically, cannibalism is discernible as an extreme form of bodily mutilation, and the Holocene is full of examples (Keeley 1996: 103). Seeing human remains treated in much the same way as prey animals constitutes evidence of cannibalism, and signatures include cutmarks, dismemberment, and other signs of postmortem processing. While it is important to remember that even in instances where a strong case for cannibalism is shown, this does not necessarily mean that someone was killed to obtain their flesh (Walker 2001: 586). However, when this indicator is combined with other clues about violent behaviors, then a stronger case for homicide is possible.

While cases like Otzi and others from the Holocene can provide a wealth of fine-grained details, the reality is that the overwhelming majority of ancient human remains do not preserve so well. And the further back in time, usually the less material there is with which to work. This is especially the case for the Pleistocene, where we rarely have complete and articulate anatomies, making cause of death all the more difficult to judge. Tantalizing clues come from cases such as an individual from the Sima de los Huesos site in northern Spain, dating to over 400,000 years ago (discussed more in the next chapter). This case indicates the intentional use of violent force, further suggesting homicide and interpersonal violence is likely as old as our species. But those sorts of cases tell us very little about why violence may be happening, and who might be involved.

In one sense, it is rather easy to identify signs of interpersonal violence in the skeleton. In fact, many examples from the mid-Holocene onward show well-defined signs of trauma and violent death, and many of these are attributed to war. However, there are several challenges associated with the archaeological visibility of social violence with human remains. First, some unhealed (i.e., perimortem or fatal) injuries are difficult to distinguish from secondary, postmortem damage. Second, any sustained injuries to soft body tissue are beyond our ability to detect. In addition, cremation was a prevalent burial practice for many societies throughout human history, thus leaving little to be recovered. Finally, archaeological sources may not be able to provide evidence of the large number of people lost in warfare battles, and of the other war casualties that could not be buried.

Let us say you excavate a cemetery and, out of one hundred burials, five of them have signs that they were killed by arrows (e.g., there is an arrowhead embedded in the pelvic bone). What can you determine from this sample? Some would suggest that violence was rather low, as only 5% of the population died from war. Others, though, would argue that this underrepresents the prevalence of violent death, as simply counting the number of traumatic marks is not enough. Archaeologist George Milner (2005) argues that to calculate mortality we need to take into account more than just the osteological evidence. By studying historical records from the 19th century Indian Wars of the American West, he shows that only one in three arrows (in this case, most of the arrowheads were made of iron, but some were made from chipped stone/wood) damaged bone, with the rest inflicting wounds in soft tissue only. Secondly, he noted that around half of the patients survived their wounds. This suggests that the 5% count from the above example would underestimate the actual amount of injury due to violence and warfare. But applying this study to earlier time periods is problematic. For one, the bow and arrow do not appear until later in the Pleistocene, so much of the earliest evidence we have would be hand-to-hand combat resulting in blunt force trauma. The weapons used in the Pleistocene were mostly made of stone and probably consisted of either thrusting or throwing spears, and it is unclear if the percentage of direct bone injuries would be similar.

Going back to our example above, let's imagine that out of the five individuals recorded as having died violently, three of them have arrowheads embedded in their bones, one has signs of recent trauma to his rib, and the last one has signs of healed femur along with an arrowhead that was buried alongside the individual. Does this last individual "count" as a victim of warfare or violence? It is hard to tell. The arrowhead could have been the object that killed him, having been implanted in the body and then recovered by an archaeologist. However, another interpretation is that the arrowhead was buried with the person as a grave good, an object buried with a person as a sign of respect or to be used in the afterlife. Or it could simply have fallen into the open grave by accident. Teasing apart these issues is very difficult. Because of the challenges in "seeing" violence in the past, Keeley (1996: 91) notes that the actual percentage of violent deaths may be much higher than the obvious examples seen in the archaeological record would tell us. If a small percentage of the ones found show trauma, he argues that traumatic events may actually be common since skeletons are rarely completely preserved and then excavated. In other words, we must account for the people who died during warfare but whose bodies do not show obvious signs of trauma, along with bodies that were not buried in a grave that would eventually be found by archaeologists.

Crossing the Streams Is Good

In the 1984 movie *Ghostbusters*, we are told that "crossing the streams" is a bad thing. Of course, the characters were wielding "proton packs," fictional energy weapons that fired a stream of protons, and the quote refers to how crossing the streams of protons would be bad. Well, in our case, we are referring not to fictional energy weapons in a movie but to streams of evidence. Here, crossing the streams is vital for our exploration of the past. It is much like the enterprise of a trial lawyer building a case. The more evidence, the more complete a cultural reconstruction and the more one can say about a society and its practices. In the end, more evidence means stronger inferences. There are many examples to illustrate how powerful the methodological tools and approaches described above can be in answering research questions, provided that sufficient information is available to bolster interpretations. Below we offer a variety of cases separated by space and time that illustrate the nature of archaeological interpretation of violence and warfare.

In 2013, archaeologists in China uncovered the skulls of more than 80 young women along the outer stone walls of an ancient city at Shimao, dating to more than 4000 years ago. The current interpretation is that these individuals were likely sacrificed as part of ancient religious rituals or related to the founding of the city and its wall construction. But, it is unclear who the victims might have been, how they were selected, and if they came from outside communities. Was this part of larger warfare-related activities? Without more data, it is difficult to say.

At the 7700-year-old site of Ofnet in Germany, researchers uncovered two pits containing the remains of 38 individuals (Frayer 1997: 185). Studies indicate that the adult males were struck across the back of the head with an axe, and cut marks were visible on skulls and vertebrae of men, women, and children, indicating decapitation. The skulls were covered in red ochre, and buried with them were

FIGURE 3.4 Drawing of the cache of skulls found at Ofnet. *Source:* Wikimedia Commons. © *Wellcome Library, London. Licensed under Creative Commons 4.0*

shells and deer teeth that had been perforated. But, is this evidence of warfare? Given the absence of additional evidence, it is difficult to conclude much else about the case aside from the fact that these individuals were killed and their heads were intentionally placed in these pits. Was this a massacre, a sacrificial offering, or some other kind of event? Was this an act of war? Was this violence and punishment within a society? Were the skulls curated and placed in the pits by the same people that performed the violence? Again, we simply do not know.

Not far away and only seven centuries later, another find comes to us with intriguing evidence and implications. A mass grave dating to 7,000 years ago was uncovered in Talheim, Germany, linked to the Linearbandkeramik Culture, discussed above. The mass grave found near Talheim had skeletal remains of 34 individuals, who appear to have been the victims of a massacre, based on the presence of numerous lethal head wounds, several arrow wounds, and the placement of all of these individuals in the same burial pit (Price et al. 2006). There were no grave goods, nor was there any sign of care or ritual connected to the mass burial, all contributing to the notion that this was a massacre event. What is striking about this time and region, in fact, is the presence of numerous cases of apparent massacre, with accompanying evidence of sacrifice, possible cannibalism, and the taking of body parts as trophy items (Price et al. 2006). For some of these early farmers of Europe, violence appears to have been a significant part of their lives. These conclusions are based on a combination of defensive features suggesting fears over attack, along with signs of blunt force trauma as the cause of death on skeletal remains from several sites across the LBK region. Very recently, archaeologists uncovered yet another site, known as Schoneck-Kilianstadten, with similarly unequivocal osteoarchaeological evidence of indiscriminate lethal violence, torture and mutilation, and disposal of corpses in a chaotic mass grave (Meyer et al. 2015).

Staying in Germany, another LBK village site known as Herxheim offers a glimpse into patterns of violence. Deposits were uncovered that contain the remains of some 500 individuals, and much of the remains appear to have undergone mutilation of some kind, with many skulls being fashioned into "calottes" (Boulestin et al. 2009). Studies show that the victims range from the newborn to the elderly, and there are signs of intentional breakage of bones, defleshing, and cannibalism. According to the researchers analyzing the site and its remains, a scenario of survival cannibalism is highly improbable, with the evidence suggesting a standard, repetitive and strongly ritualized practice (Boulestin et al. 2009: 979). Whatever the case, we can see that forms of violence would have been socially important and meaningful for the local communities.

Still in Germany and from a much later time period, a very clear case for outright warfare comes from the Tollense Valley. Chance discoveries of along a riverbank yielded numerous weapons, horse bones, and human skeletal remains with evidence of trauma from projectiles and face-to-face combat. Subsequent research has identified them as all associated with each other, strongly indicating that they are the debris from a Bronze Age battle dating to approximately 1200 BC (Jantzen et al. 2011). Though there are no historical accounts for the battle(s), the combination of material evidence provides a clear and unambiguous context for warfare, perhaps even with individuals professionally outfitted and trained to participate in war.

Anatomically modern humans were the first people to colonize Australia, and this may have happened as early as 50,000 years ago. For many researchers, the relative isolation of the continent, and the persistence of hunting/gathering lifeways and stone technologies through time up until contact with Europeans in recent centuries, combine to make Australia an important "laboratory" to observe organized violence and warfare without interference from outside "civilizations" (Gat 2006, 2015; LeBlanc 2003). Importantly, ethnohistoric accounts from the early contact period provide glimpses of warfare, including motivations, preparation, alliance building, and many other related cultural practices (Gat 2015). Using a combination of skeletal, historical, and ethnographic data, Colin Pardoe (2014) demonstrates how complementary lines of evidence can lead to very important insights about societies. The result is a comprehensive examination of regional variation in patterns of violence across different ecological zones.

Similar pan-regional studies across long chronological stretches can be seen for societies of North America (Lambert 2002; Milner et al. 2013) and South America's Andean highlands (Arkush and Tung 2013). Such studies make use of settlement patterns and cranial trauma from the material records, mapping them against large-scale cultural changes as well as shifting environmental patterns through time. Another example from the New World illustrates warfare among hunter-gatherer communities of ancient California. Archaeologists working at a precontact site called CA-ALA-554 in California uncovered a mass burial of seven people dating to 1100 years ago. Both the style of the burial and the lack of grave goods are rare for this region. This, plus the fact that many of the skeletons show signs of trauma, suggests that the individuals were victims of violent death. A recent isotopic and genetic study of these bodies provides more in-depth analysis (Eerkens et al. 2015). Isotope data suggest intergroup warfare led to the mass burial, and genetic data indicate the raiding party included sets of unrelated men, perhaps from different households.

By examining the isotopic values in the bones and teeth of those buried, researchers were able to determine that all of the skeletons interred in the mass grave were essentially "foreigners" or people from other regions. Their isotopic signatures are very different from the other, customary burials at the site, suggesting that they were non-locals and not associated with the other burials. Further analysis shows that the individuals may have moved twice, once from their place of birth when they were teenagers and the second time when they ended up at the CA-ALA-554. This suggests to the researchers that they were forced to move from their home due to population growth and expansion. The authors postulate that a group of people moved away from a village, due to population pressure, and started a new community in a different area. This move brought them into conflict with the people from CA-ALA-554, putting them into territorial disputes involving access to natural resources.

Beyond giving us a glimpse into the motivations, causes, and practices of warfare for this time and place in Central California, this case also demonstrates the power of a multi-pronged approach that uses archaeological data, ethnographic research, and anthropological concepts to reconstruct past lifeways and societies. Also put to use are complementary and cutting-edge techniques for analyzing isotopes and DNA found in these ancient individuals, allowing us to answer the more complex questions around "who" and "why" when it comes to warfare. We can put the puzzle pieces together to see that competition over territory was probably a major reason resulting in outbreaks of organized violence, and this understanding stems from various streams of evidence.

A well-known case of warfare comes from South Dakota at the Crow Creek site. Here a mass grave was uncovered in the 1970s with nearly 500 men, women, and children that appeared to have been killed in a single episode of massacre sometime in either the 1300s or 1400s (Bamforth and Nepstad-Thornberry 2007). In addition to the evidence of trauma, including scalping, mutilation, and fractures from heavy blows, there is evidence that many of the homes in their village were burned, thus suggesting attack from outsiders. The analysis of the victims' bones suggests that local populations were undergoing a time of resource stress, with signs of malnourishment. Moreover, the village had evidence of fortification construction prior to the massacre. Lastly, analysis of tree ring data indicates periods of drought marked the area in this time period. Based on all of these clues, we can make a very educated guess that the warfare seen here was related to hard times and food shortages.

Using ethnographic data from contact-era New Guinea, Paul Roscoe (2008) sheds light on the logic of settlement fortifications in terms of design and operational functioning. Most archaeologists interpret fortifications as a means to defend against intrusion and attack – to prevent access by outsiders. For certain village and tribal societies, though, Roscoe's research shows how this can be an oversimplification. The New Guinea evidence reveals that settlement fortifications were designed not just to keep attackers out but, even more important, to keep them in once they had penetrated and launched their attack. Defenders could then rally and annihilate their assailants, creating a powerful deterrent against attack in the first place. The implication here is that knowledge about this functional aspect of settlement fortifications would not have been obvious to archaeologists had they not been privy to ethnohistoric accounts describing this practice.

As demonstrated in all of these aforementioned cases, human violence and warfare are embedded within cultural practices and belief systems. Accordingly, a blend of evidence is paramount for producing the most compelling conclusions. In that spirit, we now highlight a few areas where the archaeology of violence and warfare need further refinement and development, to ensure the most complete reconstructions possible of past cultures. In some of these areas, new methods or perspectives are needed, sometimes to combat biases of our times that can affect interpretation. Moreover, because warfare is intimately connected to practices of violence, the archaeology of warfare needs to be part of a broader-based archaeology of violence, as argued by archaeologist Timothy Pauketat (2009). In that manner, all forms of violence ought to be part of the conversation.

Violence and Gender

Situated around the Yellow River Valley of China, considered to be the crucible of emerging Chinese civilization, the Shang Culture is viewed by many to be the first kingdom and dynasty for which there is both archaeological and historical evidence, dating to a period of approximately 1700 BC to 1000 BC. Its powerful elites and rulers were simultaneously shamans, religious figures, political leaders, and military commanders. They held extremely high status, and their treatment after death reflected this. Shang elites were buried with vast amounts of wealth and grave goods. One particular tomb for a high-ranking individual was found with evidence of slaves being sacrificed to accompany the individual, along with hundreds of valuable bronze artifacts, precious stone materials, thousands of cowrie shells (currency of that time), the remains of tigers, and over a hundred weapons. This was clearly the tomb of a warrior-leader-shaman. Now, a very important question we might ask is, was this individual a man or woman? We suspect many people in our society would guess "man." In fact, it is possible that many archaeologists would even make that guess if no other information were available. But, this individual was a woman by the name of Hao, and we know this because of inscriptions on some of the bronzes.

What this case illustrates is a need for researchers to approach all archaeological materials and cases with an open mind. Despite many productive studies that have explored different gender roles in warfare (Doucette 2001; Guliaev 2003; Hollimon 2001; Ness 2007; Otto et al. 2006; Vandkilde 2006), there has been a tendency in our society to equate warfare in the past with men. This should not be the default position – instead, every case needs to be approached with a critical and open eye. There is ample evidence of women playing vital roles in warfare, and this should not be a surprise since we have already established that warfare is a cultural phenomenon. It involves the participation of all kinds of people. Women are not merely passive victims or spoil. Also, there is mounting research about how female competition and aggression is undertheorized and underestimated (Cross and Campbell 2013). Globally, a combination of myths, textual accounts, and other records indicates the participation of women in warfare, and not just in auxiliary or supportive roles. According to Vietnamese history, 2000 years ago two sisters led a military uprising against Chinese colonizers. In southern Russia, archaeological research in the territory of ancient Scythia (circa 7th to 3rd centuries BC) shows dozens of suspected warrior graves to be those of young women (Guliaev 2003). These tombs contain numerous mortuary offerings indicating high status, along with weapons and military equipment. Moreover, some individuals exhibit signs of injury from violence, such as cutting blows to the head and bronze arrowheads embedded in skeletal remains.[2] More recently, hundreds of women disguised themselves as men to fight in combat during the American Civil War. As of this writing, the US military has recently announced that all combat positions will now be open to women. Just as we ought not to assume that all hunters were male, the same is true for ideas about warriors and participants in violence. In fact, the recent observations of chimpanzees fashioning and hunting with spears at the Fongoli site in Senegal are interesting because the primary participants of this behavior are mature females. If there are problems in more recent history (and prehistory) with identifying genders and sex, what about for the Pleistocene when the evidence is very slight? Extreme care must be taken, and we cannot make simple assumptions based on sometimes very subtle biases.

Structural Violence

As defined by some researchers, structural violence is harm done to certain individuals by the creation and presence of certain social structures, which can be economic, political, legal, religious, and cultural (Farmer et al. 2006; Galtung 1969, 1990; Nystrom 2015). While this type of harm does not leave obvious material signatures such as traumatic injury, there are ways we might see structural violence. Kenneth Nystrom (2015: 766) observes that archaeological documentation of socially derived disparities in access to and control over resources can result in skeletal manifestations. In other words, those that have been consistently denied basic needs, such as adequate shelter, medical attention, or nutrition, will have traces of such stresses etched into their skeletal remains. Comparing to others within the same societies who appear to have been much healthier, we might begin asking about non-overt forms of injustice and violence. Recent innovative studies have explored these aspects of violence and harm in different times and places (Klaus 2012). This sort of research needs further development, since violence is so culturally and historically specific and can thus result in many different kinds of harm (Schrader 2015).

Captives

Related to the idea of structural violence, a greater focus on the issue of captives and slaves in prehistory could help to further illuminate contexts of violence. In some cases, the taking of individuals is heavily tied to warfare between societies, and can lead to further acts of overt violence such as sacrifice and cannibalism. In other cases, captive-taking does not result in direct and immediate injury. Instead, it might lead to enslavement or other, marginalized social statuses associated with subtle, "every-day" (Scheper-Hughes and Bourgois 2004), or structural forms of violence. These actions may not leave obvious archaeological signatures, but researchers might be able to identify related cultural patterns or systems by piecing together clues about various behaviors that may seem unrelated at first. Research has shown that captives have been found in societies of all social levels throughout much of history and prehistory (Cameron 2011), often taken during raiding and warfare (Golitko and Keeley 2007; Green 2005; Junker 1999; Kusimba 2006; Parker Pearson 2005). Captives were frequently women, and as Catherine Cameron's (2011, 2016) research has pointed out, these individuals often became potent agents of culture change, playing an important role in the transmission of cultural practices. Unfortunately, far too little archaeological attention has been placed on this topic, owing in part to the difficulty in seeing captives in the material record. Part of the challenge is that the practice of captive-taking throughout world history is highly diverse and culturally specific. But, as Cameron (2011) argues, there are ways to examine the material record for evidence and more studies are needed. One way to do so, for example, would be to use bioarchaeological data to identify individuals as outsiders and potentially as captives, as demonstrated by case studies from the prehistory of North America (Hatch 2012; Koziol 2012; Martin et al. 2010).

Magical Assault and Other Social Practices

Related to notions of structural violence, it is instructive to consider other forms of assault or attack that may not result in any sort of physical or obvious forms of violence or trauma. Living in our modern, Western world, many of us see ready and empirically grounded explanations for certain phenomena. But, we ought to acknowledge that for the vast majority of human history, our ancestors lacked many of the instruments at our disposal to collect data and understand various natural phenomena. As an illustration, consider our discussion in the last chapter of ritual and magical assault of the kanaima practitioners in South America and the Gebusi in Papua New Guinea. We can imagine that past societies the world over could have had analogous belief and ritual systems within which ritual assaults by sorcerers and shamans are perceived as having real power and effects. A person's illness or sudden death may be viewed as the outcome of magical assault, with such actions requiring justice and revenge. In these sorts of situations, it is reasonable to ask if people would have created defenses against threats, whether in the form of architecture or blessing or the adornment of apotropaic talismans. Of course, getting into the heads and belief systems of prehistoric peoples is not possible. But that does not mean such beliefs were absent in the past. After all, there is plenty of ethnographic evidence showing how important beliefs can be for all kinds of societies in shaping our choices.

Recognizing the importance of past belief systems and practices, archaeologists have tried to emphasize a need to consider the interactions between people, objects, and non-human actors (e.g. supernatural forces). William Walker's (2009) work on Puebloan societies of the American Southwest makes just such an attempt, as it brings together research on warfare, witchcraft, and environmental conditions. One important activity seen in this research is the ritual abandonment and destruction of a settlement, seen as a way to cleanse areas and transition animate beings from our world to the next. Also insightful is the view of towers serving as fortification features to protect against both human and spiritual threats. Such a view helps to explain the presence of towers near water features such as springs, but placed in a way that lacked any obvious military advantage. They may have been offering protection not against human threats but against spiritual ones. This can be inferred when one looks at ethnohistoric accounts discussing springs as potential gateways to the underworld.

In the end, these sorts of cases reveal to us the importance of shedding our own biases and keeping an open mind when considering all possibilities in interpreting the material record. Furthermore, we might add to this category all other social activities not usually associated with warfare. For instance, we might consider the manufacture of certain kinds of products and how they might sometimes be tied to efforts to strengthen ties with faraway neighbors. On the surface, researchers would simply point to profiting by long-distance exchange networks. But, when combined with the right evidence, we might see that the choice in products and trading partners can also be strategic, calculated to solidify bonds and alliances with an ally against a potential common enemy. A review of pre-modern European history amply shows something analogous, with dynastic marriage functioning as a sort of foreign policy and diplomatic tool. In this light, one might wonder if many of the cultural practices devised worldwide are somehow tied to concerns over potential outbreaks of violence. *In other words, rather than seeing peace as a natural state or simply the absence of warfare, it is a condition that is produced and safeguarded through elaborate social networks and mechanisms precisely to avoid violence.* We explore this notion further in a later chapter.

What We Know About (More Recent) Ancient Warfare

Prior to the mid-Holocene, there is very little material evidence to suggest that warfare was prevalent worldwide (Ferguson 2013a). It is only later in the Holocene, which coincides with the presence of agricultural, large-scale societies, that we see more and more of the tell-tale signs of warfare (i.e., fortifications, caches of weapons, signs of massacres, extensive destruction events at settlements, and so forth). And, of course, by the time we began recording history, our reports are filled with descriptions of violence and war. Some researchers make the point that war usually leaves behind recoverable traces, enough so that when we see archaeological records absent for obvious signs of organized violence, then we must conclude warfare was absent and inconsequential (Ferguson 2013b). However, things might not be so simple. There are so many variables that need to be considered, many of them cultural. Take, for instance, the case of refuge caves seen in Hawai'i. As shown by Michael Kolb and Boyd Dixon (2002), the availability of rich ethnohistoric information was vital in allowing researchers to infer the use of lava tubes as places of refuge during times of warfare. Without such information, the use of these features as shelter from violence could have been overlooked entirely. Moreover, the ethnohistoric sources also shed insight on the uses of temples on the islands, not just as places of religious practice but also as locations for ceremonial sacrifice of enemy captives as well. Again, a reliance simply on the material record might have led to an incomplete or inaccurate interpretation about the absence or presence of warfare activities.

Along these lines, does absence of evidence from earlier time periods prove the absence of certain behaviors? Though it is true we see more evidence of warfare in the archaeological record of the later Holocene, it is also true that we see more evidence of many things in the later Holocene as well. That later material record holds much more archaeological information of all sorts of human communities and their lifeways. This is due in large part to better preservation, higher degrees of sedentary living, greater population sizes, large-scale alterations to landscapes, and many other factors. So, it should be of little surprise that we have more data available indicating violence in the Holocene. The implication is that we must challenge the notion that "absence of evidence is evidence of absence."

As discussed in this chapter, researchers are very concerned about finding evidence of warfare in prehistory to prove its existence and significance in the deeper past. In a way, this is very interesting because it suggests that a default assumption is that "peace" was an "original" or primordial condition for much of humanity's earlier pasts. But that assumption runs the risk of overlooking how humans have performed both warlike and peace-building activities. With that in mind, perhaps we should not be too quick to judge one way or another. After all, the kinds of material traces we can reasonably expect to find differ depending on contexts of events, practices, and behaviors. For instance, preparation for warfare does not necessarily leave any evidence of it. People may be concerned about threats, but there may be no material traces for such anxieties. Unless we are looking for enormous battles, we may not see much evidence of actual combat. Population size and demographic parameters can also affect these traces. An absence of weapons does not preclude the occasional or expedient use of tools for defense or deterrence against aggression. Depending on available or culturally preferred technologies, there may be absolutely no signs of preparation for warfare. Small-scale ambushes, raids, and other sorts of violent encounters may leave no traces as well, but it does not mean that organized violence was entirely absent or foreign to past societies. Also, as discussed, some forms of violence associated with warfare may be largely invisible, but there are many forms of explicit and subtle violence that need to be incorporated into the archaeology of warfare. Finally, as we have indicated in Chapter Two, our studies of warfare in the recent and ancient worlds show that practices, beliefs, and attitudes about violence and warfare are extremely variable from culture to culture, and so we can expect the material record (and the archaeological visibility of coercion, violence, and warfare) to be highly variable as well. In the end, all perspectives need to be carefully considered.

To that end, we now move our exploration into the deeper recesses of humanity's past. With a grasp of how researchers approach and evaluate the material record, let us now see what secrets the Ice Age world holds.

Notes

1 If you do not believe us, take an art history class.
2 Intriguingly, this case lends support to the classical Greco-Roman literary references to Amazon warriors.

Works Cited

Allen, Mark. 2014. Hunter-Gatherer Conflict: The Last Bastion of the Pacified Past? In *Violence and Warfare Among Hunter-Gatherers*, edited by Mark Allen and Terry Jones, pp. 15–25. Left Coast Press, Walnut Creek, CA.

Allen, Mark, and Elizabeth Arkush. 2006. Introduction: Archaeology and the Study of War. In *The Archaeology of Warfare: Prehistories of Raiding and Conquest*, edited by Elizabeth Arkush and Mark Allen, pp. 1–22. University Press of Florida, Gainesville.

Andrushko, Valerie A., A. W. Schwitalla, and Phillip L. Walker. 2010. Trophy-Taking and Dismemberment as Warfare Strategies in Prehistoric Central California. *American Journal of Physical Anthropology* 141(1), 83–96.

Arkush, Elizabeth. 2006. Collapse, Conflict, Conquest: The Transformation of Warfare in the Late Prehispanic Andean Highlands. In *The Archaeology of Warfare: Prehistories of Raiding and Conquest*, edited by Elizabeth Arkush and Mark Allen, pp. 286–335. University Press of Florida, Gainesville.

Arkush, Elizabeth, and Mark Allen (eds.). 2006. *The Archaeology of Warfare: Prehistories of Raiding and Conquest*. University Press of Florida, Gainesville.

Arkush, Elizabeth, and Charles Stanish. 2005. Interpreting Conflict in the Ancient Andes. *Current Anthropology* 46(1), 3–28.

Arkush, Elizabeth, and Tiffiny Tung. 2013. Patterns of War in the Andes from the Archaic to the Late Horizon: Insights from Settlement Patterns and Cranial Trauma. *Journal of Archaeological Research* 21(4), 307–369.

Armit, Ian. 2010. Violence and Society in the Deep Human Past. *British Journal of Criminology* 51(3), 499–517.

Bamforth, Douglas, and Curtis Nepstad-Thornberry. 2007. Reconsidering the Occupational History of the Crow Creek Site (39BF11). *Plains Anthropologist* 52(202), 153–173.

Boulestin, Bruno, Andrea Zeeb-Lanz, Christian Jeunesse, Fabian Haack, Rose-Marie Arbogast, and Anthony Denaire. Mass Cannibalism in the Linear Pottery Culture at Herxheim (Palatinate, Germany). *Antiquity* 83(322), 968–982.

Bowles, Samuel. 2009. Did Warfare Among Ancestral Hunter-Gatherers Affect the Evolution of Human Social Behaviors? *Science* 324(5932), 1293–1298.

Campbell, Roderick. 2014. Introduction: Toward a Deep History of Violence and Civilization. In *Violence and Civilization*, edited by Roderick Campbell, pp. 1–22. Oxbow Books, Oxford.

Cameron, Catherine M. 2011. Captives and Culture Change. *Current Anthropology* 52(2), 169–209.

Cameron, Catherine M. 2016. *Captives: How Stolen People Changed the World*. University of Nebraska Press, Lincoln.

Carman, John, and Anthony Harding (eds.). 2004. *Ancient Warfare: Archaeological Perspectives*. Sutton Publishing Limited, Stroud, UK.

Carneiro, Robert. 1990. Chiefdom-level Warfare as Exemplified in Fiji and the Cauca Valley. In *The Anthropology of War*, edited by Jonathan Haas, pp. 190–211. Cambridge University Press, Cambridge.

Chacon, Richard, and Ruben Mendoza (eds.). 2007. *North American Indigenous Warfare and Ritual Violence*. University of Arizona Press, Tucson.

Chapman, John. 1999. The Origins of Warfare in the Prehistory of Central and Eastern Europe. In *Ancient Warfare: Archaeological Perspectives*, edited by John Carman and A.F. Harding, pp. 101–142. Sutton Publishing Limited, Stroud, UK.

Cross, Catharine, and Anne Campbell. Violence and Aggression in Women. 2014. In *The Evolution of Violence*, edited by Todd Shackelford and Ranald Hansen, pp. 211–232. Springer, New York.

de Waal, Frans. 1996. The Biological Basis of Peaceful Coexistence: A Review of Reconciliation Research on Monkeys and Apes. In *A Natural History of Peace*, edited by T. Gregor, pp. 37–69. Vanderbilt University Press, Nashville, TN.

Doucette, Dianna. 2001. Decoding the Gender Bias: Inferences of Atlatls in Female Mortuary Contexts. In *Gender and the Archaeology of Death*, edited by B. Arnold and N. Wicker, pp. 159–177. AltaMira Press, Lanham, MD.

Eerkens, Jelmer W., Traci Carlson, Ripan S. Malhi, et al. 2015. Isotopic and Genetic Analyses of a Mass Grave in Central California: Implications for Precontact Hunter-Gatherer Warfare. *American Journal of Physical Anthropology* 125(August), 116–125.

Estabrook, Virginia. 2014. Violence and Warfare in the European Mesolithic and Paleolithic. In *Violence and Warfare Among Hunter-Gatherers*, edited by Mark Allen and Terry Jones, pp. 49–69. Left Coast Press, Walnut Creek, CA.

Farmer, Paul E., Bruce Nizeye, Sara Stulac, and Salmaan Keshavjee. 2006. Structural Violence and Clinical Medicine. *PLoS Medicine* 3(10), 1686–1691.

Ferguson, R. Brian. 1990. Explaining War. In *The Anthropology of War*, edited by Jonathan Haas, pp. 26–55. Cambridge University Press, Cambridge.

Ferguson, R. Brian. 2013a. Pinker's List. In *War, Peace, and Human Nature: The Convergence of Evolutionary and Cultural Views*, edited by Douglas P. Fry, pp. 112–131. Oxford University Press, New York.

Ferguson, R. Brian. 2013b. The Prehistory of War and Peace in Europe and the Near East. In *War, Peace, and Human Nature: The Convergence of Evolutionary and Cultural Views*, edited by Douglas P. Fry, pp. 191–240. Oxford University Press, New York.

Frayer, David W. 1997. Ofnet: Evidence for a Mesolithic Massacre. In *Troubled Times: Violence and Warfare in the Past*, edited by Debra L. Martin and David W. Frayer, pp. 181–216. Gordon and Breach Publishers, Amsterdam.

Fry, Douglas. 2006. *The Human Potential for Peace: An Anthropological Challenge to Assumptions about War and Violence*. Oxford University Press, Oxford.

Fry, Douglas (ed.). 2013. *War, Peace, and Human Nature: The Convergence of Evolutionary and Cultural Views*. Oxford University Press, New York.

Fuentes, Agustin. 2004. It's Not All Sex and Violence: Integrated Anthropology and the Role of Cooperation and Social complexity in Human Evolution. *American Anthropologist* 106(4), 710–718.

Fuentes, Agustin. 2013. Cooperation, Conflict, and Niche Construction in the Genus *Homo*. In *War, Peace, and Human Nature: The Convergence of Evolutionary and Cultural Views*, edited by Douglas P. Fry, pp. 78–94. Oxford University Press, New York.

Galtung, Johan. 1969. Violence, Peace, and Peace Research. *Journal of Peace Research* 6(3), 167–191.

Galtung, Johan. 1990. Cultural Violence. *Journal of Peace Research* 27(3), 291–305.

Gat, Azar. 2006. *War in Human Civilization*. Oxford University Press, Oxford.

Gat, Azar. 2015. Proving Communal Warfare Among Hunter-Gatherers: The Quasi-Rousseauan Error. *Evolutionary Anthropology* 24(3), 111–126.

Goldstein, Joshua. 2011. *Winning the War on War: The Decline of Armed Conflict Worldwide*. Plume, New York.

Golitko, Mark. 2015. *LBK Realpolitik: An Archaeometric Study of Conflict and Social Structure in the Belgian Early Neolithic*. Archaeopress, Oxford.

Golitko, Mark, and Lawrence Keeley. 2007. Beating Ploughshares back into Swords: Warfare in the Linearbandkeramik. *Antiquity* 81(312), 332–342.

Gordon, Valencia. 2014. Conflict and Interpersonal Violence in Holocene Hunter-Gatherer Populations from Southern South America. In *Violence and Warfare Among Hunter-Gatherers*, edited by Mark Allen and Terry Jones, pp. 133–148. Left Coast Press, Walnut Creek, CA.

Green, Miranda Aldhouse. 2005. Ritual Bondage, Violence, Slavery and Sacrifice in Later European Prehistory. In *Warfare, Violence and Slavery in Prehistory*, edited by Mike Parker Pearson and I.J.N. Thorpe, pp. 155–163. British Archaeological Reports International Series 1374. Archaeopress, London.

Guilaine, Jean, and Jean Zammit. 2001. *Origins of War: Violence in Prehistory*. Blackwell Publishing, Oxford.

Guliaev, Valeri. 2003. Amazons in the Scythia: New Finds at the Middle Don, Southern Russia. *World Archaeology* 35(1), 112–125.

Haas, Jonathan. 2001. Warfare and the Evolution of Culture. In *Archaeology at the Millennium: A Sourcebook*, edited by Gary Feinman and T. Douglas Price, pp. 329–350. Kluwer/Plenum, New York.

Haas, Jonathan. 2004. The Origins of War and Ethnic Violence. In *Ancient Warfare: Archaeological Perspectives*, edited by J. Carman and A. Harding, pp. 11–24. Sutton Publishing Limited, Stroud, UK.

Haas, Jonathan, and Matthew Piscitelli. 2013. The Prehistory of Warfare: Misled by Ethnography. In *War, Peace, and Human Nature: The Convergence of Evolutionary and Cultural Views*, edited by Douglas P. Fry, pp. 168–190. Oxford University Press, New York.

Hatch, Mallorie. 2012. Meaning and the Bioarchaeology of Captivity, Sacrifice, and Cannibalism. In *The Bioarchaeology of Violence*, edited by Debra Martin, Ryan Harrod, and Ventura Perez, pp. 201–225. University Press of Florida, Gainesville.

Hill, Paul, and Jill Wileman. 2002. *Landscapes of War: The Archaeology of Aggression and Defense*. Tempus Publishing Inc., Charleston, SC.

Hollimon, Sandra. 2001. Warfare and Gender in the Northern Plains: Osteological Evidence of Trauma Reconsidered. In *Gender and the Archaeology of Death*, edited by B. Arnold and N. Wicker, pp. 179–193. AltaMira Press, Lanham, MD.

Jantzen, Detlef, Ute Brinker, Jorg Orschiedt, et al. 2011. A Bronze Age Battlefield? Weapons and Trauma in the Tollense Valley, North-eastern Germany. *Antiquity* 85(328), 417–433.

Junker, Laura. 1999. *Raiding, Trading, and Feasting: The Political Economy of Philippine Chiefdoms*. University of Hawaii Press, Honolulu.

Keegan, John. 1993. *A History of Warfare*. Vintage Books, New York.

Keeley, Lawrence. 1996. *War Before Civilization*. Oxford University Press, Oxford.

Keeley, Lawrence. 2001 Giving War a Chance. In *Deadly Landscapes: Case Studies in Prehistoric Southwestern Warfare*, edited by Glenn Rice and Steven LeBlanc, pp. 331–342. The University of Utah Press, Salt Lake City.

Keeley, Lawrence, Marisa Fontana, and Russell Quick. 2007. Baffles and Bastions: The Universal Features of Fortifications. *Journal of Archaeological Research* 15(1), 55–95.

Kelly, Raymond. 2000. *Warless Societies and the Origin of War*. University of Michigan Press, Ann Arbor.

Kelly, Raymond. 2005. The Evolution of Lethal Intergroup Violence. *Proceedings of the National Academy of Sciences* 102(43), 15294–15298.

Kenoyer, Jonathan Mark. 2008. Indus Urbanism: New Perspectives on its Origin and Character. In *The Ancient City: New Perspectives on Urbanism in the Old and New World*, edited by Joyce Marcus and Jeremy Sabloff, pp. 183–208. School for Advanced Research Press, Santa Fe, NM.

Kim, Nam. 2012. Angels, Illusions, Hydras and Chimeras: Violence and Humanity. *Reviews in Anthropology* 41(4), 239–272.

Kim, Nam, and Lawrence Keeley. 2008. Social Violence and War. In *Encyclopedia of Archaeology*, edited by Deborah Pearsall, pp. 2053–2064. Elsevier Academic Press, San Diego, CA.

Kim, Nam, Chapurukha Kusimba, and Lawrence Keeley. 2015. Coercion and Warfare in the Rise of State Societies in Southern Zambezia. *African Archaeological Review* 32(1), 1–34.

Klaus, Hagen. 2012. The Bioarchaeology of Structural Violence. In *The Bioarchaeology of Violence*, edited by Debra Martin, Ryan Harrod, and Ventura Perez, pp. 29–62. University Press of Florida, Gainesville.

Knusel, Christopher, and Martin Smith. 2014. Introduction: The Bioarchaeology of Conflict. In *The Routledge Handbook of the Bioarchaeology of Human Conflict*, edited by Christopher Knusel and Martin Smith, pp. 3–24. Routledge, New York.

Kolb, Michael J., and Boyd Dixon. 2002. Landscapes of War : Rules and Conventions of Conflict in Ancient Hawai'i (and Elsewhere). *American Archaeology* 67(3), 514–534.

Koziol, Kathryn. 2012. Performances of Imposed Status. In *The Bioarchaeology of Violence*, edited by Debra Martin, Ryan Harrod, and Ventura Perez, pp. 226–250. University Press of Florida, Gainesville.

Kusimba, Chapurukha. 2006. Slavery and Warfare in African Chiefdoms. In *The Archaeology of Warfare: Prehistories of Raiding and Conquest*, edited by E. Arkush and M. Allen, pp. 214–249. University Press of Florida, Gainesville.

Lambert, Patricia. 2002. The Archaeology of War: A North American Perspective. *Journal of Archaeological Research* 19(3), 207–241.

Lambert, Patricia. 2007. Ethnographic and Linguistic Evidence for the Origins of Human Trophy-taking in California. In *The Taking and Displaying of Human Trophies by Amerindians*, edited by Richard J. Chacon and David H. Dye, pp. 65–89. Springer, New York.

LeBlanc, Steven (with Katherine Register). 2003. *Constant Battles*. St. Martin's Press, New York.

LeBlanc, Steven. 2014a. Warfare and Human Nature. In *The Evolution of Violence*, edited by Todd Shackelford and Ranald Hansen, pp. 73–97. Springer, New York.

LeBlanc, Steven. 2014b. Forager Warfare and Our Evolutionary Past. In *Violence and Warfare Among Hunter-Gatherers*, edited by Mark Allen and Terry Jones, pp. 26–46. Left Coast Press, Walnut Creek, CA.

Levy, Jack, and William Thompson. 2010. *Causes of War*. Wiley-Blackwell, Malden.

Martin, Debra L., Ryan P. Harrod, and Misty Fields. 2010. Beaten Down and Worked to the Bone: Bioarchaeological Investigations of Women and Violence in the Ancient Southwest. *Landscapes of Violence* 1(1), 1–19.

Martin, Debra, Ryan Harrod, and Ventura Perez. 2012. Introduction. In *The Bioarchaeology of Violence*, edited by Debra Martin, Ryan Harrod, and Ventura Perez, pp. 1–10. University Press of Florida, Gainesville.

Maschner, Herbert, and K. Reedy-Maschner. 1998. Raid, Retreat, Defend (Repeat): The Archaeology and Ethnohistory of Warfare on the North Pacific Rim. *Journal of Anthropological Archaeology* 17(1), 19–51.

McCall, Grant, and Nancy Shields. 2008. Examining the Evidence from Small-scale Societies and Early Prehistory and Implications for Modern Theories of Aggression and Violence. *Aggression and Violent Behavior* 13(1), 1–9.

Meyer, Christian, Christian Lohr, Detlef Gronenborn, and Kurt W. Alt. 2015. The Massacre Mass Grave of Schöneck-Kilianstädten Reveals New Insights into Collective Violence in Early Neolithic Central Europe. *Proceedings of the National Academy of Sciences* 112(36), 11217–11222.

Milner, George. 1999. Warfare in Prehistoric and Early Historic Eastern North America. *Journal of Archaeological Research* 7(2), 105–151.

Milner, George. 2005. Nineteenth Century Arrow Wounds and Perceptions of Prehistoric Warfare. *American Antiquity* 70(1), 144–156.

Milner, George, Eve Anderson, and Virginia G. Smith. 1991. Warfare in Late Prehistoric West-Central Illinois. *American Antiquity* 56(4), 581–603.

Milner, George, George Chaplin, and Emily Zavodny. 2013. Conflict and Societal Change in Late Prehistoric Eastern North America. *Evolutionary Anthropology* 22(3), 96–102.

Ness, Cindy. 2007. The Rise in Female Violence. *Daedalus* 136(1), 84–93.

Nystrom, Kenneth. 2015. The Bioarchaeology of Structural Violence and Dissection in the 19th-Century United States. *American Anthropologist* 116(4), 765–779.

Otterbein, Keith. 2004. *How War Began*. Texas A & M University Press, College Station.

Otto, Ton, Henrik Thrane, and Helle Vandkilde. 2006. *Warfare and Society: Archaeological and Social Anthropological Perspectives*. Aarhus University Press, Aarhus, Denmark.

Pardoe, Colin. 2014. Conflict and Territoriality in Aboriginal Australia: Evidence from Biology and Ethnography. In *Violence and Warfare Among Hunter-Gatherers*, edited by Mark Allen and Terry Jones, pp. 112–132. Left Coast Press, Walnut Creek, CA.

Parker Pearson, Mike. 2005. Warfare, Violence and Slavery in Later Prehistory: An Introduction. In *Warfare, Violence and Slavery in Prehistory*, edited by Mike Parker Pearson and I.J.N. Thorpe, pp. 19–33. *British Archaeological Reports International Series* 1374. Archaeopress, London.

Pauketat, Timothy. 2007. *Chiefdoms and Other Archaeological Delusions*. AltaMira Press, Lanham, MD.

Pauketat, Timothy. 2009. Wars, Rumors of Wars, and the Production of Violence. In *Warfare in Cultural Context: Practice, Agency, and the Archaeology of Violence*, edited by Axel E. Nielsen and William H. Walker, pp. 244–261. The University of Arizona Press, Tucson.

Pernter, Patrizia, Paul Gostner, Eduard Egarter Vigl, and Frank Jakobus Ruhli. 2007. Radiologic Proof for the Iceman's Cause of Death (ca. 5'300 BP). *Journal of Archaeological Science* 34(11), 1784–1786.

Pinker, Steven. 2011. *The Better Angels of Our Nature: Why Violence Has Declined*. Viking, New York.

Price, Doug, Joachim Wahl, and R. Alexander Bentley. 2006. Isotopic Evidence for Mobility and Group Organization among Neolithic Farmers at Talheim, Germany, 5000 BC. *European Journal of Archaeology* 9(2–3), 259–284.

Proulx, Donald. 1999. Nasca Headhunting and the Ritual Use of Trophy Heads. In *Nasca: Geheimnisvolle Zeichen im Alten Peru*, edited by Judith Rickenbach, pp. 79–87. Museum Rietberg Zürich, Zürich.

Roscoe, Paul. 2008. Settlement Fortification in Village and 'Tribal' Society: Evidence from Contact-era New Guinea. *Journal of Anthropological Archaeology* 27(4), 507–519.

Scheper-Hughes, Nancy, and Philippe Bourgois. 2004. Introduction: Making Sense of Violence. In *Violence in War and Peace: An Anthology*, edited by Nancy Scheper-Hughes and Philippe Bourgois, pp. 1–27. Blackwell Publishing, Oxford.

Schrader, Sarah A. 2015. Elucidating Inequality in Nubia: An Examination of Entheseal Changes at Kerma (Sudan). *American Journal of Physical Anthropology* 156(2), 192–202.

Thayer, Bradley. 2004. *Darwin and International Relations: On the Evolutionary Origins of War and Ethnic Conflict*. University Press of Kentucky, Lexington.

Theler, James, and Robert Boszhardt. 2006. Collapse of Crucial Resources and Culture Change: A Model for the Woodland to Oneota Transformation in the Upper Midwest. *American Antiquity* 71(3), 433–472.

Tung, Tiffiny, and Kelly Knudson. 2011. Identifying Locals, Migrants, and Captives in the Wari Heartland: A Bioarchaeological and Biogeochemical Study of Human Remains from Conchopata, Peru. *Journal of Anthropological Archaeology* 30(3), 247–261.

Underhill, Anne. 2006. Warfare and the Development of States in China. In *The Archaeology of Warfare: Prehistories of Raiding and Conquest*, edited by Elizabeth Arkush and Mark Allen, pp. 253–285. University Press of Florida, Gainesville.

Vandkilde, Helle. 2006. Warfare and Gender According to Homer: An Archaeology of an Aristocratic Warrior Culture. In *Warfare and Society: Archaeological and Social Anthropological Perspectives*, edited by T. Otto et al., pp. 515–528. Aarhus University Press, Langelandsgade, Denmark.

Vencl, Slavomil. 1984. War and Warfare in Archaeology. *Journal of Anthropological Archaeology* 3(2), 116–132.

Vencl, Slavomil. 2004. Stone Age Warfare. In *Ancient Warfare: Archaeological Perspectives*, edited by J. Carman and A. Harding, pp. 57–72. Sutton Publishing Limited, Stroud, UK.

Walker, Phillip. 2001. A Bioarchaeological Perspective on the History of Violence. *Annual Review of Anthropology* 30, 573–596.

Walker, William. 2009. Warfare and the Practice of Supernatural Agents. In *Warfare in Cultural Practice*, edited by A. Nielsen and W. Walker, pp. 109–135. University of Arizona Press, Tucson.

Webster, David. 1998. Warfare and Status Rivalry. In *Archaic States*, edited by Gary Feinman and Joyce Marcus, pp. 311–351. School of American Research Press, Santa Fe, NM.

Wendorf, Fred. 1968. Site 117: A Nubian Final Palaeolithic Graveyard Near Jebel Sahaba, Sudan. In *The Prehistory of Nubia, Vol. 2*, edited by Fred Wendorf, pp. 954–1040. Southern Methodist University Press, Dallas, TX.

Wu, Xiu-Jie, Lynne A. Schepartz, Wu Liu, and Erik Trinkaus. 2011. Antemortem Trauma and Survival in the Late Middle Pleistocene Human Cranium from Maba, South China. *Proceedings of the National Academy of Sciences* 108(49), 19558–19562.

4

THE ICE AGE WORLD

Our journey continues, and hopefully by now we have convinced our readers to consider a few key points about warfare. The first is a full appreciation of all of its cultural facets. Warfare, broadly defined, is not simply organized violence, it is not restricted to large-scale social groups, it is not restricted to young males, it does not result solely in direct physical trauma to bodies, and it is not a recent phenomenon. People in many different societies participate in various aspects of warfare, separated by vast differences in attitudes, perceptions, and cultural logics about violence. We have seen that warfare is not restricted to those eras of humanity where we had written records, with archaeological clues suggesting a deeper antiquity. Yes, the rabbit hole goes deeper, but just how deep?

To answer that question, we now turn to the very distant past, discussing the potential signs of organized violence, or even warfare, in the Pleistocene. It was during this time period, well before pottery, farming, and writing, that our ancestors began to control fire, became successful hunters of larger game, and created social institutions that would contribute to the development of highly populous and very complex societies, the kinds that most humans live in today. It is a time when our ancestors began to behave in ways that reflect a cognition and appreciation of their surroundings very similar to our own. It is also when we see the first evidence of interpersonal conflict and, perhaps, warfare. To be sure, interpersonal conflict has probably been part of human life since the dawn of our species, which makes it difficult to ascertain when warfare itself emerges. With very scant material evidence to begin with, it is difficult to separate cases of interpersonal violence from instances of larger-scale, intergroup violence. Moreover, there tends to be ambiguity in this research since terminology is not always clear. But, as noted in Chapter One, we see actions related to collective violence between distinct groups of people to be part of warfare. So, was there organized, intergroup violence before the Holocene?

In the preceding chapters we discussed the collection and interpretation of data from primatology, ethnography, and archaeology, and how such data have been put to use in answering questions about the (more recent) ancient past. These very same methodologies are used to propose and test hypotheses about the Pleistocene era, whether for modern humans, archaic humans, or populations of hominins. Modern and ethnographically-known hunter-gatherers have been interacting with state-level societies for generations, and today generally live in more marginalized environments, thus making it difficult to use them as direct proxies for Pleistocene life. This makes the material record all the more pertinent for our questions about early violence. What can the archaeological record tell us about general lifeways at a time when people lived in ways very different than many of us do today? Within the vast stretch of time known as the Pleistocene Epoch, there are a handful of cases of suspected violence, as identified through examining the remains of individuals. Whether these cases indicate a prevalence or general scarcity of violence is really up to the researcher. Without access to large-scale cemeteries (the earliest of which, mentioned in the last chapter, dates to ~12,000 years ago), it is hard to know for sure what type of behavior led to the archaeologically detected violence. In other words, the archaeology is often mute as to the exact cause of violence. Was it systematic or intergroup violence or something else, more of the interpersonal variety?

Understanding the behavior of our early ancestors is the purview of archaeology and paleoanthropology. These sciences use the material culture and the fossil record of our ancestors to learn about prehistoric cultures from around the world. By examining the remarkable discoveries of generations of scholars, we hope to shed light on the nature of violence and interpersonal conflict in the past and use this to help understand the evolutionary arc of human warfare. We also need to keep in mind the political aspects of archaeology, as oftentimes there are social implications when archaeologists argue that specific cultural groups were peaceful hunter-gatherers or were warlike and possibly cannibalistic.[1]

Before embarking on a tour of the Ice Age world cases, it would be helpful to first briefly highlight a few anthropological ideas about social organizations and the kinds of groupings people lived in during the Ice Ages of the Pleistocene. Early anthropologists, such as Lewis Henry Morgan (1877), argued that all human societies go through "stages," beginning with savagery and ending with civilization (often referred to as "unilinear" social evolution). A century's worth of archaeological research worldwide has shown this argument to be inaccurate, indicating that societies do not go through some inexorable progression or advancement of stages of social development. But while anthropologists no longer subscribe to "unilinear" ideas about social change, it is still helpful to be able to frame social groupings in general categories in order to discuss the different ways human societies can share similarities. Indeed, as we have highlighted previously, some anthropologists suggest that warfare is associated with just one category of society, specifically state-level ones. In this view, states instigate or propagate war, and any warfare practiced by smaller-scale, non-state societies that results is largely caused by the actions taken by aggressive state-level societies. This is in contrast with others who suggest that smaller-scale, non-state societies also engage in warfare apart from the influence of states. This is an important debate, since, as states did not exist until after the advent of agriculture in the Holocene, we could use these data to help us understand when organized violence could have plausibly begun. After discussing social organizations, we will present the archaeological record for violence in the Pleistocene, a time when all human societies lived as hunter-gatherers in communities without highly centralized forms of political authority.

Social Organizations

There is good reason to believe by the Middle Pleistocene (circa 200,000 years ago) people were acting in very 'modern' ways, exchanging goods with neighbors, producing body ornamentations in order to identify themselves as members of a particular group (d'Errico et al. 2001), hunting dangerous animals with tools (Milo 1998), and maybe even using raiding parties (Otterbein 2004, 2011). Furthermore, recent analysis of the archaeological data suggests that many of the supposed indicators of symbolic expression, the very traits that we today associate with modern behavior, have their roots before 200,000 years ago, predating the origins of anatomically modern humans (early human populations who, skeletally, looked the way we do today) (Kissel and Fuentes 2016). So, if we accept that there were people who were, for all intents and purposes, very much like us living in the world at 200,000 years ago and perhaps even earlier, what kinds of societies did they live in?

Anthropologists have developed numerous ways to classify human social organizations. While there has been much criticism of these classification systems (see Pauketat 2007 and Yoffee 2005), they can prove useful in order to discuss different social organizations, so long as we take care to avoid placing them in any value-based ranking. The best-known system is the "band-tribe-chiefdomstate" designation (Service 1962). Elman Service thought that human organizations went through each of these four stages in a unilinear evolutionary fashion, with the outcome being the eventual formation of a state-level society. Indeed, one of the most prominent archaeologists of the 20th century, V. Gordon Childe, surveyed archaeological data in an effort to bolster this notion, arguing that humanity underwent various "revolutions" that culminated in the rise of urbanism and civilizations. Childe even furnished a generalized list of traits and features to identify civilizations (1950). Although much of this type of research has been invaluable, certain aspects of this school of thought are no longer tenable given what we know today from the global archaeological record. For instance, while Childe argued that writing was a hallmark of civilizations, we know that the Inca Empire in the Andean highlands of South America did not make administrative use of written records, choosing instead to use other forms of communication and information storage such as the famous khipu (cords of cotton or other material used to encode information). Consequently, anthropologists today would question whether human populations go through stages of development analogous to biological evolution. Furthermore, researchers today would not claim that one kind of organization is better or more advanced than another. As such, when anthropologists use these categories, they do so largely to reflect differences in scale, usually in terms of population size and accompanying degrees of complexity. Complexity, in this sense, refers to the levels of interaction and the amount of social differentiation within a society. With these caveats in mind, it is helpful to look at the major differences between kinds of social organizations. Using Service's model as a starting point, we start by briefly describing four categories of social organizations as other anthropologists have traditionally described them. As with any attempt to classify complex human behavior, there are exceptions to the examples given here. For example, even the concept of an egalitarian society (one in which there is a general absence of formalized differences in access to power, influence, resources, or status) can be variable and debated, as the work of scholars like Polly Wiessner (2002) with the Enga peoples of Papua New Guinea shows us. In the end, though, these categories will provide you with a general idea of different types of social complexity. It is useful to think about how war and peace (or aggression and compassion) would be generally conducted in each of these different types of social organizations, as these cultural patterns would leave different kinds of material traces.

Bands are groups whose economic system is based on foraging for food.[2] They are often categorized as being relatively egalitarian, which means that there is a general absence of social inequality in terms of standards of living and access to materials and resources. Generally speaking, social status in the community comes from skill and is not inherited by birthright. Individuals gain status by being adept hunters, having skill with healing and magic, and with age. They thus do not have pronounced degrees of social stratification or unequal access to wealth and power. The classic example are the Dobe Ju/'hoansi (also known as the !Kung Bushman) from desert regions in Botswana, Namibia, and Angola. A classic ethnography comes from Richard Lee (2007), where he provides details on how this group lives. Often described as being fiercely egalitarian, the Ju/'hoansi avoid conflict and, if a situation escalates, these hunter-gatherers "vote with their feet" and the group splits. In general, population size of a band in arid regions is around 25 people (Birdsell 1958), though in regions with more rainfall, the number of individuals in a band vary from between 50 to 100 individuals; any group larger than this tends to fission due to resource stress. However, in order for a band to survive it needs to be maintained through contact with other, neighboring bands within the tribal system. Bands, though often classically described as composed of family-units (Birdsell 1973), are composed mostly from non-genetically related individuals, at least in the case of the Ache and the Ju/'hoansi (Hill et al. 2011). Foraging is considered a gendered activity, with men doing the hunting and women the gathering. However, while we tend to think of hunting as bringing in the most calories, recent research suggests that the majority of the caloric intake may come from gathering tubers and collecting honey.

Tribal societies subsist though foraging as well as the use of pastoralism and horticulture. In a tribe, authority comes through achieved status, which requires being adept at deflating arguments. The head of the tribe, often called a "big man," must be able to keep the people below him happy. The Yanomami of Brazil are one of the best known tribal societies (as described in Chapter Two), and examples of tribes are also common in the South Pacific. Tribal leaders have very little authority and must lead by example. The tribal unit is more endogamous than a band, which means that people marry within the tribe rather than outside it. As mentioned in Chapter Two, the Yanomami are considered by some scholars to be very warlike and "fierce," which some have used as support for the hypothesis that humans are warlike in their "natural" state.

Chiefdoms have political economies generally based around agriculture and the redistribution of wealth. This is a ranked society with inequalities that tend to be institutionalized and hereditary. In other words, chiefs can inherit their power through birth rather than by skill, though they need to be adept at managing conflict within the group and often are blamed when crops fail. One of their key functions is to accumulate foodstuffs as a form of tribute and then redistribute these goods at feasts and other events. There is much social ranking in these societies and individuals within them are unequal in terms of social status, power, and wealth. Modern-day examples of chiefdoms are rare, though Native American groups from the Pacific Northwest and Polynesian peoples of the Pacific have been classified as chiefdoms. Chiefdoms are often said to be constantly at war with neighboring groups, and being a successful warrior is one way to gain status in the society.

Finally, state societies generally have an economy typically based on agriculture (though there are notable exceptions as the work of William Honeychurch [2014], among others, has shown about pastoral nomadic states), a centralized political apparatus, and a division of society based on classes. State societies often have immense control over their inhabitants, often through imposing order and legitimizing their power though displays of authority, usually through the use of force. Many examples of state societies exist today and in recent history, including ancient Rome, the Inca Empire, and the United States, as well as very ancient states such as Mesopotamia, Shang Dynasty China, the Xiongnu Polity of Central Asia, and Egypt. Some scholars have suggested that modern state-level societies are less violent than their predecessors. But, others point to forms of structural violence inherent in very large and highly differentiated societies. Moreover, many would argue that state societies and their monopolies over large and highly efficient military forces can be extremely violent in both their internal (domestic) and external (foreign) policies.

While there has been much criticism over the use of ethnographic observations of modern-day smaller-scale societies for reconstructing the archaeological past (Wobst 1978), there is also much to gain (Bunn 2001; Gould and Watson 1982; O'Connell et al. 1988), as has been capably demonstrated by researchers using modern and ethnohistoric accounts and values to test ancient models of behavior. When doing so, though, we must be careful to note the environmental conditions and historical attributes under which these values were recorded. Often, anthropologists have relied on ethnographic data without critically examining the source, or without embedding them in a larger context of other evidence. Further, bands and tribes observed today come from wildly varying historical and ecological conditions, and those subsisting in the Arctic, for instance, have a different carrying capacity – the number of people that a region can support – than those living in sub-Saharan Africa. With these caveats in mind, however, ethnographic comparison is a useful starting point. For our purposes, we need to think mostly about how interpersonal violence will be seen in the smaller-scale examples of social organizations, and whether or not we can infer intergroup violence. For bands studied ethnographically, violence is often condemned and highly violent people are ostracized (Lee 2007). Some tribal societies have been described as highly warlike (Chagnon 1988), though others are less so. But, as discussed, our ethnographic depictions of these societies can only serve as a point of departure. We must engage the material record for a fuller appreciation of past cultural practices.

To be sure, there are some challenges when extrapolating our observations of recent or contemporary versions of these social organizations for modeling ancient groups. When each of these types of organization actually first appeared is highly debated. Also, some scholars suggest that there is little difference between forms of complex societies, thus blurring the lines between what we might call a chiefdom or state (see Pauketat 2007). Nevertheless, there is general consensus among researchers that human populations, for most of human history, lived as bands or tribes, and that very socially complex societies did not exist until the mid-Holocene. Regardless of how one delineates between categories of social organizations, most researchers would agree that very large-scale, highly populous, often urbanized, and politically centralized societies (generally referred to as chiefdoms, states, or civilizations) did not exist in the Pleistocene. Consequently, here we take the view that humans were living in band and tribal societies in the Pleistocene. It thus follows that if any kind of organized violence or warfare occurred in the Pleistocene, it would have looked different from how it does today in many places, or even from how it looked a few thousand years ago.

Not all of the material signatures for warfare outlined in the last chapter will be relevant, and the archaeology of emergent warfare has to rely on less material data than are generally available for larger-scale societies of the Holocene past. For instance, we would not expect to see extensive fortification architecture, such as walls, moats, or watchtowers, in the Pleistocene, nor would we expect to see evidence of a full-time, professional warrior class and highly specialized equipment for organized fighting, such as chariots or catapults. Archaeologists have demonstrated tremendous differences in the scale, conduct, and nature of organized violence and warfare between different kinds of social organizations (Kim et al. 2015). For this chapter, we are on the lookout for signs of emergent warfare, and when it comes to direct or circumstantial evidence of violence that may involve rival groups, the Pleistocene offers clues from three main buckets of data: trauma on remnant fossils and bones, artifacts, and depictions.

Early Pleistocene Contexts

It is unclear exactly how societies were organized before the advent of "civilizations," but at the moment all signs point to people living as hunter-gatherers the world over for the majority of human history. The Pleistocene Epoch dates to between 1.8 million years ago and 11,700 years ago, spanning the time from the origin of *Homo erectus* and ending around the time hunter-gathering societies begin to experiment with plant cultivation and other agricultural practices that led to domestication of floral and faunal species in various regions, such as Southwest Asia and East Asia. During this vast window of time, our earliest ancestors first left Africa, evolved into modern humans, learned to control fire, began expressing themselves through various media and art, started using language, and developed various types of technology (with durable stone being the earliest we can recover).

As we have seen in the last chapter, archaeologists have used different lines of evidence to talk about warfare, homicide, cannibalism, and interpersonal violence, highlighting various types of data. In order to study this topic, they have had to be very imaginative and creative. Scholars have fired arrows at goat carcasses, skinned pigs, and examined alleged victims of cannibalism all in the service of giving voices to the silent bones and stones we have found. As discussed in Chapter Three and as you will see, the archaeological record is (and interpretations of it are) far from perfect.

As discussed earlier in the book, there is a general and long-standing tension between proponents of either a long or short chronology of warfare, seeing warfare as either a very old or very recent activity, with many folks falling somewhere in the middle. Some scholars (Bowles 2009; Gat 2015; Guilaine and Zammit 2001; Keeley 1996; LeBlanc 2003; Pinker 2002) have advocated a long chronology of warfare, arguing for its existence well before the Holocene, something which may even come from our primate roots (Wrangham 1999). They point to archaeological data suggesting that life in the Pleistocene was full of danger due to intense competition between human groups. Lawrence Keeley, whose work has influenced many archaeologists, writes that archaeological evidence indicates "that homicide has been practiced since the appearance of modern humankind and that warfare is documented in the archaeological record of the past 10,000 years in every well-studied region" (Keeley 1996: 39). LeBlanc (2003), following Keeley's work, suggests that interludes of peace would have been short-lived and the past was non-peaceful for almost the entirety of human existence. At the heart of this debate, then, is how much Pleistocene violence can we see, and are we able to link it to warfare?

As noted in Chapter Three, many have argued that warfare is a late human invention (the "short chronology") (Ferguson 2006; Haas and Piscitelli 2013; Roper 1969; Sponsel 1996). Brian Ferguson (2006, 2013a), one of the key players in the debate about warfare's role in human history, provides a useful survey of the evidence of early warfare, suggesting that "across all of Europe and the Near East, war has been known from 3000 BC, or millennia earlier, present during all of written history" (Ferguson 2013b: 229). For him, the preconditions of war show up before war itself, suggesting that war was not inevitable. This notion generally supports Margret Mead's suggestion (1940) that warfare is a human invention, not a necessity. But, before we can talk about how warfare may be culturally invented or a natural part of our species, we must begin by reviewing the material record.

Importantly, non-anthropologists often rely on the archaeological record to support their arguments about the antiquity of human warfare and its possible relationship to the evolution of humans and human societies (Gat 2015; Pinker 2011). Pinker (2011: 1), for example, discusses "the foreign country called the past, from 8000 BC to the 1970s," in which he cites data suggestive of warlike ancestors. He notes (Pinker 2011: 3): "What is it about the ancients that they couldn't leave us an interesting corpse without resorting to foul play?" However this perspective is perhaps based on an uncritical or incomplete examination of the data (Ferguson 2013b; Kim 2012; Gray 2015). Researchers like Pinker have taken elements of the body of research to paint a very stark and vivid picture of our earliest ancestors, and their ideas have shaped much of the current popular thinking on the relationship between violence and human nature. Pinker relies heavily on the research by scholars such as Lawrence Keeley to craft an argument about the violent nature of humans in the past, but he takes the interpretations and conclusions beyond what the archaeological evidence can comfortably support (Kim 2012).

As further illustration of how people use and sometimes overstretch the reaches of archaeological data, we can return to the case of the very recent and highly significant finds of hominin fossil remains in the Dinaledi cave chamber in South Africa, mentioned in Chapter Two, which have been designated as *Homo naledi* (Dirks et al. 2015). Dating to between 230,000 and 330,000 years ago (Dirks et al. 2017) the very possibility that the *Homo naledi* remains were deliberately disposed of in the chamber by other individuals has prompted some, like science writer Michael Shermer, to conjecture that the deposits represent a case of murder, warfare, or violence (Shermer 2016). This conjecture, which is purely speculative and based on (as yet) absolutely no supporting physical evidence, largely rests on the arguments made by other non-anthropologists and their interpretations of the material record, which generally assume that our earliest ancestors were very violent.[3] But, we believe that only a highly comprehensive evaluation of the Pleistocene material record, balanced against comparative proxy data from primatology and ethnography, can provide the basis for a well-informed assessment.

Rolling in the Deep: The Paleoanthropological Record

As the story goes for some of the world's major religions, Cain kills his brother Abel in the very first act of murder in human history. Of course, we have no archaeological evidence for this story, but we do have evidence from the Pleistocene of curious activities that may qualify as homicide, interpersonal violence, and even cannibalism. Some of this evidence is linked, unsurprisingly, to modern humans, but some of it is intriguingly connected to the fossil remains of hominin populations.

Paleoanthropologists study living human societies as well as non-human primate populations to shed light on aspects of hominin behavior. There is ample primatological research indicating collective violence among select species of living primates (see Chapter Two), thus providing clues about the possible nature and patterns of violent behavior among early hominins and archaic humans (van der Dennen 1995). In studying hominin behavior of the earliest timeframe with tool use, namely the early Pleistocene era associated with the Oldowan tradition of Africa dating back some 2.5 million years ago, all we have are the remains of fossils and stone tools, which are relatively scarce in quantity when compared to the archaeological record of the late Pleistocene or Holocene. "The closest representations we have for analogical reasoning are chimpanzees and modern hunter-gatherers, and both of these models pose significant analogical difficulties" (Braun 2012: 236). Such analogical comparison through recent human communities and extant primate behavior can provide points of departure. But that kind of information must be complemented by an archaeological record. Such a complementary approach is imperative given the analogical challenges and the incompleteness of the material record. As aptly observed by Pickering (2013: 7), the "stone-and-bone witness of past action is accessible to us only in glimpses – the record is woefully incomplete, subject to the vagaries of ancient preservation and modern discovery."

Despite the incompleteness, the material evidence offers us the best means to substantiate claims and test ideas about past behavioral patterns. Some of the earliest examples from the fossil record suggest that life was hard for our ancestors: many of the fossils we find have evidence of healed fractures and broken bones, suggesting our early ancestors were more likely the hunted than the hunters (Brain 1981). However, something remarkable happens in our evolutionary lineage (though when it happened is highly debated) to vault us into the role of top apex predators. We move from being prey to becoming predators, and there is evidence of hominins practicing forms of scavenging and hunting as early as 2 million years ago (Bunn 2006). Curiously, in addition to finding the tell-tale signs of butchery through stone tool cutmarks on the bones of prey animals, we also begin to see evidence of similar cutmarks on hominin remains as well. What does the latter signify?

Cutmarks, and what they may reflect, represent some of the most intriguing aspects of research when we look at the fossil remains for some of our earliest hominin ancestors. Such trace material signatures suggest intentional defleshing and hint at possible cannibalism. Cannibalism, or the eating of one's own species, is a topic that fascinates both the public and scientists alike. A detailed review of the anthropological study of cannibalism is beyond the scope of this book but suffice it to say, cannibalism has received much attention in both the scientific and popular press. It also proves to be very telling as to how we can see evidence of systematic or collective violence in the past. Were there any cultures that used cannibalism as a form of violence in the Pleistocene, and does that evidence show us anything about intergroup violence?

One of the earliest fossil examples with intriguing signatures comes from a remarkable find at the site of Sterkfontein in South Africa, part of a region generally known as the "Cradle of Humankind" given the significant nature and amount of hominin remains found in that area over the past century. Scientists reported cutmarks left by stone tools on the upper jaw of a fossil of an australopithecine (often referred to as bipedal apes, australopithecines were some of the earliest members of the hominin line, and may have been the first to make and use stone tools) from over 2 million years ago (Pickering et al. 2000). What is unclear is why flesh was removed from the skull. It could have been related to any number of reasons, such as funerary practice, anatomical curiosity, or cannibalism. But, even if this was cannibalism, there is absolutely no way we can conclude whether this was part of a violent death, nor do we have any other information that would tell us if the individual was an "outsider" targeted for this activity. There is simply precious little information besides the cranium. All that we can say is that this is perhaps the oldest evidence of one of our ancestors intentionally defleshing the head of another.

Other evidence of potential cannibalism comes from the Bodo cranium from Ethiopia, which dates to around 600,000 years ago (White 1986). Its species designation is debated, but many think of it as an archaic member of our species, *Homo sapiens*. An interesting feature is a set of cut marks on the cheek bone and regions of the face. The cut marks left by a stone tool suggest not only scalping, but the removal of the face and perhaps the eyeballs as well (Pickering 2013)! Again, it is difficult to say why this behavior occurred. Postmortem defleshing as a sort of funerary ritual is possible, but cannibalism is plausible.

Recently, an archaeologist who studied the Sterkfontein find has suggested that cannibalism is the most reasonable hypothesis, but notes that this is mostly due to the current absence of evidence for ritual burial at this time rather than any good evidence for cannibalism (Pickering 2013). Cannibalism is not unheard of in the animal world, so we should not be too surprised to see it here. But were either of these cases the result of violent actions? And if so, were they part of group-on-group violence? At the moment, there are just too many "if's" for us to say much. We have no information about these acts being related to any sort of systematic exocannibalism, thus precluding anything more than speculation about collective violence, much less warfare. The above examples are only telling us about the remains of single individuals, and we know nothing else about the events surrounding either their deaths or their post-mortem treatment. Plus, we know little about the culture and lifeways of these early hominins, so it proves difficult to determine anything about violence at this time.

Of further interest is a recent study of a skull from the site of Sima de los Huesos (SH), in northern Spain (Sala et al. 2015). Dating to around 430,000 years ago, the site has produced a remarkable number of hominin bones (over 6,700). As the bones entered the site though a pit that was 13 meters deep, the large collection has been argued to be due to either accidental falls or the purposeful accumulation of bodies. One skull (cranium 17) is of a young adult (we know this as the third molar, or wisdom tooth, is fully erupted) and has two fractures, reminiscent of breaks seen in forensic cases due to blunt force trauma. The two fractures, which are right next to each other on the individual's forehead, are of the same size and shape, suggesting that they were caused by the same object. However, since the fractures have a different orientation, it seems that they were administered independently. The location of the trauma, which is to the left of the midline of the forehead, is similar to what is seen in modern context during face-to-face conflict with right-handed individuals. Put together, this may be good evidence of repeated blows associated with lethal interpersonal violence. Afterwards, the body was dropped down the shaft to the bottom of the pit, perhaps by members of his or her social group. Recent analysis of the SH remains suggest that other crania from the site may also exhibit signs of interpersonal violence (Sala et al. 2016). We cannot know why these fights occurred, but the evidence suggests violence was not necessarily a rare aspect of human lifeways.

Implications of Hominin Violence, Homicide, and Cannibalism

As mentioned in Chapter Two, cannibalism is not restricted to our species, as it has been observed in many species of the natural world. However, as we discussed, humans seem to take it to a new level, and many of our activities related to cannibalism can be highly political, ritual, and culturally charged. Why cannibalism was practiced is as controversial as whether it was practiced. A recent study suggests that there was a nutritional benefit to cannibalism, as the eating of human organs could have prevented certain deficiencies in omega-3 fatty acids (Guil-Guerrero 2017). Other scholars, however, have suggested that the nutritional value of humans is significantly lower than that of the majority of vertebrate meat, arguing that cannibalism would not have been nutritionally motivated (Cole 2017). At its most general level, the human consumption of human bodies can be separated into two categories: endo- and exocannibalism. The former involves the consumption of individuals within one's social group or community, while the latter involves consumption of those considered outsiders. Although both endo- and exocannibalism occur in many species, the presence of symbolic thought and cultural practices separates human cannibalism from instances seen in other species. The conscious decision to eat the flesh of one's enemy seems distinct from other kinds of non-human primate cannibalism that have been reported. While controversial (Arens 1980), recent potential cases can be instructive, such as ethnographic examples found in Hawai'i (Snow 1974) and with the Crow and Plains Indians of North America (Kantner 1999).

Endocannibalism can be related to religious, spiritual, or cultural practices rather than simply a need for sufficient caloric intake. A well-known example of endocannibalistic practice occurs within the Fore Tribe from the Eastern Highlands of Papua New Guinea, where family members are reported to have eaten the brains, meat, and viscera of deceased relatives as part of mortuary rites. Other examples come from survival situations such as the famous cases of the Donner Party or the Franklin Expedition, the latter of which set out to find the Northwest Passage in the Arctic but got trapped in ice. Archaeological study of the human remains that were recovered of the expedition back up Inuit testimony that some of the crew had resorted to cannibalism (Mays and Beattie 2015).

On the opposite side of the spectrum is exocannibalism, the practice of consuming conspecifics from outside the group. Archaeological examples of cannibalism may include the Aztec practice of human sacrifice, which some scholars believe was intended as a way to communicate with the gods (Montellano 1978), though this is not accepted by all researchers. Oftentimes when exocannibalism has been documented, it has involved acts of aggression and collective violence (Lindenbaum 2004: 478). Like endocannibalism, exocannibalism can also be tied to religious or ideological practices, and can also be a political tool. As detailed in Chapter Two, genocidal activities in Cambodia during the Khmer Rouge regime involved the evisceration and extraction of the human liver for consumption in highly symbolic acts (Hinton 2004: 180). Human cannibalism is very often intertwined with social value or function, where violence is in some way synonymous with power. It can also be an important part of warfare.

Thus if we could recognize this type of behavior in the past, especially if it can be linked to exocannibalism, it may be an indication of hostilities between communities and possible warfare. Archaeological case studies of cannibalism from the recent past include the Pueblo I (Potter and Chuipka 2010) and the Ancestral Puebloans (also known as Anasazi) (Turner and Turner 1999) societies of the American Southwest. There are instances where it may be possible to demonstrate exocannibalism occurring between groups and as a form of intimidation. Interestingly, Kantner (1999) argues that cannibalism functioned as a form of sociopolitical intimidation in the American Southwest. It seems likely that such behaviors, at least in that context, required a relatively complex socioeconomic system with some form of hierarchy and rulership. Whether these kinds of complex social organizations existed in the Pleistocene is far from certain. Some earlier examples, such as from Neandertal sites in Europe, have been argued to yield evidence of cannibalism. Cannibalism has thus been established archaeologically for numerous regions and cultures, extending from Neandertals to present-day examples.

In general, as we have shown, there is much debate about the nature of violence and warfare as recorded by archaeologists. Even when there is a lot of information and archaeological evidence, researchers arrive at different conclusions about warfare. You can imagine how challenging it becomes to answer similar questions about violence in the Pleistocene, when we have comparatively less materials to examine. For the most part, from the deepest past of humanity only fossils and stone tools remain for us to find, and as researchers have noted, studying signs of trauma on bones can be very tricky. "Of great significance from a behavioral perspective is distinguishing among injuries suffered before death (antemortem), around the time of death (perimortem), and after death (postmortem) through soil movement and other site formation processes" (Walker 2001: 576). Of course, where we can demonstrate injuries of the antemortem and perimortem variety, we can have much more to ponder about violent practices. It is telling that many of their skeletal remains show signs of either trauma or violent death. The question to which we are led is what caused this violence, and can we determine if such causes were related to warlike behaviors. At the moment, we would argue that despite all of the clues for homicide, interpersonal violence, and cannibalism, it is not possible to conclude that the causes for these material signatures are related to intergroup violence. We simply do not have enough contextual evidence to support that kind of conclusion. To illustrate this situation, let us turn our attention to a very important case study.

The Gran Dolina Case: c. 800,000 BP

There is an especially intriguing case from a cave in present-day Spain that has generated much debate about the origins of both culinary cannibalism and warfare. Recent work on the hominin remains from Gran Dolina Cave in the Atapuerca Mountains (identified as *Homo antecessor* by some authorities, though whether it is actually a separate species is quite controversial) has suggested that some of the hominin remains exhibit signs of having been subject to cannibalism (Carbonell and Mosquera 2006; Carbonell et al. 2010; Fernandez-Jalvo et al. 1996; Fernandez-Jalvo et al. 1999). In identifying a pattern of cannibalism, researchers noted four specific characteristics: 1) similar butchering techniques for both hominins and animal remains; 2) similar breakage patterns; 3) identical pattern of discard; and 4) a similarity between the hominin remains in this assemblage and that of butchered human assemblages (suggested to have been victims of cannibalism) from other archaeological sites. Specifically, it is argued that the butchery techniques used to deflesh the hominins at Gran Dolina were "aimed at meat and marrow extraction" (Fernandez-Jalvo et al. 1999: 620). Is this simply opportunistic meat consumption, or a "culinary tradition," or other cultural practice with symbolic meaning, such as a ritual treatment of deceased kin or the killing and consumption of enemies? If the latter, this may fit some definitions of warfare (Otterbein 2004, Otterbein 2011).

Researchers Eudald Carbonell and colleagues argue that this was not simply a dietary choice, but also a conscious decision on the part of the hominins living at the site to prevent their rival groups from outcompeting them. In making their case about cultural cannibalism, the authors imply that the cannibalistic behavior associated with the Gran Dolina hominins may have been part of a system of values and beliefs within that society, perhaps connected to a symbolic component (Carbonell et al. 2010: 540). Intriguingly, though, the authors also write that the butchery techniques show the "primordial intention of obtaining meat and marrow and maximally exploiting nutrients" (Carbonell et al. 2010: 545). For us, the latter observation sounds more congruent with the notion of predation rather than any form of cultural system or culinary tradition of cannibalism.

Ultimately, without an extensive material record it is also not altogether clear how ancient forms of cannibalism can be readily distinguished from each other. What took place with this case may have been solely for nutrition through predation, or perhaps an example of endocannibalism without any sort of "modern" beliefs or practices (see Saladie et al. 2012 for a detailed discussion of Pleistocene intergroup cannibalism). The absence of direct signs for distinct social groups and communities prevents us from eliminating the possibility that endocannibalism can account for the pattern of remains. Further, it is possible individuals who had died of natural causes were eaten due to resource stress, or that children were killed by adults due to population stress. Non-human populations are believed to regulate their population through the killing of the young, such as brown bears (Young and Ruff 1982) and polar bears (Taylor et al. 1985). Even in cases with more evidence, it is still challenging to infer a context of inter-community violence. For instance, with Gough's Cave, dating to 15,000 BP (see Chapter Two), we have bones of people with signs of processing to extract nutrients and the curation of skullcaps. Though these are symbolically meaningful actions, we would still require more data to infer organized violence. The fact that such behaviors occur in non-human animals suggests that it is difficult to interpret the occurrence of exocannibalism from the currently available data alone.

Overall, if we are to take cues from comparisons with primate or non-primate behaviors, it would appear that some degree of equifinality marks the material signatures of the Gran Dolina case when it comes to culinary cannibalism. The currently available evidence makes it challenging to demonstrate the occurrence of either some kind of exocannibalism or culinary cannibalism, as suggested by researchers. Juxtaposing the Gran Dolina case against other known cases of hominin or human cannibalism seen in the archaeological, historical, and ethnographical records, it would appear that an interpretation of either cultural cannibalism or exocannibalism would overstep the bounds of the currently available data. Ultimately, it becomes extremely difficult to conclude that this is a form of organized violence between groups.

Violence and Our More Recent Ancestors

As noted in Chapter Two, the totality of current evidence suggests that anatomically modern humans (AMH) and forms of modern behavior, marked by complex cognition and symbolic thinking, existed by around 200,000 years ago in Africa, if not earlier. The suspicion held by many researchers is that these populations first originated in Africa, and then proceeded to migrate into other areas of Eurasia. Increasingly, the story of AMH is tied to the story of other archaic human populations, as indicated by the evidence that various lineages not only overlapped in time and space, but also exchanged genes. As we have noted, there were at least five populations of archaic humans in Eurasia during the Late Pleistocene (AMH, *Homo naledi, Homo floresensis,* Neandertals, and Denisovans). Given the evidence now available, it is reasonable to start comparing datasets in an exploration of behaviors of the Mid- to Late Pleistocene.

A very interesting case comes to us from southern China, at a site known as Maba. A lesion on the frontal bone of the Maba cranium, a late archaic human, seems to have been created by traumatic impact (Wu et al. 2011). Dated to between 250–100 thousands of years ago (kya), this cranium has a semicircular lesion on its surface. The concentric rings around the depression suggest blunt force trauma, and the general size indicates an injury from a small, hard missile, rather than a fall or impact on a larger object. While non-lethal, the trauma was most likely caused by a human agent. Interestingly, the lesion appears on the right side of the face. Recent cases of interpersonal violence show that the majority of these injuries appear on the left side, which fits with the predominance of right-handed individuals. However, Xiu-Jie Wu and colleagues show that 50% of the "sided" injuries from before 13,000 years ago are on the right, which is above what is expected for the proportion of right-handedness in the modern era. What this means is unclear.

Our perceptions of Neandertals have undergone a sea change in recent years. Many decades ago, we viewed them as brooding ape-people (the quintessential "cave man"), with more in common with other primates than with us. We now know that they were probably much more like us than previously believed, given the newly available evidence from genetic studies and archaeological remains. They may have acted and looked at the world in similar ways to modern humans. Also of interest for this book is how Neandertals as a group have often been "accused" of various atrocities, notably in the context of cannibalism. The site of Krapina in Croatia seems to provide evidence of cannibalism but it may also reflect burial practices (Russell 1987a, 1987b). For a Neandertal group at El Sidron in Spain dating to approximately 50 kya, researchers have presented evidence indicating both possible cannibalism as well as genetic evidence of a patrilocal mating behavior (Lalueza-Fox et al. 2011). Though, again, there is the question of whether cannibalism in this context is related to warfare.

One of the better known examples comes from St. Cesaire, France, where a Neandertal skeleton dating to ~36,000 years ago was discovered with a healed fracture on the top of its cranium (Zollikofer et al. 2002). The shape of the injury suggests it was caused by a sharp implement. Interestingly, the individual lived for at least a few months after receiving the wound, suggesting s/he received some sort of care. This, plus the presence of shells found near the body, suggests the individual was intentionally buried. The cause of the blow is, of course, unknown, but may have been due to intergroup conflict. But, due to low population densities, it has been hypothesized that regional groups would have practiced mutual avoidance of other groups rather than engage in direct competition with one another.

Another contender for Neandertal violent death is Shanidar 3, an older male (40–50 years) from the Zagros Mountains in Iraq. This skeleton is radiocarbon dated to around 50 kya.[4] He has a lesion on his left ninth rib that most likely was due to a weapon attack. Steven Churchill and colleagues (2009) suggest that he was struck by a low-energy projectile weapon rather than a high-energy thrusting weapon, though they note that this is far from certain. As many scholars have argued that Neandertals did not have projectile weaponry and relied mostly on thrusting spears, this might suggest that he was attacked by a modern human. Since the tip of the weapon was not recovered (leaving some to suggest it was a wooden-tipped spear), it is hard to say for certain how he was killed. If the burial does date to 50,000 years ago, it could be at the time when modern humans were entering southwest Asia. Genetic evidence tells us human and Neandertal populations were in contact with one another, exchanging both cultural and genetic material. With all of the interactions that occurred between groups, it is not out of the question that fighting could have occurred from time to time. However, it also must be recalled that we do not know for certain that it was caused by a throwing weapon and we cannot rule out accidental death.

You may have noticed a significant issue with the above cases. While they may show interpersonal violence, they are for the most part single instances of violence devoid of a larger context of data.[5] One reason for this is that, with very few exceptions, early human fossils tend to be found in single occurrences. It is difficult to extrapolate from this to more general views. Moreover, the cultural aspects of archaic human populations are difficult to know, as much of the material record has been lost to us. And so, the skeletal evidence alone is not sufficient in revealing the presence of emergent warfare in the Early or Mid-Pleistocene. However, we would point out a couple of observations here. First, given the rarity of fossils in the corpus of Pleistocene records, the fact that we see evidence of trauma means we should not be hasty in dismissing violence, which in turn means we should be open to the possibility that groups sometimes had reasons and motivations to use aggression and violence in attacking members of other groups. And this brings up a second and related point, that we cannot simply assume a default position that warfare was wholly absent or not yet "invented" in the Mid- to Late Pleistocene. If groups did find occasion to compete or fight, for whatever reasons, these behaviors would have approximated forms of human warfare (emergent warfare) even if they would have looked different from what we may be familiar with today. In that regard, we argue that the default assumption should be a more neutral one. Maybe there was warfare 100,000 years ago, maybe not.

The Late Pleistocene

As should be clear, archaeologists often face a major challenge in distinguishing between intergroup conflict and interpersonal violence or homicide (Kim and Keeley 2008). Skeletal trauma only suggests the possibility of violence, which could have been homicidal and interpersonal in scale, and do not necessarily demonstrate collective violence. Many signs (some more equivocal than others) of interpersonal violence do exist within the Pleistocene record, but one or several violent and contemporaneous deaths do not necessarily mean warfare was involved. When it comes to Pleistocene contexts, we have to rely almost exclusively on osteological remains for signs of violence, but these findings cannot tell us much about the participants, their intentions and planning, and scales of violence. As illustration, we can return to the case of Otzi the "iceman." What could we infer had we only been able to recover his skeletal remains and not any of the other artifacts and ecofacts associated with his body? With the other materials, researchers are able to offer stronger conclusions about the violence contributing to his death.

While the fossil and archaeological records for much of the Pleistocene largely hint at violence and organized violence, the evidence becomes more compelling as we get closer to the Holocene. From the Late Pleistocene comes a case associated with the fascinating site of Les Rois, in southwestern France (Ramirez Rozzi et al. 2009). This cave site yielded stone tools attributed to the Aurignacian industry, a stone tool tradition associated with anatomically modern humans and dating to ~30,000 years ago. What makes the site interesting is that two jaw bones were found at the site: one which looks like a modern human jaw and the other, a juvenile mandible of a Neandertal. Interestingly, the Neandertal jaw has cutmarks on the interior surface (similar to marks seen on the faunal remains at the site). One provocative interpretation of these data is that the Neandertal child was consumed by modern humans. Of course, there are other plausible interpretations, such as biological contact between the two groups. As genetic evidence indicates that Neandertal and modern humans did mix (Green et al. 2010), this is also a possibility.

The Upper Paleolithic period in Europe, which roughly spans a period of 50,000 to 10,000 years ago, provides additional evidence of some interpersonal conflict and perhaps war deaths. A child from an Upper Paleolithic site (c. 32,000 BP) in Italy has a point embedded in the vertebrae, which would likely have been lethal (Kim and Keeley 2008). A female pelvis from San Teodoro Cave, Italy, has a flake embedded in it that may have been an arrowhead (Bachechi 1997). Keeley (1996) suggests the presence of warfare-related victims at the Upper Paleolithic sites of Predmosti (27,000–25,000 BP) and Dolni Vestonice, though Ferguson (2006) discounts this, suggesting that the data are not sufficient to make a strong determination.

One problem with assessing the record is that not all traumas lead to death, which means that it is often quite hard to tease apart the reasoning behind the recorded injuries. In the recent study about the Maba cranium mentioned above, Wu and colleagues (2011) provide a listing of all the known traumatic lesions on *Homo* fossils that predate the Late Glacial Maximum of 13,000 years ago. Interestingly, all but one of the 79 fossils show some level of healing (in the form of bone remolding), suggesting perhaps some form of compassion. Some of these are relatively minor injuries, though others show serious injuries that could have resulted in loss of function or death. The authors suggest that these data support the assertion of both high risk of injury and the ability to survive these incidences for many of these contexts.

In another overview of the fossil record for interpersonal violence, only three out of the 69 examined cases were considered to be lethal (Sala et al. 2015). These include the Neandertal skeleton from Shanidar Cave, Israel, with the potentially grievous rib injury, and a *Homo sapiens* from Sunghir, Russia with a traumatic injury to his backbone that may have been the cause of death. It is not clear, outside of some sort of *CSI: Paleolithic*, if these cases represent interpersonal violence or if, instead, they are examples of hunting accidents or other mishaps. Again, the equifinal nature of many archaeological finds makes interpreting past events very difficult.

As may be clear, good data for lethal conflict are rare. The best, and most often cited, evidence for collective violence comes from the previously discussed site of Jebel Sahaba located on the east bank of the Nile River in Sudan (Wendorf 1968).

The cemetery is often reported as being the earliest evidence of warfare as it has multiple occurrences of skeletons with trauma. There is no occupation area nearby, which is surprising since many cultures tend to bury their dead near their campsites. It is possible that the campsite was washed away by the Nile (the cemetery is ~1 km away from the river). The burials are covered by sandstone slabs, which made locating the skeletons easy. Some burials have only one individual, while others have up to four people in one burial pit. Originally dated to 13,740 BP +/− 600 years, recent redating has produced a minimum date of at least 11,600 years ago, though possibly older. This, along with a diagnostic tool called a lunate, would put the site as being part of what archaeologists call the Qadan Culture. Importantly, of the 61 skeletons, 45% are said to show signs of traumatic death, including points and barbs directly associated with burials (and a few artifacts embedded in the bone fragments themselves). While archaeologists often interpret objects buried with skeletons as a form of grave good, in this case it was argued that the stone tools were directly responsible for the individual's death. Interestingly, analysis of body shape suggests they are more similar to sub-Saharan Africans rather than Egyptians or Nubians (Holliday 2013). Recent work on the skeletal material suggests there are even more makers of violent death in the form of arrow impact marks, suggesting that the individuals succumbed to attacks from archers (Keys 2014). There are also healed injuries on the bones, which some argue suggest sustained violence over an individual's lifetime.

A reanalysis of parts of the collection also indicates traumatic deaths. The ulnae (the lower arm bone) of a few of the individuals (~11%) shows signs of what are known as 'parry marks,' which are left when trying to avoid a direct blow to the head (Judd 2006). Unfortunately, the bones that were originally reported as having embedded lithics in them could not be located, though a recent study reports on embedded microliths in six of the individuals. As compelling as this case might be, there are some important points to keep in mind. For instance, while the artifacts found associated with the bodies are often referred to as arrowheads, they could also be microliths that were attached to shafts. Secondly, some of the artifacts are found inside skulls that have no recorded entry wounds (Ferguson 2013b). Finally, the suggestion that 45% of the individuals died a traumatic death comes mostly from the artifact data. However, of the 24 individuals counted to show signs of trauma, only four have embedded fragments of tools. The rest are just in association with the bodies. This suggests to some researchers that trauma is closer to 10% rather than ~50% (Jurmain 2001). In the end, it seems clear that some form of intergroup and systematic violence occurring at 12,000 years ago can account for some of the trauma found. And this appears to have occurred at a time when there were no large-scale, complex societies or populous settlements known as cities.

A paper by Lahr and colleagues (2016) discusses a case from Kenya, dating to ~10,000 years ago. At a site located along the banks of what would have been a lagoon, researchers uncovered evidence of what may have been a massacre. Of nearly 30 individuals found at the site of Nataruk, a dozen individual skeletons were found partly preserved and articulated. Of these 12, ten show signs of lethal trauma.

This includes sharp-force trauma on the head, most likely due to arrow wounds. Others show sign of blunt-force trauma to the head, and two have hand fractures. The two skeletons who do not show signs of trauma (one male and one pregnant female) are oriented in such a way as to seem like they were bound. Most tellingly, three artifacts were found within the skeletons. One is an obsidian blade embedded in a cranium. Based on its raw material likely coming from a source far away, this blade is suggested to have been made by the aggressors. Of further interest is that the skeletons were not ritually placed into burials, unlike the case of Jebel Sahaba. The burials were not all placed in the same orientation, and do not have any grave goods. The embedded projectile points and fractures clearly indicate violent trauma of an intergroup variety. The researchers suggest possible scenarios, such as raiding between groups, and state that "the deaths at Nataruk are testimony to the antiquity of inter-group violence and war" (Lahr et al. 2016: 397). The interpretations about a single massacre event continue to be debated (see Stojanowski et al. 2016), but if intergroup violence is occurring at this time in this region, the Nataruk case provides further support for the notion that intergroup violence need not be restricted to larger-scale, complex societies or civilizations.

Tool Technologies Through Time

So, we can see that the fossil records of the world show us that violence is not a recent phenomenon, and that forms of organized violence are discernible at the end of the Pleistocene, if not earlier. But the fossil record constitutes only one stream of evidence. We need more, and as we stated earlier, we must "cross" or combine multiple streams. We now turn to the material record for artifacts – the products of human tinkering. When it comes to weapons, there is much ambiguity in the prehistoric record. Even for time periods when we know warfare was extant and prevalent, implements in the archaeological record can often demonstrate multiple possible functions, which can sometimes include violence and warfare. One can imagine how much more difficult interpretations become when we consider the earliest kinds of tools.

The earliest stone tool tradition, the Oldowan, does not have anything that resembles a weapon in a strict functional sense, but instead yields simple chopping tools, perhaps used to process animal carcasses.[6] The later Acheulian period (which dates from ~1.8 mya – 100 kya) is typed by the Acheulian hand axe, but this too does not seem to have been a hunting weapon, though its function has been hotly debated (McNabb et al. 2004). Of course, anything can be used as a weapon if one were properly motivated, and this could include any sort of material, such as stone, wood, or bone. For the last, you might picture the iconic opening sequence of the film *2001: A Space Odyssey*. However, we simply do not have enough evidence to conclude that tools, such as those of the Oldowan, were being fashioned with an intended use as a weapon for conspecific attack. As noted in Chapter Three, it can be very challenging to determine possible weaponry functions from utilitarian tools of everyday living. Suffice it to say, a branch or bone could be used wielded as a shock weapon or club very easily for use in threatening displays or outright interpersonal violence. Or for that matter, even human extremities such as the hand can function well in violent behavior (see Morgan and Carrier 2013 for a controversial and highly debated argument about the evolution of the hominin hand and its efficacy in striking performance).

But did our ancestors make and use tools for the express purpose of causing harm? The answer is yes. We have clear evidence of implements used to injure prey animals. The oldest recorded implements that could also have been weapons date to between 400 and 300,000 years ago from Europe and are made of wood (one reason we do not find many examples of spears is wood degrades quite quickly and it is only under specific circumstances, such as waterlogged sites, when it preserves). One set of spears was uncovered from Schöningen, Germany. Made from spruce trees, these implements date to around 300,000 years old and were likely used to hunt horses given the proximity of remains for butchered horses and other large animals (Kuitems et al. 2015). Elsewhere, a spear from a site south of Ipswich, England, dates to 400,000 years ago and is of uncertain function (Allington-Jones 2015). Which species of early hominin to assign to both these finds is debatable, with some arguing they represent an early version of Neandertals. In any event, it is difficult to tell the exact function of many of these artifacts. Due to the nature in the archaeological record, we will not be able to find most wooden spears, as they degrade too quickly. These few examples, then, may indicate that spears were more common, likely used to hunt, and possibly could have been used in interpersonal conflict. But, the use of spears as weapons for warfare for much of the Pleistocene is highly speculative.

Since wooden artifacts most likely will not preserve under most conditions, archaeologists have studied stone artifacts that may have been used as weapons or as the tip to a composite tool. Some of the earliest evidence of a projectile weapon comes from a series of sites in Ethiopia, where scientists have found "pointed-tool" artifacts (Sahle et al. 2013) dating to over 280 kya. The shape of the tools suggests they were used as part of a thrown projectile weapon such as a javelin. They also have fracture marks indicating impact from being used against targets. Jayne Wilkins and colleagues (2012) reported evidence for the hafting of stone points on to spears in southern Africa by ~500 kya and note that hafted spear tips appear to be common later in time after ~300 kya. This hints at the possibility that stone-tipped spears could have been manufactured by hominins prior to 500 kya. While much more recent in time, a study found a poison applicator dating to some 24,000 years ago (d'Errico et al. 2012), perhaps indicating that we will soon find evidence of the use of poison at an even earlier date. It is also important to note that even without any stone tip hafted at the business end of a spear, it can be hardened by fire to increase its potency.

Weapons that allow an individual to affect a wound on someone (animal or human) from a far distance are very useful in warring conditions but they seem to show up late in the archaeological record. A recent review of the evidence (Shea 2006) concludes that there is little support for the use of projectile points before 50 kya, suggesting that the technology only became widespread after 50 kya. This study suggests one reason for this may have been climate change, which resulted in human populations packed into smaller regions, which could have increased *coalitionary* killing. However, that study was written before the discoveries noted above were made. With the recent evidence for projectile technologies being produced earlier and by some of our hominin ancestors, we might now revisit the notion that the infliction of injury from distance is a relatively late development, challenging the idea that it is restricted to the past 50,000 (or even 100,000) years. As a corollary, we might then say that the possible existence of such technologies could have opened the door for our ancestors to consider using such technologies against people, and not just hunted animals.

Iconography

The evidence from art is even less definitive, though some examples prove to be quite interesting. As always, we often run into issues of interpretation. For example, if we were to find an image engraved on a rock that clearly shows a human figure with an arrow embedded in him, does that mean he was the victim of interpersonal violence? Perhaps, but we would have to know that a) both the person and arrow were drawn at the same time, b) that it is depicting a historic event rather than a symbolic one, and c) was not showing a hunting accident but rather the intentional infliction of harm on someone. Another difficulty is dating these objects. For cave art in particular, dating these paintings is often difficult and, until recently, destructive, so we often have to rely on very broad dates.

That being said, there are simply very few depictions of human figures at all before 10,000 years ago. Until cave art appears, much of the artwork we find are geometric patterns engraved on eggshells or other media and a few anthropomorphic figurines. Cave art has been reported from over 340 sites in Europe alone, making it an important source of knowledge for archaeologists who want to reconstruct the behavior and beliefs of Upper Paleolithic peoples (Nomade et al. 2016). The earliest cave art date to around 40,000 years ago and is found in both Europe and Southeast Asia, though there are undated examples from Africa and Australia that may be this old as well. Most cave art is of non-human animals such as bison, reindeer, and horse, so the few anthropomorphic figures have received much attention. Interestingly, the human-like figurines are often more abstract than the animals.

Of these, only a handful has been reported as showing signs of violent death caused by other humans.[7] Cave sites such as Cougnac, Pech Merle, and Cosquer record instances of human-like figures being pierced by arrows and other weapons (Bachechi 1997). One example of what may depict a murder is from Cosquer Cave in southern France. The artwork depicts a figure on its back being struck by various projectiles. Describing this figure, Jean Guilaine and Jean Zammit (2001: 54) argue that:

> a spear pierces his chest and a javelin, complete with two barbs, enters his back, going right though his body and head ant out the other side . . . it

seems, therefore, that murder and capital execution played an important part in both the thoughts and customs of the day.

Skeptics, however, suggest that the figure looks more like a chamois (a goat-antelope) than a human (Haas and Piscitelli 2013). Indeed, these skeptics question whether any of these images depict actual humans or human–animal hybrids (some of them have tails), thus associated with magical animals and fertility. Furthermore, it is possible that the "spears" seen in some Paleolithic art that makes it look like the animals or humans are being killed could have been painted later, perhaps during a different ceremony (Guilaine and Zammit 2001).

Also relevant is a pebble from Paglicci Cave, Italy, which is reported as having an engraved image of a "human-like" figure being struck by spears (Guilaine and Zammit 2001). This artifact is dated to ~20,000 years ago, though not much has been published on this artifact. It does suggest a possible depiction of homicide.

At the very end of this time period, at ~12,000 years ago, someone or some people at an Italian site near Monte Pellegrini painted a complex scene with animals and humans. The nine humans are in various positions, and scholars have debated what the scene depicts. Two of the figures in the center of the image may represent victims based on the pose they are shown in, which would have been very painful (legs bent back, arms tightly folded behind the shoulder) (Guilaine and Zammit 2001). If so, could this represent a sort of initiation/torture event, perhaps with captives?

Captives, as noted in Chapter Three, are often the result of warlike or raiding actions, though discovering evidence of this in the archaeological record is very difficult. A Venus figurine from Kostienki in southern Russian dating to around 23,000 years ago has been argued to depict a captive (Taylor 2005). Tim Taylor argues that the statue has its wrists bound together, suggesting it could be evidence of slavery. He has further argued that the reason the more famous Venus of Willendorf is faceless may be that she represents a captive/slave, a faceless category. If true, perhaps such figurines correspond to war captives. While very tentative, it is important to keep these ideas in mind as we continue to gather evidence. The Venus figurines as a group could indeed represent captives, but this hypothesis requires more data in order for it to be better accepted. At the very least, these kinds of material data suggest that we need to be mindful that there are different possibilities for cultural practices and logics around appropriate or acceptable forms of human–human relationships throughout the Pleistocene.

Conclusions About the Ice Age World

What can we tell about the existence of warfare and violence in the Ice Age world? As we have been arguing in this book, looking at the question from the perspective of the emergence of warfare and of peacefare can help to situate the question in an evolutionary context.

By its very nature, it can be hard to find positive evidence for peaceful societies in the archaeological record, unless we expand the definition of peace. If peace is

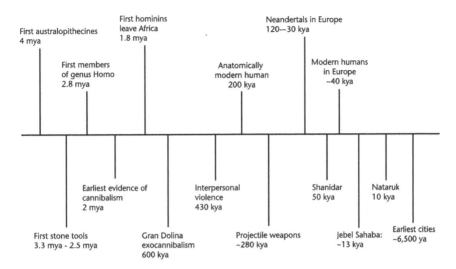

FIGURE 4.1 Timeline of major events and developments referenced in the chapter. *Produced by the authors*

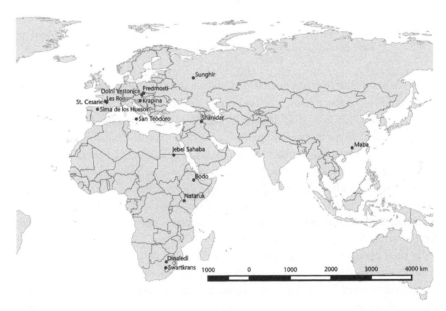

FIGURE 4.2 Map of selected sites referenced in the chapter. *Produced by Marc Kissel*

simply the absence of war then the concept becomes almost meaningless for archaeological investigation. Essentially, any time period without evidence of war can qualify as a peaceful period. On the other side of the coin, even if we fail to find good evidence of a violent past, this does not mean our ancestors were not warlike or wholly unfamiliar with warfare. As we have shown, conflict and violence do not

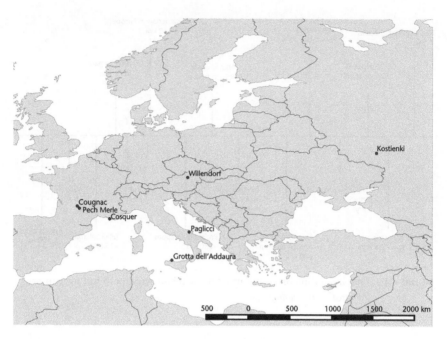

FIGURE 4.3   Map of selected sites described in the text where iconography or figurines have been uncovered. *Produced by Marc Kissel*

always leave indelible traces in the material record. Just because we do not find bodies with blunt force trauma or embedded projectile points in a settlement wall does not mean life was absolutely tranquil. We need to think of peace as the involvement of cultural activities, preferences, ideologies, and interactions that help people to cooperate and either avoid or resolve conflict. Even then, finding archaeological evidence of peacemaking behaviors can have its challenges. For instance, we won't find diplomacy in the Pleistocene material record. But we might find hints of such efforts, such as evidence of trade and exchange between groups, especially if the exchanges are happening not so much out of material necessity but for the strengthening of social relationships.

Is the notion of a natural history of peace more or less likely than that of a natural history of war? The anthropologist Leslie Sponsel (1996: 96) writes that the phrase "natural history of peace" refers to "the possibility of a holistic and dia-chronic description of peace as the norm in most societies, which in this and other respects means that peace is natural." Sponsel further notes that most of the work, even in journals devoted to the study of peace, concentrates in fact on war and violence. Penny Spikins and colleagues (2010) argue that the human fossil record demonstrates that compassion is a very human trait, and tracking the evolution of collaboration, trade, and exchange suggests that humans are better than most non-human primates at collaborating with each other (Fuentes 2013; Oka and Fuentes 2010). Taken together, these sorts of views emphasize the abilities of our ancestors to get along and cooperate. One pattern seems clear: the majority of the evidence for highly organized and complex warfare comes late in human evolution, not occurring until the Upper Paleolithic or earlier. A reason for this may be that certain kinds of warfare require a complex social organization in which those in power are able to control others. This type of social organization is often considered to be present in state-level societies, which did not arise until well after 10,000 years ago.

But, does this mean that all forms of organized violence only arose when societies became more complex? What can we say about interpersonal violence and the possibility of emergent warfare in the Pleistocene? The fossil record provides clear examples of individuals who received serious injuries caused by others. Teasing apart whether these are signs of intergroup violence is more difficult. When it comes to the material record, the data lend themselves to a fair amount of ambiguity. We can see signs of violence, some of which may have been between groups, but the majority of material signatures are fairly equivocal when it comes to the question of intergroup violence. Accordingly, we cannot say there is conclusive material evidence of warfare throughout the majority of the Pleistocene. With the exception of cases such as the Jebel Sahaba cemetery or the Nataruk site, it is difficult to find definitive examples of warfare before the Holocene.

However, we argue that a concept of emergent warfare, one involving socially cooperative violence, allows for a more nuanced view. In this perspective, we complicate the argument that warfare was only invented at the start of the Holocene (or later), and we then ask if that argument makes sense when we consider the full range of independent variables that may have led to warfare's "invention" or "emergence." Just as symbolic expression, previously thought to only be associated with anatomically modern humans, is now known to be found with pre-modern populations such as Neandertals, *Homo erectus*, and other archaic populations, so too can we see early expressions of behaviors we can link to both warfare and peacefare. Earlier scholars compared the wondrous Upper Paleolithic art to the apparently boring Middle Paleolithic technologies, arguing that the dearth of art suggested that the modern humans associated with the Upper Paleolithic were more cognitively complex. However, we should not expect all forms of complex cognation to appear the same (McBrearty 2013). The fact that late Pleistocene Australia was populated by modern humans, with material culture that does not seem to fit many of the expectations of modern human behavior, suggests that variation is key (Brumm and Moore 2005). Similarly, we should not expect to see modern warfare in the Pleistocene, or even warfare akin to that seen in the Mesolithic era of regions like Europe. The presence of interpersonal violence (along with other behaviors like hunting) suggests the presence of a key building block for emergent warfare. Likewise, we simultaneously see the origins of compassion and sociality (Spikins et al. 2010). The evidence of healed trauma on many Pleistocene individuals speaks to a world sometimes fraught with danger, with threats that may come from both other species but also one's own. It also speaks to the care and compassion given to individuals by their communities. What we can see, then, is that the crucial ingredients for various kinds of complexly organized human action are certainly present in the Pleistocene. At the crux of the matter, then, is when they surface.

We need to combine the streams of evidence in order to understand the role that war plays in human evolution. Was there emergent warfare deep in the Pleistocene? It depends on one's perspective and how much weight one assigns to various kinds of evidence. Using analogy, many would argue that our earliest ancestors in the Early and Middle Pleistocene would have engaged in intergroup violence approximating rudimentary forms of human warfare. For the Late Pleistocene, when we begin to see greater evidence for symbolic thought and modern behavior, the use of analogy with extant human societies comes to the fore, and again, many promote the view that our Late Pleistocene ancestors would have been just as capable of warfare as we are today. At the moment, we would postulate that violence for pre-AMH might have been analogous to that seen with some of our contemporary primate relatives, such as chimpanzees, but we caution against an overreliance on this analogy. There are other possible models (e.g. bonobos and other primates) that paint different pictures, and we should also remember that we are dealing with many different lineages (sometimes overlapping, sometimes isolated) through millions of years of evolutionary change. To make a blanket generalization that all of these hominin populations in all times, places, and environmental conditions would have behaved exactly the same way would be too simplistic. Rather, we might be on safer empirical ground in saying that a capacity for forms of violence would have been there, and we have some physical evidence to support this notion.

Ultimately, there are no unequivocal signs of group-on-group violence or warfare in the Early and Middle Pleistocene fossil or archaeological records, though there are some indications of interpersonal violence, homicide, and cannibalism. Where does this leave us? Well, if we were to imagine a map with clues, the arrows seem to be pointing to the Pleistocene Epoch for finding emergent warfare. After all, this is where we can see gradual changes associated with our ancestors as they took on new physical traits that enabled novel behavioral patterns. Although we have not physically identified hard evidence of emergent war- or peacemaking, we can still postulate about emergent capacities surfacing as our ancestors moved along their evolutionary trajectories. The clues we have today suggest that cooperation, compassion, group identity, symbolic thinking, and higher cognition all take shape in the Pleistocene, and so we see no reason to preclude the possibility that emergent forms of war- and peacemaking also began to develop. This is where we would need to concentrate our efforts in exploring notions of emergent warfare and peacefare. It is during this time when we are able to really cooperate and communicate in ways we can today, when very complex and sophisticated abilities for planning ahead and thinking in abstract terms allow forms of cooperation and sociality to take off – even if it means cooperating to use violence against members of other groups. It was also a time where we could think ahead to devise ways to resolve and avoid conflict. And, as we will discuss, it was a time when language became a fundamentally vital tool to make all of these interactions possible.

We will return to the ideas about emergent warfare, peacefare, and language later in the book. But first, we ponder the question of whether violence is in our genes.

Notes

1 On the social aspects of archaeology see Abu El Haj (2001).
2 While sometimes referred to as hunter-gatherers, it is important to note that the majority of the calories in most bands come from foraging.
3 For a critical evaluation of Shermer's argument, see a post on the weblog of John Hawks (http://johnhawks.net/weblog/fossils/naledi/shermer-naledi-murder-2016.html).
4 These are older dates, though, and could be biased and are not "corrected."
5 The exception to this is Atapuerca, where numerous crania show signs of trauma (Sala et al. 2015), though it is unclear if these trauma are human-derived or not.
6 Recently archaeologists in Kenya have announced an earlier stone tool tradition, the Lomekwian, but its functions are not currently known (Harmand et al. 2015)
7 There are also some examples of humans who were apparently killed during encounters with animals, but these too are hard to interpret.

Works Cited

Abu El Haj, Nadia. 2001. *Facts on the Ground: Archaeological Practice and Territorial Self-Fashioning in Israeli Society.* University of Chicago Press, Chicago, IL.

Allington-Jones, Lu. 2015. The Clacton Spear: The Last One Hundred Years. *Archaeological Journal* (June), 1–24.

Arens, William. 1980. *The Man-Eating Myth.* Oxford University Press, Oxford.

Bachechi, L. 1997 An Arrow-caused Lesion in a Late Upper Palaeolithic Human Pelvis. *Current Anthropology* 38(1), 135–140.

Birdsell, Joseph. 1958. On Population Structure in Generalized Hunting and Collecting Populations. *Evolution* 12(2), 189–205.

Birdsell, Joseph B. 1973. A Basic Demographic Unit. *Current Anthropology* 14(4), 337–356.

Bowles, Samuel. 2009. Did Warfare Among Ancestral Hunter-Gatherers Affect the Evolution of Human Social Behaviors? *Science* 324(5932), 1293–1298.

Brain, C K. 1981. *The Hunters or the Hunted?: An Introduction to African Cave Taphonomy.* University of Chicago Press, Chicago, IL.

Braun, David. 2012. What Does Oldowan Technology Represent in Terms of Hominin Behavior? In *Stone Tools and Fossil Bones: Debates in the Archaeology of Human Origins,* edited by Manuel Dominguez-Rodrigo, pp. 222–244. Cambridge University Press, Cambridge.

Brumm, Adam, and Mark W. Moore. 2005. Symbolic Revolutions and the Australian Archaeological Record. *Cambridge Archaeological Journal* 15(2), 157–175.

Bunn, Henry. 2001. Hunting, Power Scavenging, and Butchering by Hadza Foragers and by Plio-Pleistocene Homo. In *Meat-eating and Human Evolution,* edited by Craig Stanford and Henry Bunn, pp. 199–218. Oxford University Press, Oxford.

Bunn, Henry. 2006. Meat Made Us Human. In *Evolution of the Human Diet: The Known, the Unknown, and the Unknowable,* edited by P. Ungar, pp. 191–211. Oxford University Press, Oxford.

Carbonell, Eudald, and Marina Mosquera. 2006. The Emergence of a Symbolic Behaviour: The Sepulchral Pit of Sima de los Huesos, Sierra de Atapuerca, Burgos, Spain. *Comptes Rendus Palevol* 5(1–2), 155–160.

Carbonell, Eudald, Isabel Caceres, Marina Lozano, et al. 2010. Cultural Cannibalism as a Paleoeconomic System in the European Lower Pleistocene. *Current Anthropology* 51(4), 539–549.

Chagnon, Napoleon. 1988. Life Histories, Blood Revenge, and Warfare in a Tribal Population. *Science* 239(4843), 985–992.

Childe, V. Gordon. 1950. The Urban Revolution. *The Town Planning Review* 21(1), 3–17.

Churchill, Steven E., Robert G. Franciscus, Hilary A. McKean-Peraza, Julie A. Daniel, and Brittany R. Warren. 2009. Shanidar 3 Neandertal Rib Puncture Wound and Paleolithic Weaponry. *Journal of Human Evolution* 57(2), 163–178.

Cole, James. 2017. Assessing the Calorific Significance of Episodes of Human Cannibalism in the Palaeolithic. *Scientific Reports* 7(7), 44707. DOI:10.1038/srep44707.

d'Errico, Francesco, Christopher Henshilwood, and Peter Nilssen. 2001. Engraved Bone Fragment from c. 70,000-year-old Middle Stone Age levels at Blombos Cave, South Africa: Implications for the Origin of Symbolism and Language. *Antiquity* 75(288), 309–318.

d'Errico, F., L. Backwell, P. Villa, et al. 2012. Early Evidence of San Material Culture represented by Organic Artifacts from Border Cave, South Africa. *Proceedings of the National Academy of Sciences* 109(33), 13214–13219.

Dirks, Paul, Lee Berger, Eric Roberts, et al. 2015. Geological and Taphonomic Context for the New Hominin Species Homo *naledi* from the Dinaledi Chamber, South Africa. *eLife*; 6:e24231. DOI: 10.7554/eLife.24231.

Dirks, Paul H.G.M., Eric M. Roberts, Hannah Hilbert-Wolf, et al. 2017. The Age of Homo Naledi and Associated Sediments in the Rising Star Cave, South Africa. *eLife*, 6, 1–59.

Ferguson, R. Brian. 2006. Archaeology, Cultural Anthropology, and the Origins and Intensifications of War. In *The Archaeology of Warfare: Prehistories of Raiding and Conquest*, edited by E. Arkush and M. Allen, pp. 469–523. University Press of Florida, Gainesville.

Ferguson, R. Brian. 2013a. Pinker's List. In *War, Peace, and Human Nature: The Convergence of Evolutionary and Cultural Views*, edited by Douglas P. Fry, pp. 112–131. Oxford University Press, New York.

Ferguson, R. Brian. 2013b. The Prehistory of War and Peace in Europe and the Near East. In *War, Peace, and Human Nature: The Convergence of Evolutionary and Cultural Views*, edited by Douglas P. Fry, pp. 191–240. Oxford University Press, New York.

Fernández-Jalvo, Y., P. Andrews, and C. Denys. 1999. Cut Marks on Small Mammals at Olduvai Gorge Bed-I. *Journal of Human Evolution* 36(5), 587–589.

Fernández-Jalvo, Yolanda, J. Carlos Diez, José María Bermúdez de Castro, Eudald Carbonell, and Juan Luis Arsuaga. 1996. Evidence of Early Cannibalism. *Science* 271(5247), 277–278.

Fuentes, Agustin. 2013. Cooperation, Conflict, and Niche Construction in the Genus *Homo*. In *War, Peace, and Human Nature: The Convergence of Evolutionary and Cultural Views*, edited by Douglas P. Fry, pp. 78–94. Oxford University Press, New York.

Gat, Azar. 2015. Proving Communal Warfare Among Hunter-Gatherers: The Quasi-Rousseauan Error. *Evolutionary Anthropology* 24(3), 111–126.

Gould, Richard A., and Patty Jo Watson. 1982. A Dialogue on the Meaning and Use of Analogy in Ethnoarchaeological Reasoning. *Journal of Anthropological Archaeology* 1(4), 355–381.

Gray, John. 2015. Steven Pinker is Wrong about Violence and War. *The Guardian*, March 13.

Green, Richard E., Johannes Krause, Adrian W. Briggs, et al. 2010. A Draft Sequence of the Neandertal Genome. *Science* 328(5979), 710–722.

Guil-Guerrero, J.L. 2017. Evidence for Chronic Omega-3 Fatty Acids and Ascorbic Acid Deficiency in Palaeolithic hominins in Europe at the Emergence of Cannibalism. *Quaternary Science Reviews* 157, 176–187.

Guilaine, Jean, and Jean Zammit. 2001. *Origins of War: Violence in Prehistory*. Blackwell Publishing, Oxford.

Haas, Jonathan, and Matthew Piscitelli. 2013. The Prehistory of Warfare: Misled by Ethnography. In *War, Peace, and Human Nature: The Convergence of Evolutionary and Cultural Views*, edited by Douglas P. Fry, pp. 168–190. Oxford University Press, New York.

Harmand, Sonia, Jason Lewis, Craig Feibel, et al. 2015. 3.3-million-year-old Stone Tools from Lomekwi 3, West Turkana, Kenya. *Nature* 521(7552), 310–315.

Hill, Kim R., Robert S. Walker, Miran Bozicević, et al. 2011 Co-residence Patterns in Hunter-gatherer Societies Show Unique Human Social Structure. *Science* 331(6022), 1286–1289.

Hinton, Alexander. 2004. The Poetics of Genocidal Practice. In *Violence*, edited by Neil Whitehead, pp. 157–183. School of American Research Press, Santa Fe, NM.

Holliday, T. W. 2013. Population Affinities of the Jebel Sahaba Skeletal Sample: Limb Proportion Evidence. *International Journal of Osteoarchaeology* 25(4), 466–476.

Honeychurch, William. 2014. Alternative Complexities: The Archaeology of Pastoral Nomadic States. *Journal of Archaeological Research* 22(4), 277–326.

Judd, Margaret. 2006. Jebel Sahaba Revisited. In *Archaeology of Early Northeastern Africa*, edited by Karla Kroeper, Marek Chlodnicki and Michal Kobusiewicz, pp. 153–166. Poznan Archaeological Museum, Poznan, Poland.

Jurmain, R. 2001. Paleoepidemiolgical Patterns of Trauma in a Prehistoric Population from Central California. *American Journal of Physical Anthropology* 115(1), 13–23.

Kantner, J. 1999. Survival Cannibalism or Sociopolitical Intimidation? Explaining Perimortem Mutilation in the American Southwest. *Human Nature* 10(1), 1–50.

Keeley, Lawrence. 1996. *War Before Civilization*. Oxford University Press, Oxford.

Keys, David. 2014. Saharan Remains May Be Evidence of First Race War, 13,000 Years Ago. *Independent*, July 13.

Kim, Nam. 2012. Angels, Illusions, Hydras and Chimeras: Violence and Humanity. *Reviews in Anthropology* 41(4), 239–272.

Kim, Nam and Lawrence Keeley. 2008. Social Violence and War. In *Encyclopedia of Archaeology*, edited by Deborah Pearsall, pp. 2053–2064. Elsevier Academic Press, San Diego, CA.

Kim, Nam, Chapurukha Kusimba, and Lawrence Keeley. 2015. Coercion and Warfare in the Rise of State Societies in Southern Zambezia. *African Archaeological Review* 32(1), 1–34.

Kissel, Marc, and Agustin Fuentes. 2016. From Hominid to Human: The Role of Human Wisdom and Distinctiveness in the Evolution of Modern Humans. *Philosophy, Theology, and the Sciences* 3(2), 217–244.

Kuitems, M., H. van der Plicht, Dorothée G. Drucker, Thijs van Kolfschoten, S.W.L. Palstra, and Hervé Bocherens. 2015. Carbon and Nitrogen Stable Isotopes of Well-preserved, Middle Pleistocene Bone Collagen from Schöningen (Germany) and Their Palaeoecological Implications. *Journal of Human Evolution* 89(December), 105–113.

Lahr, M. Mirazón, F. Rivera, R.K. Power, et al. 2016. Inter-group Violence among Early Holocene Hunter-gatherers of West Turkana, Kenya. *Nature* 529(7586), 394–398.

Lalueza-Fox, Carles, Antonio Rosas, Almudena Estalrrich, et al. 2011. Genetic Evidence for Patrilocal Mating Behavior among Neandertal Groups. *Proceedings of the National Academy of Sciences of the United States of America* 108(1), 250–253.

LeBlanc, Steven (with Katherine Register). 2003. *Constant Battles*. St. Martin's Press, New York.

Lee, Richard B. 2007. *The Dobe Ju/'Hoansi*. 4th ed. Wadsworth, Belmont, CA.

Lindenbaum, Shirley. 2004. Thinking About Cannibalism. *Annual Review of Anthropology* 33(1), 475–498.

Mays, S., and O. Beattie. 2015. Evidence for End-Stage Cannibalism on Sir John Franklin's Last Expedition to the Arctic, 1845. *International Journal of Osteoarchaeology* 26(5), 778–786.

McBrearty, Sally. 2013. Advances in the Study of the Origin of Humanness. *Journal of Anthropological Research* 69(1), 7–31.

McNabb, John, Francesca Binyon, and Lee Hazelwood. 2004. The Large Cutting Tools from the South African Acheulean and the Question of Social Traditions. *Current Anthropology* 45(5), 653–677.

Mead, Margaret. 1940. Warfare Is Only an Invention, Not a Biological Necessity. *Asia* 15(8), 402.

Milo, Richard G. 1998. Evidence for Hominid Predation at Klasies River Mouth, South Africa and Its Implications for the Behaviour of Early Modern Humans. *Journal of Archaeological Science* 25(2), 99–133.

Montellano, Bernard R. Ortiz de. 1978. Aztec Cannibalism: An Ecological Necessity? *Science* 200(4342), 611–617.

Morgan, Lewis. 1877. *Ancient Society*. D. Appleton, New York.

Morgan, Michael, and David Carrier. 2013. Protective Buttressing of the Human Fist and the Evolution of Hominin Hands. *The Journal of Experimental Biology* 216, 236–244.

Nomade, Sébastien, Dominique Genty, Romain Sasco, et al. 2016. A 36,000-year-old Volcanic Eruption Depicted in the Chauvet-Pont d'Arc Cave (Ardèche, France)? *Plos One* 11(1), e0146621.

O'Connell, James F., Kristen Hawkes, and Nicholas Blurton Jones. 1988. Hadza Hunting, Butchering, and Bone Transport and Their Archaeological Implications. *Journal of Anthropological Research* 44(2), 113–161.

Oka, Rahul, and Agustín Fuentes. 2010. From Reciprocity to Trade: How Cooperative Infrastructures Form the Basis of Human Socio-economic Evolution. In *Cooperation*, edited by Robert Marshall, pp. 3–28. AltaMira Press, Walnut Creek, CA.

Otterbein, Keith. 2004. *How War Began*. Texas A & M University Press, College Station.

Otterbein, Keith. 2011. The Earliest Evidence for Warfare?: A Comment on Carbonell et al. *Current Anthropology* 52(3), 439.

Pauketat, Timothy. 2007. *Chiefdoms and Other Archaeological Delusions*. AltaMira Press, Lanham, MD.

Pickering, Travis. 2013. *Rough and Tumble: Aggression, Hunting, and Human Evolution*. University of California Press, Berkeley.

Pickering, Travis, Tim D. White, and Nicholas Toth. 2000. Brief Communication: Cutmarks on a Plio-Pleistocene Hominid from Sterkfontein, South Africa. *American Journal of Physical Anthropology* 111(4), 579–584.

Pinker, Steven. 2002. *The Blank Slate: The Modern Denial of Human Nature*. Viking, New York.

Pinker, Steven. 2011. *The Better Angels of Our Nature: Why Violence Has Declined*. Viking, New York.

Potter, James M., and Jason P. Chuipka. 2010. Perimortem Mutilation of Human Remains in an Early Village in the American Southwest: A Case for Ethnic Violence. *Journal of Anthropological Archaeology* 29(4), 507–523.

Ramirez Rozzi, Fernando V., Francesco d'Errico, Marian Vanhaeren, Pieter M. Grootes, Bertrand Kerautret, and Véronique Dujardin. 2009 Cutmarked Human Remains Bearing Neandertal Features and modern human remains associated with the Aurignacian at Les Rois. *Journal of Anthropological Sciences = Rivista di antropologia : JASS / Istituto italiano di antropologia* 87, 153–185.

Roper, Marilyn Keyes. 1969. A Survey of the Evidence for Intrahuman Killing in the Pleistocene. *Current Anthropology* 10(4), 427.

Russell, M.D. 1987a. Bone Breakage in the Krapina Hominid Collection. *American Journal of Physical Anthropology* 72(3), 373–379.

Russell, M.D. 1987b. Mortuary Practices at the Krapina Neandertal Site. *American Journal of Physical Anthropology* 72(3), 381–397.

Sahle, Yonatan, W. Karl Hutchings, David R. Braun, et al. 2013. Earliest Stone-tipped Projectiles from the Ethiopian Rift Date to >279,000 Years Ago. *PLoS ONE* 8(11), 1–9.

Sala, Nohemi, Juan Luis Arsuaga, Ana Pantoja-Perez, et al. 2015. Lethal Interpersonal Violence in the Middle Pleistocene. *PLoS One* 10(5), e0126589. DOI: 10.1371/journal.pone.0126589.

Sala, Nohemi, Ana Pantoja-Perez, Juan Luis Arsuaga, Adrian Pablos, and Ignacio Martinez. 2016. The Sima de Los Huesos Crania: Analysis of the Cranial Breakage Patterns. *Journal of Archaeological Science* 72, 25–43.

Saladie, Palmira, Rosa Huguet, Antonio Rodriguez-Hidalgo, et al. 2012. Intergroup Cannibalism in the European Early Pleistocene: The Range Expansion and Imbalance of Power Hypotheses. *Journal of Human Evolution* 63(5), 682–695.

Service, Elman Rogers. 1962. *Primitive Social Organization: An Evolutionary Perspective*. Random House, New York.

Shea, John. 2006. The Origins of Lithic Projectile Point Technology: Evidence from Africa, the Levant, and Europe. *Journal of Archaeological Science* 33(6), 823–846.

Shermer, Michael. 2016. Did This Extinct Human Species Commit Homicide? *Scientific American* 314(1), 75.

Snow, Charles Ernest. 1974 *Early Hawaiians: An Initial Study of Skeletal Remains from Mokapu, Oahu*. University of Kentucky, Lexington.

Spikins, Penny, Holly Rutherford, and Andy Needham. 2010. From Homininity to Humanity: Compassion from the Earliest Archaics to Modern Humans. *Time and Mind* 3(3), 303–325.

Sponsel, Leslie. 1996. The Natural History of Peace: The Positive View of Human Nature and Its Potential. In *A Natural History of Peace*, edited by Thomas Gregor, pp. 95–125. Vanderbilt University Press, Nashville, TN.

Stojanowski, Christopher, Andrew Seidel, Laura Fulginiti, Kent Johnson, and Jane Buikstra. 2016. Contesting the Massacre at Nataruk. *Nature* 539(7630), E8–E10. DOI: 10.1038/nature19778.

Taylor, Mitch, Thor Larsen, and R.E. Schweinsburg. 1985. Observations of Intraspecific Aggression and Cannibalism in Polar Bears (*Ursus maritimus*). *Arctic* 38(4), 303–309.

Taylor, Tim. 2005. Ambushed by a Grotesque: Archaeology, Slavery and the Third Paradigm. In *Warfare, Violence and Slavery in Prehistory*, edited by Mike Parker Pearson and I.J.N. Thorpe, pp. 225–232. BAR, Oxford.

Turner, Christy, and Jacqueline Turner. 1999. *Man Corn: Cannibalism and Violence in the Prehistoric American Southwest*. University of Utah Press, Salt Lake City.

van der Dennen, J.M.G. 1995. *The Origin of War: The Evolution of a Male-coalitional Reproductive Strategy*. Origin Press, Groningen, Netherlands.

Walker, Phillip. 2001. A Bioarchaeological Perspective on the History of Violence. *Annual Review of Anthropology* 30, 573–596.

Wendorf, F. 1968. Site 117-A Nubian Final Paleolithic Graveyard near Jebel Sahaba. In *The Prehistory of Nubia*, edited by F. Wendorf, pp. 954–995. Southern Methodist University, Dallas, TX.

White, Tim D. 1986. Cut Marks on the Bodo Cranium: A Case of Prehistoric Defleshing. *American Journal of Physical Anthropology* 69(4), 503–509.

Wiessner, Polly. 2002. The Vines of Complexity. *Current Anthropology* 43(2), 233–269.

Wilkins, Jayne, Benjamin Schoville, Kyle Brown, and Michael Chazan. 2012. Evidence for Early Hafted Hunting Technology. *Science* 338(6109), 942–946.

Wobst, H. Martin. 1978. The Archaeo-Ethnology of Hunter-Gatherers or the Tyranny of the Ethnographic Record in Archaeology. *American Antiquity* 43(2), 303–309.

Wrangham, Richard. 1999. Evolution of Coalitionary Killing. *Yearbook of Physical Anthropology* 42(S29), 1–30.

Wu, Xiu-Jie, Lynne A. Schepartz, Wu Liu, and Erik Trinkaus. 2011. Antemortem Trauma and Survival in the Late Middle Pleistocene Human Cranium from Maba, South China. *Proceedings of the National Academy of Sciences* 108(49), 19558–19562.

Yoffee, Norman. 2005. *Myths of the Archaic State: Evolution of the Earliest Cities, States, and Civilizations.* Cambridge University Press, Cambridge.

Young, Barry, and Robert Ruff. 1982. Population Dynamics and Movements of Black Bears in East Central Alberta. *The Journal of Wildlife Management* 46(4), 845–860.

Zollikofer, Christoph, Marcia S. Ponce de Leon, Bernard Vandermeersch, and François Lévêque. 2002. Evidence for Interpersonal Violence in the St. Césaire Neanderthal. *Proceedings of the National Academy of Sciences* 99(9), 6444–6448.

5
INSIGHTS FROM GENOMIC RESEARCH

We used to think our fate was in our stars. Now we know, in large measure, our fate is in our genes.

James Watson Quoted in Time *"The Gene Hunt,"*
by Leon Jaroff, March 20, 1989

By now on our journey, you have seen that violence is not restricted to humans, nor is it restricted to the recent past. In our reviews of the material evidence, we can see that violence extends well into the Pleistocene, linked to our earliest ancestors, though it is unclear how much of it can be clearly connected to warfare. But, before we return to the question of warfare's origins, we would like to present a new class of data that has been increasingly brought to bear on the larger research topic – genetics. Such research is increasingly being used by scholars inside and outside of biology to better understand human evolution and behavior.

Is there an innate drive for humans to be warlike and aggressive, as argued by many researchers? If so, where does this behavior come from? Is it part of our primate heritage (see Chapter Two) or is it unique to humans? As we have discussed, different cultures (both past and present) have conceptualized violence differently. If cultural differences explain the differences we see, then we would have to assume that it is not innate after all. Yet, some scientists suggest this view is overly naive (Pinker 2002), which suggests that there must be some biological drive to aggression that is deep in our nature. Indeed, some researchers have argued that there is a genetic component to aggression and that certain genes can make a person more aggressive (McDermott et al. 2009). The most famous instance of this is the so-called "warrior gene" (Gibbons 2004) which has been the source of much research over the last 20 years. Is it true that some people, by virtue of their genes, are more likely to respond with violence than others when put in the same situation? Have these genes been selected for over evolutionary times?

More provocatively, do these genes show up in greater frequencies in certain populations?

In recent years scientists, journalists, and the public have focused increased attention on the field of behavioral genetics. As the name implies, this is the study of the role genes play in behavior. Some studies have argued for links between specific genes and dancing prowess (Bachner-Melman et al. 2005), or for the likelihood of going to college (Shanahan et al. 2007), as well as cooperation levels (Mertins et al. 2011). While some genetic studies are based on human subjects, other, more invasive tests are based on non-human primates and mammals such as mice and rats. As may be expected, much research has been focused on the search for particular genes that play roles in the types of human behavior people are most interested in. Thus, studies have centered on the genetic background for sexual preference, political ideology, IQ, athleticism, and, importantly, violence and aggression.

Yet, the question of what causes aggression is a complex one. The reason two individuals may react to the same situation in different ways does not have an easy answer. Why, for example, will one person turn to violence while the other will turn the other cheek? The answer, perhaps, lies partly in our genetic makeup. Many readers are probably familiar with the concept of a "Flight or Fight" response, which supposedly is the basis for how an animal reacts in a dangerous situation. In high stress situations, an individual's nervous system and hormones react and affect how she deals with the event. As the regulation and production of these hormones is controlled partly by our genes, it makes sense to investigate what our genetic dispensations may be. If we are evolved to be warlike and aggressive, there should be clear signs of this in our genetic makeup. Indeed, many scholars and writers have argued that this is the case. In this chapter, we investigate these ideas and discuss how genetic studies are performed, how to correctly interpret their results, and how to apply them to the question of human aggression. In order to investigate this, we must first understand how genes function, how and why they can differ, how genes affect behavior, and how scientists study these phenomena.

Background on Genetics

Humans are diploids, which simply means that we inherit one copy of a gene from our biological mother and one from our biological father. Chromosomes are where DNA is found. DNA's job is, in part, to tell the cell how and when to make specific proteins. The part of the DNA that tells the cell to make a specific protein is called a gene. One set of chromosomes that deserves mention are the sex chromosomes, X & Y. Men have one X and one Y, while females are XX.

In order to understand how this works, let's use a simple example. Imagine that there is one gene for eye color (there isn't). On a particular part of the DNA, called the locus, we would find the gene for eye color. But not everybody has the same eye color. So that means that people have different types of that eye color gene. The reason for this is in the coding of the DNA. DNA consists of four nucleotide bases: adenine (A), thymine (T), cytosine (C), and guanine (G). Each gene is composed of a subset of these bases. Within a gene are the As, Ts, Cs, and Gs that provide instructions on how to take a bunch of smaller compounds (called amino acids) and put them together to make a protein. As different combinations of amino acids lead to the formation of different proteins, mutations or changes within the genetic code of a specific gene can lead to differences in the protein itself. This is, in theory, the reason why eye color differs (in fact, a number of genes control eye color so the story isn't that simple. Very few complex human traits are controlled by only one gene). We call different versions of the same gene an *allele* (so an allele for green eyes, one for blue, one for green, etc.). You get one copy of an allele from your biological mother and one from your biological father. An individual's *genotype* is the organism's alleles while the *phenotype* is the observable characteristic (thus, identical twins have the same genotype but often different phenotypes). An individual whose genotype consists of two of the same alleles on a pair of chromosomes is called *homozygous*, and an individual who has two different alleles is called *heterozygous*. Finally, some alleles are *dominant* over others. What this means is that if you inherit one copy of the dominant allele from a parent, you will express that trait phenotypically. However, the only way to express a recessive trait phenotypically is if your genotype has both *recessive* alleles. Using these terms, we can recast the nature and nurture debate as a debate about how genotype affects phenotype.

Traits that are controlled by only one gene are called Mendelian traits and, while there are many of them in humans, the majority of the traits that we tend to think of as Mendelian are in fact caused by more than one gene.[1] However, for most traits, even supposedly simple ones such as eye color and height, the situation is more complex. If a trait is continuous, by which we mean that the trait can take on almost any value (such as height), it is not Mendelian. Many behavioral traits are influenced by genes (Goldsmith and Bihun 1997). Behavioral traits, then, are most likely also the result of multiple genes (even the strongest supporters of the "genes for violence" admit to this).

Genes affect our phenotype in myriad ways. However, the role of environment cannot be forgotten. To understand this, we need to introduce the concept of *heritability*. Heritability is the proportion of the phenotypic variance that is explained by the genotypic variance within a population that has the same environment. The last part of this definition is extremely important. Heritability measurements are only relevant to the population being investigated. If a study is undertaken on a large group of undergraduate students it may indeed be relevant to the population at large, but this is not always the case.

A trait that has a high heritability is a trait that is caused mostly by genetic variation, while one that has a low heritability is controlled mostly by the environment. Geneticists often want to know if the *variation* in a trait is due to people having different *alleles* or having different *environments* (furthermore, the interaction between genes and the environment, or between nature and nurture, is of fundamental importance). In fact, we will see that oftentimes it is the interplay between the environment and the genes, rather than either the environment or the genes, which is the critical factor in behavior.

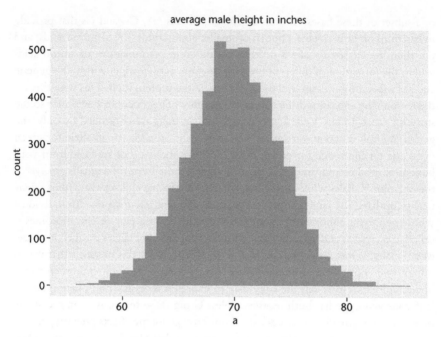

FIGURE 5.1   Average male height in inches

The most important concept here is *variance*. We see variance in all sorts of traits, such as height and weight. Figure 5.1 shows how a trait may vary. In this case, it shows hypothetical data on the height of males from a population. While the average value is around 70 inches, note that there is a great deal of variation around this height. Variance tells us something about how that trait varies in the population. Phenotypic variance is the variation that is observable, such as skin color, weight, and height. We know at least two aspects explain phenotypic variance: the fact that not everyone has the same genes (genetic variance) and that not everyone is under the same environment (environmental variance). Whenever you hear about a study that says scientists have found a gene that explains something complex (political belief, sexual orientation, aggression, and so on) think about the population they studied. Oftentimes this consists of college students at major universities. Do you think that 18-year-olds who take part in a study in order to get beer money are a good representation of humans as a whole?

Heritability is a trait of a population. What we mean by this is that when we measure the heritability of a trait, we need to clear whom we are studying. For example, say we examined the height differences between everyone in Madison, Wisconsin. Some are tall and some are short. Both the genes you have and the environment you grew up in control how tall you are. Heritability for height is high, so we might think that most of the differences we see in height are due to differences in genes for height. But recall that this is only true when comparing individuals within the same environment. If we assume that everyone in Madison has access to a similar diet then this would indeed be the case. However, say we compared people from Madison to people from another country. Now, we are comparing people who have different environments (differing access to food, health care, etc.) and thus the differences we see are due to difference in the environment. If you have genes that make you tall, but do not have access to high quality food, you might end up being shorter than your genes would predict. In the end, we can see how physical traits can be the outcomes of highly complex sets of interacting variables. The same can be seen for behaviors – as outcomes of biological heritage along with environmental and cultural conditions. At the heart of this is the notion of plasticity (which we return to in the coming chapters), which sees enormous range in possible outcomes when it comes to our traits and behaviors.

We must keep these caveats in mind, since in the case studies discussed in this chapter this important fact is often overlooked or forgotten when reported by journalists, or when people set policy, or defend a particular view of human innate behavior. We also must keep in mind that genetic influences are not static, but dynamic (Goldsmith and Bihun 1997). What we mean by this is that genes play a key role not just in development, but also throughout an organism's life. The questions this chapter will now investigate are if there are indeed predispositions in our genetic makeup that make humans warlike and aggressive, and prone to forming coalitions to fight each other.

Warrior Genes

You probably know people whose first reaction when confronted is to fight, while others may choose to try to find a more peaceful solution. The reason why some people are aggressive, while others are not, can be traced to multiple causes. In this section we investigate studies that suggest genes hold the answer to why some people are violent.

Some of the first studies on aggression linked it to serotonin (SR), a neurotransmitter that plays a major role in many behaviors, from sleep to general happiness. Neurotransmitters are chemicals that transmit information between nerve cells and control numerous functions (the neurotransmitter norepinephrine, for example, controls the rate at which your heart contracts, as well as the flight-or-fight response). As they are very important in understanding behavior, research centers on these chemicals and how they affect us. SR, like other neurotransmitters, has many functions, including allowing for "communication" between different parts of the brain. SR not only influences brain development, but plays a role in many complex behaviors including impulsiveness and aggression (Lesch and Merschdorf 2000).

Importantly, there may be a link between low levels of serotonin in the brain and heightened aggression. Evidence of this comes from studies that have shown that changes in diet can affect aggression. SR is derived from tryptophan, one of the essential amino acids that humans must obtain from their diet. By manipulating the diets of subjects, scientists were able to show heightened anger and a lower ability to control emotions among individuals who lacked tryptophan in their diets and thus had lower serotonin levels (Umukoro et al. 2013). (While it does not have

Synapse

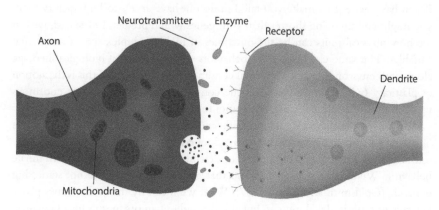

FIGURE 5.2 Illustration of brain synapse showing the role of neurotransmitters.
Source: Medical Labeled/Alamy Stock Vector

significantly higher amounts of tryptophan than other foods, you could suggest to your family that they eat lots of turkey at Thanksgiving dinner, thus making them less angry and less prone to arguing about politics at the dinner table.) What may be happening is that in individuals with lower SR, the communication between the amygdala (which deals with emotions) and that of the prefrontal cortex is lowered, making it hard for the brain to "control" the responses coming from the amygdala.

How do compounds like SR function? To understand this, we will focus on the role SR plays in depression. Many antidepressants work by increasing the amount of SR in the brain (either by preventing SR from being removed once it has been used or by stopping SR from being broken down, both of which leave more SR in the brain). In general, these drugs allow neurotransmitters to remain active longer (they are kept in between the neurons rather than being reabsorbed). By keeping the neurotransmitters in place, it allows for greater communication between the brain's functional centers. In the brain, there are chemicals whose job it is to prevent the neurotransmitters from accumulating. One such natural enzyme is Monoamine oxidase A (known to its friends as MAOA). Its job is to regulate certain neurotransmitters (including norepinephrine, serotonin, and dopamine) by removing them when no longer needed. To put it in scientific terms, MAOA's job is to catalyze various neurotransmitters (Shih et al. 1999).

However, if MAOA does not function properly, SR may be built up in the brain rather than be removed. The best-studied case of this involves a gene located on the X-chromosome which codes for MAOA. MAOA's effect on behavior stems from research done by a team from the Netherlands led by Han Brunner. In two articles (Brunner, Nelen, Breakefield, et al. 1993; Brunner, Nelen, van Zandvoort, et al. 1993) the team described a Dutch family in which 14 males exhibited an increase in violence (including rape and arson). Interestingly, it was a female family member who brought this case to the attention of Brunner and colleagues. She was concerned about the fate of many of her male family members, one of whom had run someone over with his car and another that had stabbed a warden with a pitchfork. The scientists discovered a genetic mutation close to the vicinity of the MAOA gene on the X chromosome and hypothesized that perhaps this mutation decreased the amount of MAOA in the men and led to an increase in violence.

You may be wondering why this condition occurred in males. Recall that, biologically speaking, women have two X chromosomes while men have an X and a Y. This means that females have to inherit two copies of the faulty allele in order for them to express the trait, so are much less likely to demonstrate this condition. This is also the reason why many studies on violence and its link to MAOA are only done on males, as the inheritance patterns are easier to understand and to predict mathematically. As we will discuss, the notion that men are more violent than women is a commonly held belief. However, this is not necessarily true. Teasing apart biological from cultural aspects of human behavior is not simple, and assumptions that males are inherently more violent need to be scrutinized carefully.

In the Dutch case, it was learned that a single change in the genetic code (a cytosine was replaced with a thymine at the 936th position) caused the MAOA molecule to stop forming, thus rendering it useless. Males who have this faulty MAOA gene are more aggressive. They also have elevated levels of serotonin, dopamine, and norepinephrine in their brain. However, the role of this MAOA allele would not seemingly be too important, as the mutation described by Brunner and colleagues is very rare. MAOA deficiency is uncommon in humans as a whole (Schuback et al. 1999). Indeed, we must be careful in linking the MAOA gene as a gene for violence since, as discussed above, there are no genes for specific behaviors. Besides, the types of aggression humans undertake are numerous and thus hard to subsume all under one gene. There are almost 300 SNPs[2] on the MAOA gene alone (Charney and English 2012). This did not stop the researchers from suggesting they had found an "aggression gene" (Morell 1993) or a "warrior gene" (Gibbons 2004).[3]

Since the Dutch study appeared, however, more work has revealed some interesting patterns. Scholars have noted that while maltreatment in youth can lead to violence as an adult, not all children who experience such abuse become violent (i.e., most maltreated children do not become criminals, but maltreatment is a predictor of such behavior). Psychologist Avshalom Caspi and colleagues (2002) asked why some maltreated children developed antisocial behaviors, while others seem to behave in "normal" ways. Maltreatment in youth can affect levels of SR and norepinephrine and may lead to aggressive behavior in adults. With this in mind, the scholars hypothesized that children who have a faulty MAOA gene would be more at risk for hyper-reaction due to the lack of MAOA activity. Caspi and colleagues wanted to investigate if there were any underlying genetic differences between these different groups. Fortunately, there existed a "perfect" study population from New Zealand, where over 1,000 children were studied from birth to adulthood. These participants had life history events recorded as well as different psychological traits, criminal records, and the results of IQ tests. Eventually, genetic data were also obtained from some of the participants (for an overview of this study, and indeed a good primer on the entire history of the study of the interaction between genes and the environment, see James Tabery's *Beyond Versus* [2014]). Scientists have since mined these data, looking for clues as to how genes and the environment interact to form behaviors.

In order to understand their results, which form the basis of subsequent work, recall that genes make proteins. Sometimes, when DNA is copied, there are copying errors that can lead to what are known as Variable Number Tandem Repeat (VNTR). These occur when small parts of the DNA code are duplicated, which can change the gene's product. For example, the DNA sequence ATGATGATGATGATG is a tandem repeat of "ATG" five times. Often these repeats have no phenotypic effect but are useful for identification purposes in forensic cases. Other times, they can have catastrophic effects. One well-known example of a VNTR is Huntington's disease. A tandem repeat located within the huntingtin gene leads to the production of a different protein than is necessary for proper function and causes neurological problems.

Humans are variable in the number of repeats in the MAOA gene (when the Caspi study was written, the number and type of repeats were not yet known. There are known to be at least five different versions of this gene, in which a 30 base pair sequence is repeated either 2, 3, 3.5, 4, or 5 times [Sabol et al. 1998; Deckert et al. 1999]). Caspi and colleagues showed that young males who have low MAOA activity are more likely to respond violently as adults. Their conclusion is that while individuals with low-activity MAOA account for only 12% of the cohort, they make up 44% of the groups violent convictions (a risk factor of ~11%). This study received a lot of attention and was one of the first to document a gene-environment interaction (G*E.) G*E occur when a response to the environment is based upon a certain genotype. It also brought more awareness to the gene itself and thus more studies began to concentrate on variants of the MAOA gene.

Figure 5.3 is from the original publication and is a "norm of reaction" graph. It shows how different phenotypes react under different settings. The figure is comparing high and low MAOA expression under different levels of childhood mistreatment, with the Y-axis recording levels of antisocial behavior. Individuals with the low-activity allele who were raised under severe mistreatment have a higher likelihood of antisocial behavior than those with the high-activity variant. Often missed, however, is that when there is no mistreatment, which is the most likely outcome, the converse is true. We will come back to this point soon.

Using fMRI data, psychiatrist Andreas Meyer-Lindenberg and colleagues (2006) examined the difference in brain function due to differences in the MAOA gene. fMRI measures brain activity by detecting changes in blood flow (increased activity in the brain = increased blood flow). They note that carriers of the low-expression variant have a reduction in their amygdala, hypothalamus, and other brain regions compared to the high-expression allele. Importantly, they note increased activity in

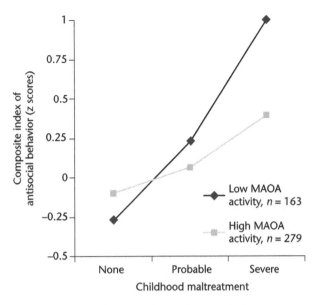

FIGURE 5.3   The effect of an individual's genotype on antisocial behavior is influenced by that person's treatment in childhood. *Adapted from Caspi et al. (2002)*

the amygdala which has been previously associated with anger (stimulating the amygdala in animals can produce violent behavior).

However, one must be careful in interpreting these results for two reasons. Firstly, there is no way to say for certain that it is the MAOA variant causing these differences, as there could be other factors at play. Secondly, and more importantly, is how researchers separate low- and high-activity versions of the gene. In this study, low-activity is represented by 2, 3, and 5 repeats while high-activity is 3.5 and 4. The original papers describing these variants (Sabol et al. 1998) argued that individuals with the 3.5 and 4 copies have the gene transcribed 2–10 times more efficiently than people with the 3 or 5 version. Other researchers have found that the 3.5, 4, and 5 alleles transcribed higher amounts than the 3 type (Deckert et al. 1999). This discrepancy seems to be unexplained. One reason may be that the first study looked at males and the second one looked at females. It does, however, show the difficulty in these studies, especially when applied to human subjects. Summaries of the various studies linking MAOA to aggression have to keep these differences in mind, but it is not always clear which breakdown is being used.

Since publication of the study by Caspi and colleagues, there have been studies both confirming the results and others that question parts. A tool scientists use to analyze data from different studies is called a meta-analysis. Often referred to as conducting research about previously existing research, meta-analysis is an important tool for genetic studies. A recent meta-analysis of MAOA, stress, and aggression reports that there is a small effect recorded on the interaction between being mistreated as a child and having low MAOA and subsequent aggression (Weder et al. 2009).

The effect of MAOA on aggression may not be as great as originally presented (this phenomenon, in which the effect size[4] is smaller as more studies are completed, is well known [Ioannidis et al. 2001]). The point here is that the more studies that were undertaken, the smaller the effect of MAOA variants on violence became. This does not show that it has no effect, but rather that we need to be careful when relying on only a single study.

Careful readers may have noted a contraction in the studies discussed above. If MAOA functions in part to remove free serotonin from the brain, individuals who have a less effective MAOA gene would have *more* serotonin. However, previous work on SR has suggested that it is people with *less* serotonin that are more aggressive. How can we reconcile these discrepancies? Perhaps high SR levels can also cause aggression (Seif and de Maeyer 1999). MAOA also metabolizes dopamine and norepinephrine. Increases in these NTs increase the 'fight-or-flight" response, making individuals have trouble in high stress situations. Perhaps the increase in SR is offset by the increase of dopamine and norepinephrine. Whatever the case, it does point to the complexity of these studies.

The label of MAOA as a "warrior gene" comes from a report on a paper given at the American Association of Physical Anthropologists meetings in 2004 by reporter Anne Gibbons (2004). Gibbons reports on work done by Tim Newman on an MAOA gene variant found in macaques. She notes that their work dates the low-activity allele to 25 mya and suggests it must have had some reproductive payoff for it to have stayed in the gene pool. Gibbons suggests that aggressive and risk-taking men must have had a selective advantage in order for the gene to stay in the gene pool.

Interestingly, a later paper by biological anthropologist Timothy Newman and colleagues (2005) paints a different picture. They studied the VNTRS in the MAOA gene of macaques. Macaques that have the short-repeat version have higher activity, and thus better removal of the neurotransmitters, as compared to the long version. Mother-reared macaques with the low-activity variant were more aggressive (in terms of food competition) than the nursery-reared macaques with the low allele. What does this mean? It does not conform to what would be expected based on results observed in humans, as the researchers expected the nursery-reared individuals to have experienced more stress in their youth. What could be taken from this is that environment matters more than perhaps is often noted since what is really important here is how a monkey is raised.

Another set of studies has linked MAOA and criminality directly. Criminologist Kevin Beaver and colleagues (2013) examined the National Longitudinal Study of Adolescent Health (Add Health survey) data to conclude that African–American adult males who have the 2-repeat allele are more likely than others to engage in a shooting or stabbing event. Specifically, African-Americans in the study group who did not have the 2-repeat allele had a chance of shooting or stabbing someone with a probability of .07% while those with the allele had a probability of 50%. However, once again we must investigate the population being studied. As they removed the Caucasian sample since the allele was too rare, they are left with an African-American sample size of 133. They report that 7% of this sample has the 2-repeat allele, which means that 8 individuals have that allele, so 4 were involved in a shooting stabbing. On the other hand, the group that does not have it would have about 9 people involved in a shooting/stabbing event.

How can we interpret these results? Not much is known about the individual history of the people involved in the specific aggression, so it is hard to know how the environment affected them. Secondly, "shooting/stabbing" is a pretty specific example. We need to consider the context of these studies. Are the differences in the brain the cause of anti-social behavior, is the environment of violence that is endemic in some populations producing these changes, or is it something else? Moreover, we must remember that the living conditions of poverty can have large effects on gene expression. The interaction of unfair treatment/discrimination and SNPs suggests that gene-environment interactions can have significant effects on historically disadvantaged populations (Quinlan et al. 2016). Poverty and inequality may lead to more violence for reasons removed from genetics. We must remember that heritability is a measure of a population, not an entire group. Furthermore, what are the ramifications if the results from the study by Beaver and colleagues are accurate? The field of bioethics is a relatively new discipline that examines such questions.

Other studies have suggested that people with low variants are simply more aggressive in general. In one instance individuals who participated in a psychological study were found to be more likely to dole out punishments if they had the low variant (McDermott et al. 2009). Interestingly, the researchers concluded by asking why low production alleles would stay in the population if they led to aggression. Some suggest that in general people are not prone to violence but rather that, under certain circumstances, a subset of the general population is more likely to react violently than others (McDermott et al. 2012).

The best example of the anthropological implications of this research comes from a study of the Maori people of New Zealand. In a paper presented at a genetics conference in 2006, scientists reported on the frequency of the 3-repeat version of the MAOA allele in different populations (see Perbal 2013 for an overview). Specifically, they noted that it was common in the Maori population (56%). It was argued that the reason Maori males were more violent (as seen in crime statistics) was due to the prevalence of this allele in the population. However, the same researchers also report heavy frequency in other, non-Maori populations.

The news media reported on this study and it received a lot of attention. As discussed by a variety of authors, there are numerous issues with this interpretation. For one, it does not take into account poverty and other factors that are also associated with certain Maori communities. As pointed out by bioethicist Laurence Perbal (2013) the notion that this gene explains why Maori are violent fits the stereotype associated with this population but does not take into account the context.

Table 5.1, adapted from work by biochemist G. Raumati Hook (1999), lists some of the behavioral traits that have been linked to MAOA deficiencies. Would any of these traits be useful in a small population? Hook (1999: 4) notes,

TABLE 5.1 Behavioral traits that have been linked to MAOA deficiencies

Anxiety
Personality disorders
Antisocial behavior
Violence and risk taking
Risk taking
Antisocial behavior
Aggressive behavior
Impulsive aggression
Mental disorders
Obesity
Impulsivity
Depression and suicidality
Impaired impulse control
Mental retardation (Brunner syndrome)
Mental retardation, autism, seizures, sleep disturbances (Norrie disease)
Panic disorder

> None listed are traits that, anyone would consider, confers advantages in terms of survival and in fact probably serve the exact opposite. That is, possession of these traits would pose severe disadvantages especially in the ancient world of the voyaging and war-like Polynesians.

Perhaps the most important takeaway from these studies is one which may have been obvious at the outset: behavior is conditioned by both genes and the environment, as well as the interaction between these two. This is true in both humans and non-human primates. While there are some long-term studies of humans, it is hard to test behavioral genetic hypotheses in human populations due to the problems of different environmental settings.[5] As noted in the aforementioned study, rhesus macaques reared by mothers and those reared in a nursery express differing responses to stresses (Newman et al. 2005). The researchers examined variation in a gene (5-HTTLPR) that is associated with SR. Scientists separated out monkeys who were homozygous for the longer version of the gene with those who were heterozygous. Their prediction was that the heterozygotes would respond differently and show high stress levels. However, they also wanted to tease apart the effect of environment. Some of the macaques were raised in a nursery setting while others were raised by mothers. Interestingly, the nursery reared infants with the heterozygote genotypes, but not the mother-reared ones, were more aggressive than the ones with the homozygote genotype. Perhaps the "good genes" protect monkeys against earlier adverse conditions or perhaps the "bad genes" effects are mitigated by a mother's presence (Dettmer and Suomi 2014).

Studies have also been done with monkeys raised in different types of deprivation from social contact. In some cases, monkeys are peer-reared (they spend the first few months of their lives with same-aged peers but no adults), others are surrogate peer-reared (monkeys are alone in cages but spend a small part of the day in peer groups), and the third group is raised by their biological mothers. While complex, the data suggest that when a monkey is exposed to adverse conditions early on in life they are at greater risk for excessive aggression. Interestingly, they have also shown differences in neurochemicals depending upon how the baby was reared (Dettmer et al. 2014). Another interesting recent development is the study of epigenetics. Monkeys that experience peer-rearing versus surrogate peer-rearing show different patterns of gene expression in the prefrontal cortex. In other words, their social environment affected how specific genes are expressed.

Nature, Nurture, and the Plasticity of Behavior

The major issue here is how nature interacts with nurture, and how the complex interaction of variables (whether biological, cultural, or environmental) can result in a wide range of possible behaviors. As discussed by philosopher of science James Tabery (2014), this question can be restated in genetic terms as how different genotype groups respond differently to various environments. Since the early 20th century, scientists have attempted to parse out the role that genes and environment play in producing behaviors. It is also true that these debates (about mental health, IQ, serotonin transporter genes, and others) are interlaced with larger political and social issues of the day. For those who feel that heredity and environment are mostly independent, it is argued that those who believed there is an interaction had the burden of proof on them. Likewise, scholars who suggest that traits such as violence are affected by the environment argue that the other side does not fully comprehend how genotype interacts with the environment to produce the phenotype.

As Lawrence Keeley suggests (1996: 158), the "incredible plasticity of human conduct" means that there is no strictly biological explanation for warfare. Perhaps the most important aspect to remember in all of this, at least from an anthropological stance, is the interplay between genes and the environment. As the studies of MAOA suggest, differences in the amount of the SR in the brain can produce aggressive tendencies, but only in individuals who were exposed to specific environments. This is a very interesting result, which perhaps can be used to help treat patients. Taking an anthropological perspective on the studies (that link stress, MAOA deficiency, and aggression) involves thinking about the context. Recall that the majority of children in the study were not abused. This would mean that, based on the Caspi study, the individuals with low MAOA are actually less likely to be aggressive than those with the high-activity version. Thus claims that children with the low-allele variant should be carefully watched and perhaps given hormone shots fail to account for the role environment plays.

However, this is far from being the "warrior gene" that has been argued to be at the heart of human aggression. We must critically examine the evidence. For one, as noted above it is not entirely clear how the different polymorphisms of the MAOA gene affect the expression of neurotransmitters in the brain. This leads to the confusing situation in which some papers use different alleles to stand for the high- and low-versions of the gene.

Secondly, studies proposing to link behavior to specific genes are complicated by many issues that are rarely addressed. In one example, political scientists James Fowler and Christopher Dawes (2008) looked at two genes (MAOA and 5-HTT, a gene that encodes a serotonin transport protein) and argued that individuals possessing the high-variant version of MAOA are more likely to vote than those with the low-producing version. A subsequent study examined whether MAOA variants explained credit card debt (De Neve and Fowler 2014). As political scientists Evan Charney and William English (2012) point out, both the MAOA and the 5-HTT genes are found at different proportions in different populations. For example, white Americans carry the "high" MAOA variant at a higher percentage than Asian Americans do (53% compared to 32%). However, proportionately speaking white Americans vote in more elections than Asian Americans do. Could it be that instead of this being a genetic trait it is a reflection of cultural differences? In fact, the link between high MAOA and voting disappears when the results are broken down by cultural group (Charney and English 2012).

More importantly, though, we need to be critical of how these studies are performed from an anthropological perspective. The aforementioned work done by Beaver and colleagues as well as by others is based on the "National Longitudinal Study of Adolescent Health" (Add Health) survey, which, alongside taking quantitative data, includes some genetic information. However, they looked at less than a dozen genes. Yet these handfuls of genes have been argued to account for all sorts of behaviors. As Charney and English (2012) point out:

> The Third Wave of the Add Health study contains well over a thousand survey questions covering a vast range of behaviors. If one considers the entirety of the Add Health data sets, many thousands of behavioral variables are associated with each individual, and if one introduces interaction terms and multivariable controls, the quantity of variables available for genetic "prediction" could quickly surpass ten thousand. The standard statistical criterion for any individual study of a gene-behavior correlation is significance at an alpha level of .05. The problem with this criterion becomes clear if researchers embark on what collectively amounts to a blind fishing expedition in search of correlations between a handful of candidate genes and a wide array of behaviors.
>
> *Charney and English 2012:14*

Psychiatrist Niklas Langstrom and colleagues (2015) report on a study from Sweden showing that, for men, having a father or brother who was convicted of a sexual offense increases the odds of that individual also being convicted (4–5 times more likely). While news coverage focused on the apparent genetic predispositions for sexual crimes, there is more to the story. As discussed by Emily Underwood (2015) there are a number of complications. For one, we know nothing about the criminal's early life exposure to abuse. Secondly, if a family member is convicted of sexual offense, the rest of the family is likely to be under higher scrutiny. Likewise, a wide range of offenses are included in this study, from rape to indecent exposure, making it hard to attribute a genetic basis to such a wide variety of crimes.

Conclusions

Over the last few years, a series of three meta-analyses about the role of serotonin and environment in causing depression has been published (Karg et al. 2011; Munafò et al. 2009; Risch et al. 2009). Two (Munafò et al. 2009; Risch et al. 2009) out of the three meta-studies were unable to confirm a link, while the third, which used less strict guidelines for inclusion, but also had a larger sample size, did see a link between 5-HTTLPR, stress, and depression. The question for non-experts thus becomes whom to believe. Do we choose studies such as the first two which involve a smaller number of studies, but only include those that fit specific parameters, or do we look at meta-analyses with larger samples but may conflate different study types? There are no easy answers here. In a commentary published alongside one of these studies, neuroscientist John Hardy and psychiatrist Nancy Low sum up the problem well:

> The reader is therefore entitled to ask, "What should I believe? Which explanation is true?" Unfortunately, the answer is unclear, and a long time will pass before questions can be resolved because all the studies so far can be interpreted in opposing ways.
>
> *Hardy and Low 2011: 455*

One difficulty in understanding the causes of human behavior is that the word "behavior" can have a different meaning depending on the approach used to study the phenomena. As discussed by Helen Longino (2012), sometimes it is applied to a population, other times to a specific individual's mental history, or to a specific disposition to respond in a certain way to a situation, or to a more complex pattern of interactions (for a combination of the above techniques).

Given the uncertainties and the complexities involved in shaping behavior, we can safely say at the moment that there is simply no conclusive evidence for a specific gene or hormone which will make someone more aggressive. The effect of a gene is mediated though, and influenced by, the environment. Indeed, the situation is even more complicated than that, as we can see that environments (both of the social and environmental varieties) can impact the effects of combinations of genes, not merely single genes. In this sense, there is no magic bullet – we cannot recognize the existence of a "warrior gene." Rather, a multitude of genes act in tandem. "Ask not what a gene does. Ask what it does in a particular environment and when expressed in a particular network of other genes" (Sapolsky 2017: 265). Think back to the study of the effect of different variants of the MAO-A gene by Caspi and colleagues (2002). One version of the gene partially explained antisocial behavior in adults, but *only* when the individual had a history of childhood abuse. The same gene in an adult with a healthy upbringing had little to no effect. The primary lesson from this chapter is that any complex behavior is influenced by a multitude of genes, each probably only having a small effect. To put this into perspective, a study on the genetics of human height found ~180 genes that potentially influence height. The one that had the greatest effect explained about 0.4% of the variation in height (Allen et al. 2010; Sapolsky 2017). As with much of anthropology we need to know the fuller context to understand the specific causes of a behavior. And even in cases where we have a plethora of data, it is usually quite difficult (and sometimes impossible) to isolate specific causes for human behaviors and cultural practices. It is difficult, then, to say that we can ascertain the genetic roots of aggression. Instead, we can simply conclude that genes affect us but do not control us. They help provide some parameters for a range of possible behavioral outcomes, and other factors are thus implicated as we consider the plasticity of human behavior.

What can we gain from diving down the rabbit hole of genetic studies? In order to understand the nature of warfare in the human past, we must "cross the streams" of data. We also must understand the limitations of each dataset. As we noted in Chapter Four, the more we critically examine data the more complex the question becomes. This does not mean that there are no genetic causes for violence, nor does it mean that we are strictly responding to our genetic predispositions. Current research suggests that there may indeed be some individuals predisposed to violent actions under certain conditions. But we must remember that heritability is a measure of a group, not an entire population. Recognizing humans as products of both biological and cultural evolution is a key step in understanding emergent peacefare and warfare in our evolutionary history. This recognition also speaks to the enormous variability and plasticity that mark human behavior.

Notes

1 A good source for this is the website: http://udel.edu/~mcdonald/mythintro.html.
2 SNP stands for "Single Nucleotide Polymorphism," and refers to places in the genome where people vary based on a single nucleotide base. For example, some people might have a thymine while others have a cytosine. Oftentimes, SNPs have no effect on health but can be used to track lineages though time.
3 You may have noticed an apparent contradiction. If this mutation prevents MAOA from removing serotonin it will lead to a higher amount of SR in the brain. But, previous research suggested that it is individuals with lower SR that are more prone to aggression.
4 An effect size is a way of determining the difference between two groups. The larger the effect size, the greater the difference between the two populations.
5 Some ways around this have been proposed, including looking at identical twins reared apart, but even these studies have problems.

Works Cited

Allen, Hana Lango, et al. 2010. Hundreds of Variants Clustered in Genomic Loci and Biological Pathways Affect Human Height. *Nature* 467(7317), 832–838.

Bachner-Melman, Rachel, Christian Dina, Ada H. Zohar, et al. 2005. AVPR1a and SLC6A4 Gene Polymorphisms Are Associated with Creative Dance Performance. *PLoS Genetics* 1(3), 394–403.

Brunner, H.G., M. Nelen, X.O. Breakefield, H.H. Ropers, and B.A. van Oost. 1993. Abnormal Behavior Associated with a Point Mutation in the Structural Gene for Monoamine Oxidase A. *Science*, 262(5133), 578–580.

Brunner, H.G., M.R. Nelen, P. van Zandvoort, et al. 1993. X-linked Borderline Mental Retardation with Prominent Behavioral Disturbance: Phenotype, Genetic Localization, and Evidence for Disturbed Monoamine Metabolism. *American Journal of Human Genetics* 52(6), 1032–1039.

Caspi, Avshalom, Joseph McClay, Terrie Moffitt, et al. 2002. Role of Genotype in the Cycle of Violence in Maltreated Children. *Science* 297(August), 851–854.

Charney, Evan, and William English. 2012. Candidate Genes and Political Behavior. *American Political Science Review* 106(01), 1–34.

De Neve, Jan Emmanuel, and James H. Fowler. 2014. Credit Card Borrowing and the Monoamine Oxidase A (MAOA) Gene. *Journal of Economic Behavior and Organization* 107(Part B), 428–439.

Deckert, J., M. Catalano, Y.V. Syagailo, et al. 1999. Excess of High Activity Monoamine Oxidase A Gene Promoter Alleles in Female Patients with Panic Disorder. *Human Molecular Genetics* 8(4), 621–624.

Dettmer, Amanda, and S.J. Suomi. 2014. Nonhuman Primate Models of Neuropsychiatric Disorders: Influences of Early Rearing, Genetics, and Epigenetics. *ILAR Journal* 55(2), 361–370.

Dettmer, Amanda M., Ruth Woodward, and Stephen J. Suomi. 2014. Reproductive Consequences of a Matrilineal Overthrow in Rhesus Monkeys. *American Journal of Primatology* (July), 77(3), 1–7.

Fowler, James H., and Christopher T. Dawes. 2008. Two Genes Predict Voter Turnout. *The Journal of Politics* 70(3), 579–594.

Gibbons, Ann. 2004. Tracking the Evolutionary History of a "Warrior" Gene. *Science* 304(5672), 818–819.

Goldsmith, H.H., and J.T. Bihun. 1997. Conceptualizing Genetic Influences on Early Behavioral Development. *Acta Paediatrica. Supplementum* 422(S422), 54–59.

Hardy, John, and Nancy Low. 2011. Genes and Environment in Psychiatry. *Archives of Genetic Psychiatry* 68(5), 455–456.

Hook, G. Raumati. 1999. "Warrior Genes" and the Disease of Being Māori. *MAI Review* 2, 1–11.

Ioannidis, John, Evangelia Ntzani, Thomas Trikalkinos, and Despina Contopoulos-Ioannidis. 2001. Replication Validity of Genetic Association Studies. *Journal of Experimental Psychology. Human Perception and Performance* 29(3), 306–309.

Jaroff, Leon. 1989. The Gene Hunt. *Time Magazine* March 20, pp. 62–67.

Karg, Katja, Margit Burmeister, Kerby Shedden, and Srijan Sen. 2011. The Serotonin Transporter Promoter Variant (5-HTTLPR), Stress, and Depression Meta-Analysis Revisited: Evidence of Genetic Moderation. *Archives of Genetic Psychiatry* 68(5), 444–454.

Keeley, Lawrence. 1996. *War Before Civilization*. Oxford University Press, Oxford.

Langstrom, N., K.M. Babchishin, S. Fazel, P. Lichtenstein, and T. Frisell. 2015. Sexual Offending Runs In Families: A 37-year Nationwide Study. *International Journal of Epidemiology* 44(2), 713–720.

Lesch, Klaus Peter, and Ursula Merschdorf. 2000. Impulsivity, Aggression, and Serotonin: A Molecular Psychobiological Perspective. *Behavioral Sciences and the Law* 18(5), 581–604.

Longino, Helen. 2012. *Studying Human Behavior.* University of Chicago Press, Chicago, IL.

McDermott, R., C. Dawes, E. Prom-Wormley, L. Eaves, and P. K. Hatemi. 2012. MAOA and Aggression: A Gene-Environment Interaction in Two Populations. *Journal of Conflict Resolution* 57(6), 1043–1064.

McDermott, Rose, Dustin Tingley, Jonathan Cowden, Giovanni Frazzetto, and Dominic D.P. Johnson. 2009. Monoamine Oxidase A Gene (MAOA) Predicts Behavioral Aggression Following Provocation. *Proceedings of the National Academy of Sciences of the United States of America* 106(7), 2118–2123.

Mertins, Vanessa, Andrea B. Schote, Wolfgang Hoffeld, Michele Griessmair, and Jobst Meyer. 2011. Genetic Susceptibility for Individual Cooperation Preferences: The Role of Monoamine Oxidase A Gene (MAOA) in the Voluntary Provision of Public Goods. *PLoS ONE* 6(6), 1–9.

Meyer-Lindenberg, Andreas, Joshua W. Buckholtz, Bhaskar Kolachana, et al. 2006. Neural Mechanisms of Genetic Risk for Impulsivity and Violence in Humans. *Proceedings of the National Academy of Sciences of the United States of America* 103(16), 6269–6274.

Morell, V. 1993. Evidence Found for a Possible "Aggression Gene." *Science* 260(5115), 1722–1724.

Munafò, Marcus R., Caroline Durrant, Glyn Lewis, and Jonathan Flint. 2009. Gene × Environment Interactions at the Serotonin Transporter Locus. *Biological Psychiatry* 65(3), 211–219.

Newman, Timothy K., Yana V. Syagailo, Christina S. Barr, et al. 2005. Monoamine Oxidase A Gene Promoter Variation and Rearing Experience Influences Aggressive Behavior in Rhesus Monkeys. *Biological Psychiatry* 57(2), 167–172.

Perbal, Laurence. 2013. The "Warrior Gene" and the Māori People: The Responsibility of the Geneticists. *Bioethics* 27(7), 382–387.

Pinker, Steven. 2002. *The Blank Slate: The Modern Denial of Human Nature.* Viking, New York.

Quinlan, Jacklyn, Laurel N. Pearson, Christopher J. Clukay, et al. 2016. Genetic Loci and Novel Discrimination Measures Associated with Blood Pressure Variation in African Americans Living in Tallahassee. *PLoS ONE* 11(12), 1–22.

Risch, Neil, Richard Herrell, and Thomas Lehner. 2009. Interaction Between the Serotonin. *Jama* 301(23), 2462–2472.

Sabol, S.Z., S. Hu, and D. Hamer. 1998. A Functional Polymorphism in the Monoamine Oxidase A Gene Promoter. *Human Genetics* 103(3), 273–279.

Sapolsky, Robert. 2017. *Behave.* Penguin Press, New York.

Schuback, Deborah E., Evan L. Mulligan, Katherine B. Sims, et al. 1999. Screen for MAOA Mutations in Target Human Groups. *American Journal of Medical Genetics* 88(1), 25–28.

Seif, Isabelle, and Edward De Maeyer. 1999. Knockout Corner: Knockout Mice for Monoamine Oxidase A. *The International Journal of Neuropsychopharmacology* 2(3), 241–243.

Shanahan, Michael J., Lance D. Erickson, Stephen Vaisey, and Andrew Smolen. 2007. Helping Relationships and Genetic Propensities: A Combinatoric Study of DRD2, Mentoring, and Educational Continuation. *Twin Research and Human Genetics: The Official Journal of the International Society for Twin Studies* 10(2), 285–298.

Shih, M., T.L. Pittinsky, and N. Ambady. 1999. Stereotype Susceptibility: Identity Salience and Shifts in Quantitative Performance. *Psychological Science* 10(1), 80–83.

Tabery, James. 2014. *Beyond Versus: The Struggle to Understand the Interaction of Nature and Nurture.* MIT Press, Cambridge, MA.

Umukoro, Solomon, Aderemi C. Aladeokin, and Anthony T. Eduviere. 2013. Aggressive Behavior: A Comprehensive Review of Its Neurochemical Mechanisms and Management. *Aggression and Violent Behavior* 18(2), 195–203.

Underwood, Emily. 2015. Reality Check: Is Sex Crime Genetic? *Science*. Available at: www.sciencemag.org/news/2015/04/reality-check-sex-crime-genetic (accessed October 1, 2017).

Weder, Natalie, Bao Zhu Yang, Heather Douglas-Palumberi, et al. 2009. MAOA Genotype, Maltreatment, and Aggressive Behavior: The Changing Impact of Genotype at Varying Levels of Trauma. *Biological Psychiatry* 65(5), 417–424.

6

THE ONSET OF HUMAN VARIABILITY AND EMERGENT WARFARE

The very controversial anthropologist Napoleon Chagnon suggests that, "Violence is a potent force in human society and may be the principal driving force behind the evolution of culture" (1988: 985). But, does the weight of evidence bear this out? At the moment, there is insufficient material evidence from the bulk of the Pleistocene to conclude that warfare has been the principal driving force for the evolution of culture. Concurrently, the absence for clear signs of warfare from much of the Pleistocene makes it difficult to say that warfare has been the driving force for human biological evolution.

However, does that mean forms of violent social interactions were wholly insignificant and absent until recent eras, and that they played absolutely no role in humanity's earliest history? If we accept that the relationship between social and biological evolution was significant for human evolution, then any social behaviors could have played a role in humanity's evolutionary trajectory. Along this line of thinking, then, cooperative actions using violence (whether within or between groups) could have thus been important in social life.

At the moment, the earliest material evidence that most researchers accept as strong support for warfare comes from the terminal Pleistocene, from cases such as Jebel Sahaba and Nataruk (see Chapter Four). The presence of warfare at the end of the Pleistocene forces us to ask the question: why then and why not earlier or later? We clearly see it later in highly variable social and environmental contexts all over the globe. Of course, the evidence becomes stronger in areas where more people live and are interacting, and this would suggest that the more people intermingle, the more opportunities there would be for people to both get along peacefully and not so peacefully. As for the other part of the question, why not earlier, let us consider this point.

What would have been the potential independent variables for the onset of warfare behaviors at the end of the Pleistocene? We can now eliminate the presence of farming societies, states, cities, or analogous social phenomena and cultural practices as the causes leading to an innovation or invention of warfare. We must then ask if there are other variables. Could it be sedentism? Could it be changing patterns of climate? The end of the Ice Ages saw gradual warming climates, with new patterns of distribution for wild animals and plants. It is possible that these shifting patterns played a role in how people lived in different places. But, what we might ask ourselves is what independent variable is common to all of the known cases of people participating in warfare. The answer is people. The capacity to have human culture, to think and act like a human being means that when it comes to having the aptitude to participate in violence, it really does not matter if you live in a state, a band, subsist off of farmed foodstuffs, fish, or hunt. Living in the Holocene or the Pleistocene is of secondary significance. Possessing human cognition is of primary significance. This raises the possibility of another variable to consider, one related to archaeological "visibility."

Perhaps it is only at the end of the Pleistocene that demographic and settlement patterns take on forms more conducive to leaving obvious signs of organized violence. After all, we can use the same logic about warfare in the Holocene. We see undisputed signs of warfare in regions with larger-scale, complex societies in the Holocene not because people suddenly evolved to be more warlike or more capable of making war. We see warfare at that point because the densities of population, interactions, and residual material traces for all kinds of social activities become more prevalent and durable. And recent decades of archaeological research has yielded enough evidence to indicate that smaller-scale, non-state societies of the Holocene also participated in forms of warfare as well. The evidence is not as obvious, but the clues are there nonetheless. Rather than massive city walls of stone, a settlement may have a simple palisade and ditch. Instead of massive quantities of products being made and transported across long distance between culturally distinct societies, we see in the Pleistocene fainter clues and signals of goods being transported across geographic expanses. But, most people would accept the likelihood that our Pleistocene forebears had the wherewithal to be participants in long-distance exchange. The common denominator, of course, is humans being human.

And so, take this logic further. Would humans living in the mid- to Late Pleistocene be all that different from humans in the Holocene? Biological evolutionary research tells us the answer is "no." Accordingly, we have to be open to the possibility that our cultural practices could have included warfare, among a gamut of social, group behavioral patterns that mark humans today. But how far back can we trace warfare?

Let's take a moment to catch our breath and take stock. We have been on a whirlwind tour of evidence, from the material records of the recent and distant pasts to an exploration of our current understanding of how our genes can influence our behaviors. A few things should be clear by now. We have been on a very long (i.e., millions of years!) journey to becoming "human," and, along the way, our bodies and our cultural patterns have picked up and dropped off certain tools and accompaniments, whether physical traits or cultural behaviors. Researchers are still learning the how, why, when, and where for this enormously complex and fascinating journey. But it should be abundantly clear by now that we are the current outcome of two parallel processes of biological and cultural evolution, and we are still evolving. As Fuentes (2012) argues, we are the product of "naturenurtural" development. From that perspective, we see enough evidence currently to indicate that determining the onset of humans engaging in warlike activities can only be understood in terms of other, more macro-level changes in humanity's biological and cultural evolution. To put it in different terms, we might view warfare as an epiphenomenon of developing human nature, as a sort of outcome or byproduct. We base this perspective on the idea that to become fully human resulted in a wide and tremendously plastic range of thinking and behaviors that allowed cooperation in ways quite unprecedented in nature.

So, what does that mean about our original questions about the onset of warfare? Well, it means that the answers are intimately linked to questions about human evolution. Although we set out in this book to explore the advent of warfare, our research journey has taken us down a path to understanding the onset of human variability and cultural modernity, and how this developmental process affected changing patterns of human violence. We can see clues in the fossil record that our earliest ancestors did, on occasion, find reasons to act in violent ways. This includes violence to one another as well as to other species (i.e., hunting). The behavior is discernible with different hominin populations throughout the Old World, well back into the early days of the Pleistocene. Of course, the evidence does not indicate much about the nature of those violent behaviors. How common was it? Was it between distinct groups or communities? Why was it happening? We have no satisfying answers, really, for these questions. Hence, we cannot say much about "warfare" in these murkiest of time depths. When it comes to organized behaviors that employ physical force to cause harm or violence, the best we can conclude about the populations of hominins (at least the pre-anatomically modern human ones) is that they likely had the tools to do so. We know that they had the capacity to thrive in different environments, fashion tools of stone (and other materials), could control and harness fire, and could cooperate to hunt other species of animals. Presumably, this meant that they could occasionally direct such aggressive stances toward each other as well, whether between members of the same or of different communities. But the capacity to do so does not mean they had a biological tendency or predisposition for violence.

From the earliest days of crude stone tools, the material record shows advancements in technology, suggesting that hunting became more and more effective with the manufacture and uses of longer-range weapons, such as thrusting or even throwing spears. In that respect, we suspect evolving abilities related to hunting would have been an important foundation for any kind of warfare that would eventually emerge. But even if hominin groups were purposefully hunting and killing members of other groups, and this is a very big "if," we argue that those forms of organized violence did not equate with human categories of violent practice. As we argued earlier in the book, human forms of violence are so embedded with symbolic meaning and abstract planning that we see only superficial similarities with those of other species, including primates. So, in that sense, evolving hunting behaviors would have been a necessary condition, but not a sufficient one, for the emergence of warfare. *Modern or variably human behavior had a beginning, and so too, then, did various behavioral strategies and patterns made possible by the same underlying physical and biological changes that made modern behavior possible.* Warfare as we see it today, and as we can recognize it archaeologically throughout the course of the Holocene, is marked by ritual, institutionalized, and cultural practices. It is within the material record of the Holocene that we see clear evidence for warrior identities or ideology, institutionalized violence within societies. We see evidence around specific causes and motivations for violence, including revenge and "moralistic violence" (Armit 2010). In effect, our ways of harming one another, and the reasons behind such harm, go well beyond any violence elsewhere in the natural world.

We have not always practiced violence and warfare in these culturally complex ways. So, when did a human brand of warfare really begin, and would it have looked the same in its earliest manifestations? Although the archaeological record is not sufficiently robust to document warfare practices earlier than the Holocene, our assumption is that the culturally-laden ideas and practices related to group violence certainly could have been extant well before the violence indicated at Jebel Sahaba, Nataruk, or by some of the iconographic depictions of intergroup violence dating to the Upper Paleolithic.

Hominin communities may have had some of the key ingredients for organized fighting, in ways that are qualitatively different than other species. But, though they possessed sophisticated tools for living and hunting, were they capable of warfare? In our 50,000-foot view of the journey, it looks as though violence approximating our kinds today would have required important capacities to socialize, organize, and cooperate, to communicate symbolic ideas and view worlds and people in creative ways. These would have been part of the sufficient conditions needed for our ancestors to be able to perform warfare in the highly complex ways we might see today. What many researchers refer to as modernity or variability in behavior and culture pertains to symbolic thinking and expression, marked by complex cognition. We argue that such capacities were fundamentally necessary for emergent warfare. But that is just one side of the story. The construction of peace through peacemaking behaviors and cultural practices is the other, equally significant, side of the story, to which we will return in the next chapter. In this chapter, we present some ideas about emergent warfare. We paint a somewhat abstract picture with very broad brushstrokes. We can only offer a "just-so" story, conjecture on what we perceive as the likely key building blocks of behaviors that contributed in some fashion to both emergent warfare, and, in many similar ways, emergent peacefare. In the end, we present our interpretations of available data, noting that some of our conclusions are more speculative than others. There is still much room for debate and contrasting opinions.

Our Earliest Ancestors

What was life like for the last common ancestor (LCA) of humans and chimpanzees (see Figure 6.1)? We have already talked about primate violence and the evidence of interpersonal conflict in hominins, but what do we know about the culture, if we can call it that, of the species from which chimpanzees and humans evolved?

As we have discussed, some read the primatological record as supporting the assertion that violence and warfare have very ancient and primordial roots. Wrangham and Peterson (1996: 64), for instance, argue that "chimpanzee-like violence preceded and paved the way for human war, making modern humans the dazed survivors of a continuous, 5-million-year habit of lethal aggression." Others, looking at a similar dataset, suggest the opposite (Sussman and Marshack 2010; Sussman et al. 2005). In this book, we have expressed some skepticism that chimpanzee warfare is analogous to early human warfare, as we emphasize the evolutionary arc of human warfare as being distinctive to the human niche. Just as talking about "slavery" in ants does not mean that it is similar to the Middle Passage, we must be careful to not confuse the science of the metaphorical for that of the biological (Marks 2002).

Moreover, even if chimpanzees are violent, does that mean that the Last Common Ancestor of humans and chimps was also violent? The surprising answer is no. While scientists are still unsure of exactly when humans and chimps split (estimates range from 12 to 5 million years ago), it gives ample time for chimpanzees to have evolved new behaviors, especially as their habitats shrunk. In fact, as noted in Chapter Two, some researchers suggest that the reason chimps are violent has to do with human

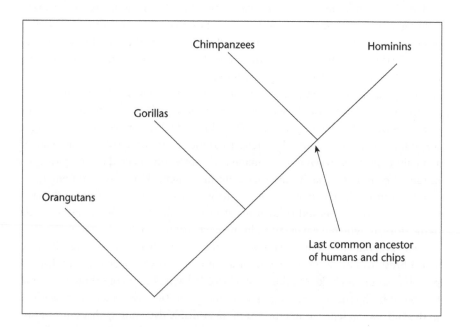

FIGURE 6.1 Phylogeny showing suspected position of the Last Common Ancestor (LCA). *Produced by Marc Kissel*

provisioning and encroachment on their land (Sussman and Marshack 2010). Secondly, as the anthropologist Jonathan Marks (2015) has noted, we are not apes, we are ex-apes. The adaptive landscape humans evolved from is unique, making us different from primates in both biology and culture (Fuentes 2012).

The fossil evidence is also equivocal. *Ardipithecus ramidus*, a ~4.4 million year old species of early hominin, may provide some answers. Its body design is said to be much more "human-like" than "ape-like," indicating that the LCA was more hominin and less like a chimp (White et al. 2009). Some take this to mean that members of the Ardi species engaged in pair-bonded relationships, and that there was potentially less male competition for mates than seen in chimpanzees (Lovejoy 2009). If true, this suggests that chimpanzee-level aggression may be distinctive of chimpanzee niches. In other words, chimps may be the derived ones. These issues make it difficult to reconstruct what the LCA would have been like behaviorally.

Some Key Building Blocks

The interplay between biological and behavioral changes, leading to modern human nature, may be far too complex to really talk about causality. This is why there is so much debate about what "sparked" humanity (see Fuentes 2017), or propelled developments leading to humanity. Even if we were not dealing with precious few fossils and artifacts in a record of millions of years, even if we had many more complete specimens and traces of technology and lifeways, there would still be disputes over what really made us human.

One of the reasons why it is so difficult to pinpoint the "spark" is that we are often blinded by our assumptions of how evolution works. Recent work in biology has suggested that scientists need to incorporate what has become known as the Extended Evolutionary Synthesis (EES). This allows anthropologists a more nuanced approach. The EES emphasizes constructive development, the ability for an individual to respond to, as well as alter, internal and external states (Laland et al. 2015). This allows the organism to shape its own developmental trajectory. As biologist Kevin Laland and colleagues note, the layout of the blood vessels is not determined strictly by genetic predetermination, but rather they are distributed to regions that have a need for more oxygen and thus the layout is influenced by development. Thus, these pathways are quite important parts of phenotype construction and need to be considered alongside genetic ones.

As a second theme, "EES views reciprocal causation to be a typical, perhaps even universal, feature of evolving and developing systems, characterizing both the developmental origin of phenotypic variation and its evolution in response to changeable features of its environment" (Laland et al. 2015: 7). The idea of the genes as a "blueprint" belies the more nuanced approach currently accepted by most biologists. We need to recognize the role non-genetic inheritance, which includes both behavioral and symbolic behaviors, plays in human evolutionary history.

FIGURE 6.2 Images of various so-called "Venus" figurines, which date to some 20,000–30,000 years ago. Traditionally, artifacts such as these, along with cave art, were used to suggest that modern human behavior evolved fairly recently and rather quickly (in what is referred to as the "Upper Paleolithic Revolution"). Today, much evidence is available to challenge this perspective. *Source: The Natural History Museum / Alamy Stock Photo*

Perhaps the most salient aspect of the ESS is niche construction (Laland et al. 2014; Whiten and Erdal 2012; Odling-Smee et al. 2003), which anthropologists have applied to the origins of farming (O'Brien and Laland 2012) and other aspects of human evolution (Fuentes 2014, 2015). Put simply, this theory notes that an organism has the ability to change the way that the environment, via natural selection, affects its fitness by changing its own environment. Beavers, for example, construct dams. How is this relevant to our challenge of understanding the origins of human warfare? Many theories of human evolution link changing environment with key events in the evolution of our species. However, these are often framed as hominins responding to environmental pressures. While this is true, we must also be aware of how humans, along with other animals as well, affect the environment. If a beaver builds a dam, this affects the fitness of the organism, and this changed environment gets passed down, non-genetically, to the next generation.

Seen in this light, emergent warfare and cooperation are aspects of a distinctively human niche that has its origins in the distant past. We needed the physical capacity for language (speech) but also the cognitive ability to think in abstract ways to express symbols, concepts, and so forth. With these tools, we began to identify more complex networks of affiliation and affiliate bonds – direct kinship ties might have been broadened into larger tribal networks and more complex kinds of kinship bonds. If we think in terms of niche construction, the building blocks we discuss below are elements of this complex interplay between biology, culture, and the environment.

When it comes to organized fighting and killing that we would expect with emergent warfare, there are a few key building blocks that would have been vital. Overall, this suite of evolutionary developments need not be part of a package that emerged in some pivotal moment in human history. Rather, the evidence now hints at the appearance of certain signals and traits throughout the history of hominin evolution, that eventually combine to allow certain biological and cultural changes to occur (Kissel and Fuentes 2016). These ultimately resulted in very sophisticated behavioral patterns of sociality and communication. Greater intelligence simultaneously resulted in better innovations for group activities and cooperation, such as hunting, with tools that become increasingly sophisticated over time. Ultimately, our brains, bodies, and cultural patterns made use of language (i.e., both symbolic representation and speech) to vastly improve our ways of socializing and cooperating. We suspect that these developments would have opened the door for recognition of near and distant kin, along with complex notions of group identity. This, in turn, would have allowed for such ideas to be communicated and put into service for cultural lifeways. As argued by anthropologist Raymond Kelly (2000), such notions of identity could have been very important for societies to apply a concept of social substitutability or segmentation to cultural logics related to violence. Once we began expressing and recognizing contrasting group affiliations in highly complex manners, we would have been quite capable of engaging in emergent forms of warfare.

Hunting

This is obviously an important behavior for us to consider, as hunting not only contributed to developments in the *Homo* genus, but hunting-related activities and innovations lie at the foundation of intergroup violence. Were the first arrows created to hunt animals or other humans? This is a question that we currently cannot answer. Yet, the acquisition of caloric-rich foods that could be shared between members of a community, and the various forms of sociality and cooperation that would have necessitated successful hunting strategies, were unquestionably significant for early human evolution.

In 1968, Sherwood Washburn and Chert Lancaster suggested (1968: 303),

> The biology, psychology, and customs that separate us from the apes – all these we owe to the hunters of time past . . . for those who would understand the origin and nature of human behavior there is no choice but to try to understand "Man the Hunter."

Since that suggestion was made, the paradigm of "Man the Hunter" has received much attention, with anthropologists suggesting that meat-eating was a key part of human evolution. In a classic paper written decades ago, the archaeologist Glynn Isaac (1978) argued that early hominins at 1.7 million years ago in East Africa were successful hunters who were able to not only obtain meat from animals, but could also bring this food back to camp where it was shared with others. This "home base" model has received a lot of attention. While some scholars critique it because it makes early humans look "too human" (Binford 1981; Blumenschine 1987; Cavallo and Blumenschine 1989), others have supported much of this argument through ongoing research, demonstrating that early members of our genus were successful hunters (Bunn 2001; Dominguez-Rodrigo and Pickering 2003; Pickering 2013). They do so while noting how we must be careful in our conclusions to avoid overly projecting our behaviors into the patterns of these early humans.

Ongoing and recent research on this question has suggested that ambush hunting and power scavenging were key behaviors of hominins in the early Pleistocene (Bunn and Gurtov 2014). This leads us to wonder about the possible link between the hunting of other animals and the hunting of conspecifics. As highlighted in Chapter Four, there are clues suggesting the defleshing of hominins by other hominins. Though we do not know why such actions took place, plausible explanations, of course, can include homicide and cannibalism. As human adaptations for obtaining meat are more technological than biological, could the evolution of meat-eating and the emergence of warfare be tied together? Bunn (2001) argues that one of the reasons for a large brain was to help solve problems of obtaining meat. In turn, meat allowed for hominins to have, and maintain, larger brains. Given evidence of possible hunting of large prey by certain hominin groups, and evidence of spears (see Chapter Four), it is fair to ask the question whether such cooperative hunting behaviors could have also involved intraspecies violence between communities as well. If so, this could constitute a form of lethal intergroup violence. But at what point does it approximate human warfare? It may be more accurate to call it lethal organized violence, but not quite human warfare as we have defined it. As argued by Pickering (2013: 4) (emphasis present),

> It's true that some nonhuman animals use tools to hunt, others target prey larger than an individual hunter, and a few even share food—but none, other than the human animal, possesses these traits as a *behavioral complex* used in combination to both satisfy their caloric and nutritional requirements *and* to build social cohesion.

Is there evidence of the very early use of hunting implements that could have, on occasion, functioned as weaponry for intra-species violence? The answer is a very strong maybe. At the moment, there is no evidence for arrows or stone-tipped spears being used by *Homo erectus* or earlier hominin species, but that still leaves rocks, clubs, and pointed sticks as plausible implements for both hunting and intra-species violence (Pickering 2013: 83–84). As detailed in Chapter Four, the earliest wooden spears that we have recovered come from the Schöningen site in Germany, dating to some 300,000 years ago (Conard et al. 2015). However, microscopic use-wear analyses on stone tools used 1.6 million years ago at the site of Koobi Fora in Kenya show signs of possible woodworking activities, making the production and uses of spears plausible (Keeley and Toth 1981). In recent studies, analysis of stone handaxes of the Acheulian tradition from the Peninj site (Tanzania) also shows possible woodworking activities. Archaeologist Manuel Dominguez-Rodrigo and colleagues (2001) recovered and analyzed plant remains known as phytoliths found preserved on the working edges of the tools. Their analyses show that the phytoliths were probably derived from acacia trees, which are extremely sturdy (Pickering 2013: 84). The combination of clues suggests that hominins were using stone tools to cut down acacia trees, or at least parts of them. While this does not mean that spears were being manufactured, one need only consider the recent Fongoli evidence of chimpanzees making and using spears to hunt small mammals (Pruetz and Bertolani 2007) to open our minds to the possibility that our hominin ancestors, equipped with a bigger brain, could have been doing the same thing over a million years ago.

In sum, the case can be made that early representatives of the *Homo* genus were capable of producing tools and hunting large mammals. This indicates the capacity for aggressive behavior and the use of violence. But, does it mean that they were bearers of complex cultural ideas around violence? That, at the moment, is unsubstantiated. Nor does their hunting behavior mean that our evolutionary history is marked by a fundamentally aggressive make up. We are in agreement with Pickering's assessment when he notes (2013: 2):

> Recognizing the circumstantial utility of aggression is not the same as arguing that humans are fundamentally aggressive. Instead, it is the simple acknowledgment that aggression is a behavioral tactic – one among many along a broad spectrum of human behavioral potential – that can be recruited to satisfy (or, at least, attempt to satisfy) the innate human dispositions to dominate and to resist being dominated.

For Pickering, hunting was a primary factor in our becoming fully human.

Though Pickering is not referencing intergroup violence or warfare, we can glean some insights. In a manner somewhat akin to Pickering's view on how human hunting underlies "humanness," we suggest that both humanness and hunting underlie emergent forms of human warfare. This is not to say that warfare definitively existed during the Pleistocene, but it does imply that many of the features of warfare had roots within other behavioral patterns that were extant earlier. In our opinion, just as human culture and modern behavior appear to have emerged gradually, the same may be applicable for human warfare. Cooperative group behavior in organizing and communicating for hunting activities would have been vital for any possible instances of premeditated, intergroup violence. In such fashion, human warfare would have been developed in sort of piecemeal fashion, with various strategies, tactics, and practices being selectively incorporated and discarded by people over time. We discuss these ideas and the implications for theories on evolutionary fitness in the concluding chapter.

For Pickering, there is also an important shift in the evolution of hunting that reflects an important milestone in human evolution. For him, successful human hunting emerges only after it is decoupled from human aggression (Pickering 2013: 8). This perspective is relevant to our argument about the uniquely human aspects of warfare. We do not simply engage in warfare due to aggression or aggressive tendencies. Violence is not simply a reflex, especially when it comes to human groups. Our motivations, justifications, and risk assessments around acts of organized violence are based on a complex host of decision-making criteria.

Raymond Kelly (2005) notes major transitions throughout the Pleistocene, with shifting social, environmental, and demographic conditions influencing decisions to engage in, and thus shaping the evolution of, lethal intergroup violence. In his argument, the introduction of long-distance weaponry such as the javelin-like throwing spear, likely eradicated potential gains for coalitionary or cooperative killing. This may have occurred up to a million years ago. It was with this transition, he argues, that selective factors favoring such coalitionary killing gave way to those favoring more positive relations between neighboring communities. This ushered in, according to Kelly (2005: 15297), a

> period of Paleolithic warlessness, grounded in low population density, an appreciation of the benefits of positive relations with neighbors, and a healthy respect for their defensive capabilities, lasted until the cultural development of segmental forms of organization engendered the origin of war.

This was the transition to an "era of intrinsic defensive advantage" (Kelly 2005: 15298). The emergence of segmented societies coincided with the next marked shift, one in which advantages and perceived social benefits for raiding and intergroup violence were high enough to bear the costs associated with intercommunity violence. We return to the idea of social segmentation below.

Language

In the late 19th century, both the Linguistic Society of Paris and the London Philosophical Society banned discussion of the origins of language as it was seen to be lacking any concrete evidence. While we no longer want for data on this subject, the study of language origins is still a hotly debated topic. A host of research has centered on the origins and evolution of language, generating a diverse range of perspectives on what constitutes language, its developmental processes, when or over what time span these processes occur, and how they are tied to human evolution (Barnard 2012; Deacon 2010; Dor et al. 2014; Dunbar 1998; Lieberman 2007; Noble and Davidson 1991; Seyfarth and Cheney 2008; Tallerman 2005). Researchers come from all kinds of disciplinary backgrounds, including anthropologists, neuro-scientists, linguists, biologists, computer scientists, and many others. Presenting the full scope of this field is not possible here, but suffice it to say that many researchers view the development of full human language as a movement beyond the commu-nication systems of other species, the latter of which can include vocalizations of non-human primates or intricate "dances" of honeybees to communicate informa-tion about nectar sources (Tallerman 2005: 2). In the end, though, much debate still surrounds questions about language origins.

Some argue that the differences between non-human primate languages and that of our own are not as significant as others would believe, while others see human language as vastly more complex and unique. These divergent views play out in many related debates over the ability to see and use grammar and syntax. Closely tied to language origins are notions about the cognitive abilities of language users, such as possession of a theory of mind (an ability to understand the mental state of others as distinct from one's own) and categories of intentionality. These questions and their answers have serious implications for when we became (or started becoming) human, and which of our earliest ancestors possessed language or rudimentary forms of fully human language.

For our present purposes, we simply wish to acknowledge the general notion that language was vital in aiding and propelling our arcs of both cultural and biological evolution. We see it as likely having played an important role in the evolution of our patterns of behavior and sociality, which, of course, would include cooperative behaviors related to intergroup violence. The origins of linguistic complexity are probably linked to the origins of cultural complexity, or even behavioral modernity (Barnard 2012), and given our stance on what constitutes warfare, we would place a strong emphasis on language. We would stress the significance of the acquisition of language, as a means to communicate through symbolic thought, in fostering complex forms of sociality and cooperation, all of which would have been instru-mental for emergent warfare. That being said, it would seem that answering the "when" and "why" for acquiring language would shed light on emergent warfare.

For some researchers, such as anthropologist Alan Barnard (2012: 3), a quintessential part of being human is our ability to think and communicate in symbols, which allows us to create metaphors and conjure mystical ideas that can be shared. "These things differentiate not only chimpanzees from humans, but also early humans, like *Homo erectus*, from ourselves" (Barnard 2012: 3). It should be noted, however, that the distinctions between humans, hominins, and other related primates are sometimes blurred. For instance, it is hard to know for sure that *H. erectus* did not create symbols. While symbolic thought is often seen as the marker of modern human origins, discoveries of engraved objects associated with *H. erectus* sites in Java (Joordens et al. 2014) suggest a more complex behavioral pattern than previously suggested. Moreover, experiments with chimpanzees have demonstrated a theory of mind and some degree of intentionality, and this is especially the case when experimentation involved situations of competition over food (Hare and Tomasello 2004). However, in the end we can plainly see that non-human primates lack the total package of cognitive and physical traits that confer possession and use of full language.

In the wild, chimpanzees do vocalize their excitement when working together in hunting, for instance. But as psychologist Michael Tomasello and colleagues (2012: 677) write, their vocalizations

> are mostly hardwired to particular stimulus and motivational states, so what is being expressed is general excitement (with the same vocalizations used when excited about other things) and not anything about the content of what is happening or what the vocalizer wants to happen. There are no reported vocalizations (or gestures) specifically associated with hunting or coordination.

This stands in contrast with the ways in which humans coordinate and communicate intentions and decisions in situations requiring cooperation for a common objective. For Tomasello and colleagues (2012: 680), the data suggest that when chimpanzees do hunt in small groups for monkeys, they do this with cognitive and motivational mechanisms not specifically evolved for the task.

> In contrast, humans, as already evident in young children, have evolved a suite of cognitive and motivational mechanisms for sharing food co-operatively, coordinating and communicating toward joint goals with complementary roles, and engaging in various kinds of reputation-based social selection (including a concern for self-reputation as a cooperator) — what we have called skills and motivations for joint intentionality.
>
> *Tomasello et al. 2012: 680*

Recognizing these important differences, the logical question to now ask is when did we first possess the cognitive and motivational mechanisms to cooperate, coordinate, and communicate toward joint goals, with skills related to joint intentionality?

Moving back to our hominin past, language, whether in the form of gesture, pantomime, or speech, cannot be directly detected or measured in the fossil or archaeological record. We must rely on indirect methods of discovery. Scientists have tried to use skeletal indicators that suggest a fossil species had the capability to use language. Much research has been spent studying the placement of the larynx, also known as the voice box. In humans, the larynx sits low in the throat, allowing us to produce more complex sounds than our ape cousins. Interestingly, a human baby's larynx is higher up, which allows them to drink milk and breathe at the same time. However, it is difficult to assess the position of the larynx in a fossil. One way forward is to examine the hyoid bone, which resides in the throat, as its size and shape is influenced by the larynx. A Neandertal hyoid from 60,000 years ago is morphologically very similar to hyoids of modern people, leading some to suggest that Neandertals could speak (Arensburg et al. 1989). Interestingly, a hyoid from a 400,000-year-old hominin from Italy (Capasso et al. 2008) differs from both that seen in Neandertals and in modern humans, suggesting that this population did not yet develop full human speech.

However, we also must note that there is more complexity here. W. Tecumseh Fitch (2000) notes that many mammals change the position of their larynx when vocalizing, suggesting that its position, and thus the vocal tract itself, is flexible. Due to this observation, some have suggested other markers, such as the size of the thoracic canal, which is linked to the ability to control breathing – a prerequisite of speech. Once again, it seems that Neandertals were similar to modern humans in this skeletal trait, but that *Homo erectus* lacked this ability (Fitch 2009). Additional evidence comes from the study of the inner ear bones. Ear ossicles from Neandertals (Quam and Rak 2008) and from hominins found at Sima de Los Huesos dating to 500,0000 BP (Martínez et al. 2013) suggest they were adapted to the range of sounds produced by modern humans, which may thus indicate a capacity for language at this time.

Equally as controversial is the search for a genetic basis for language. Much work has concentrated on the FOXP2 gene, often referred to as a "language gene." A faulty version of the gene causes people to have severe impediments to language, prompting some speculation about its possible role in language. But, as is often the case, the story is much more complex than that. FOXP2 is not really a language gene. The gene, which is found in all mammals, differs by only two amino acids between chimpanzees and Neandertals (as a comparison, the difference in the gene between humans and mice is three amino acids). Interestingly, the human version of the gene is found in Neandertals (Krause et al. 2007). Whether this means that Neandertals could talk, though, is unclear.

We can also try to detect language by exploring various "behavioral innovations preserved in the archaeological record" (d'Errico et al. 2003: 56). For d'Errico and colleagues (2003: 50), there are certain material signatures that can operate as proxies for language, allowing us to trace the process of language diversification. This process might be reflected in different activities, such as mortuary practices, decoration of objects, and other sorts of symbolic behaviors. Traditionally, many researchers saw the advent of behavioral modernity and symbolic thought occurring in a revolutionary fashion some 40,000 years ago, as reflected by archaeological evidence from Europe (Renfrew 1996). But, as we discussed in Chapter Two, research in recent years has largely overturned this perspective, recognizing that complex cultural systems and associated practices are visible in the archaeological record of different world regions and far earlier in time (McBrearty and Brooks 2000). Today, there are some interesting questions being explored about the relationship between such behaviors and different species of hominins and archaic humans. For instance, there is an apparent chronological overlap and connection between anatomically modern human populations, appearing as early as 200,000 years ago in parts of Africa, and signs of behavioral modernity. It must be noted, though, that there are even earlier signals as reflected by various cases, though many of these are highly debated and still lack consensus. For the time being, many researchers would agree that the evidence from the past 200,000 years strongly supports the notion that symbolic thought and language were around and important for archaic humans in different world regions.

Given the challenges in detecting the earliest presence of spoken language, are there other ways to "see" the earliest instances of symbolic thinking? As noted by researchers, there is a significant difficulty in discerning symbolic thought in the archaeological record. A major reason, for instance, is the ambiguity over what is actually meant or symbolized (Kissel and Fuentes 2017). Symbols are signs and hold meaning for objects due to conventional agreement. The only reason that a green light means "go" is that everyone agrees that is the meaning. It is difficult to ascertain exactly if something is a symbol without knowing the cultural system that produced that object. For this reason, archaeologists often debate whether specific artifact types are legitimate evidence for symbolic thought. Despite this challenge, however, we might still hypothesize that a certain material signature reflects the intent to convey messaging or communication through a symbol of some kind.

Such evidence includes, for instance, the production and suspected uses of bodily adornment items, such as beads (Bouzouggar et al. 2007). The argument is that early humans were intentionally manipulating and decorating objects in order to possess them and possibly wear and display them. We may not know what the objects meant or actually symbolized, but we can see evidence of collection, transport over long distances, and manipulation. In recent years, groundbreaking discoveries in various locations throughout Africa have demonstrated a very early use of items for extrasomatic adornment, well before the end of the Pleistocene. We can point to suspected beads found at Blombos Cave in South Africa, dating to approximately 75,000 years ago (Henshilwood et al. 2004), as well as similar artifacts dating to 82,000 years ago recovered from northern Africa, which were likewise covered in red ochre for pigmentation (Bouzouggar et al. 2007). These finds intriguingly point to a possible existence of "interlinking exchange systems or of long-distance social networks" (Bouzouggar et al. 2007: 9969). According to archaeologist Christopher Henshilwood and colleagues (2004: 404), "Fully syntactical language is arguably an essential requisite to share and transmit the symbolic meaning of beadworks and abstract engravings such as those from Blombos Cave." Though some researchers question the link between beads and language, the manipulation and uses of beads offer strong indications, at a minimum, that people were thinking symbolically. Even earlier shell beads have been found in Israel and Algeria, dating to between 100,000 and 135,000 years ago, indicating symbolic human behavior (Vanhaeren et al. 2006). Indeed, bead technology may date to as early as 300,000 years ago, though these claims need to be critically examined (Bednarik 2005). Other scholars have suggested that the complex Neandertal toolkit, which includes hafting, control of fire, sewn clothing, burial of the dead, body decorations, and hunting a diverse array of animals, would suggest some sort of language capacity (Dediu and Levinson 2013).

Significantly, the capacity for and uses of language may have also been a vital means to differentiate between groups as well, since different communities may have plausibly been engaged in different languages. According to Francesco d'Errico and colleagues (2003: 55) regional variability in stone tool styles from approximately 70,000 BP and later may reflect linguistic borders. In this manner, perhaps the earliest, rudimentary instances of ethnic difference and variable identity would have been tied to these ways in which groups looked, acted, and spoke differently from each other. Accordingly, language acquisition may have been a crucial component for powerful notions of ethnolinguistic identity and complex forms of interaction, which in turn could have fostered ever more sophisticated kinds of cooperative relations. At the same time, language and identity could have also contributed to cooperative behavior within groups as they plausibly engaged in intermittent outbreaks of organized violence between groups. If so, we might consider these interactions in a larger context of emergent warfare.

Wrangham and Peterson (1996: 257) recognize the importance of breaking through the "language barrier" for evolving practices of organized aggression and violence. But, in contrast, whereas they see aggressive and violent tendencies as inextricably linked to human (especially male) evolution, we would de-emphasize that link. Language and symbolic thought permit so much more than competition and warfare, and, arguably, these other social behaviors made possible by language and higher intelligence may be more vital as drivers of human evolution than warfare. As we will argue in the next chapter, having the cognitive and symbolic ways of thinking that permitted language, coupled with the use of language as a communication tool, would have been instrumental not only for organizing to fight for very complex reasons, but also for creating new ways to avoid and resolve conflict – to make peace. As argued by anthropologist John Terrell (2014), a fundamental part of our journey to becoming human was our "talent for friendship." In other words, human nature benefitted from our ways of cooperating and finding common ground with one another. Such a "talent" would have been arguably instrumental for people to make and keep the peace both within their communities and with those from outside their own social groups.

Kinship Recognition and Group Identity

As warfare involves fighting between groups, it goes without saying that group identity, along with ways to perceive both ingroup and outgroup members, is crucial. As illustrated in recent research on the formation of Viking Age (c. AD 750–1050) war bands and armies, the construction and fusion of ingroup identity and fusion contributed to the cohesiveness and success of military groups (Raffield et al. 2015). Researchers argue how kinship and pre-existing social relationships could have been very important, but they note that armed groups could also consist of individuals from diverse origins (Raffield et al. 2015: 38–40). Such heterogeneity would have necessitated strong mechanisms of ingroup identification and identity fusion.

So much has been researched, theorized, and published by anthropologists about kinship and kinship systems within human societies, more than can be covered here. But for our purposes, we would point out that while other species can easily recognize kin as well as members of their group and community, they are not able to do so in highly complex ways. "Compared to all other species, humans exhibit by far the most extensive domain of kin recognition in terms of differentiated kin types" (Chapais 2014: 751). Not only do we have the cognitive and linguistic capacities to reckon kinship systems more extensively than other species, we can also create fictive bonds of kinship (which, for many people, can be just as important as genetically-based kinship), and having language meant possessing ways to also express complicated ideas about relationships between individuals and groups. Consider again the Viking war bands, or warriors and soldiers in large fighting forces where comrades-in-arms may initially be strangers with no blood relations whatsoever. Our abilities to forge group cohesion and manufacture bonds allow us to be cooperative on levels unprecedented in nature (see Turchin 2016). Beyond cooperation, the rise of languages likely provided an important means to differentiate groups. As noted in the previous section, it is during the time of proto-languages that we might start to expect the surfacing of tangible ethnolinguistic differences.

All of these developments would have meant that identity and identity politics, how one might negotiate one's identity in relation to others, or the identity of one's group in relation to others, would have been very important and subject to discussion. Notions of inclusivity and exclusivity can become fluid and also subject to negotiation and creative manipulation. This, we believe, would have been an important building block or necessary condition for emergent warfare, even if it is difficult to pinpoint when this would have begun based on the state of presently available evidence. But, seeing the use of personal adornment as a sign of symbolic thinking and possibly even indicative of oral communication, we might also think about the production and uses of such items as social currency and markers for identity. The presence of artifacts thus suggests that the expression of identity may have been both plausible and important, and it follows that groups of individuals could have easily distinguished themselves from others not only within their groups but from those in outside communities as well. This would have been an important and permissive condition for any kind of emergent warfare to occur.

Social Substitution

Related to the idea of kinship and group identity is the notion of social substitution or segmentation. In very important research, anthropologist Raymond Kelly (2000, 2005) outlines an evolutionary pathway for warfare. One of the crucial elements contributing to the appearance of warfare is the human ability to recognize and use notions of social substitution. According to this argument, social substitution pertains to how desires for revenge against perceived affronts can be satisfied through targeting of any member of the offender's community, beyond just the primary offender. This idea, of course, ties in well with a notion of identity. New cognitive and communicative abilities may have been a very pivotal factor for emergent warfare. These abilities would have entailed new ways for people to clearly conceive of different identities in complex ways, as well as to also begin actively fashioning and manipulating identity, especially through sophisticated outward cultural expressions. Competition (and occasional violence) between groups requires notions of identity – of inside members and of those deemed outside. Such notions could have been heavily tied to cultural expressions and perceptions, as seen in adornment, decoration of the body, types of materials and tools being used, and so forth. How we wear clothing, paint our bodies, or other actions that differentiate ourselves constitute messages that are clearly broadcasted and transmitted to members of our own community as well as those outside of it.

In this way, Kelly's model of segmentation offers insights for both the rise of warfare as well as the beginnings of more sophisticated sociopolitical organization, though, as pointed out by Jones and Allen (2014: 364), finding direct archaeological evidence of lineage-based social organization and social segmentation is quite challenging, making it extremely difficult to test Kelly's model. Nevertheless, in our search for potential building blocks, we suspect social substitutability would have been vital for more sophisticated and complex forms of organized fighting and violence in our evolutionary past. As Kelly compellingly argues (2000: 7, emphasis present), the advent of a human ability to use a calculus of social substitution is

> clearly a watershed event in human history in that it creates the preconditions for a more general deployment of lethal violence *as an instrument of the social group* and a legitimate means for the attainment of group objectives and interests.

It should thus be noted that anyone can participate in the instigation of war or participation in various aspects of it, and it should be obvious that there are many possible roles and practices related to warfare. This requires highly complex cooperation and social rules, norms, or cues of interaction within a community or group, especially as the groups get larger and the motivations all the more complicated. Men, women, young, or old – all people are potential participants.

Complex Cooperation

> Within societies all across the planet, be they small nomadic groups of kin wandering through the grasslands or millions of unrelated individuals living in a metropolis, whether modern or prehistoric, cooperation is the glue that binds us together. It is difficult to even imagine a society in which cooperation, at some level or another, has not been integral.
>
> *Dugatkin 1999: 2*

For the majority of this book, we have, by design, been talking about violence. After all, warfare is a violent, repugnant practice that seems to be part of the dark side of human behavior. However, we also must keep in mind that peaceable cooperation is equally important for both modern humans and our hominin ancestors. As the quote by Dugaktin above suggests, cooperation is found in all societies. Without it, modern life would not function.

What you may have noticed is that some of the key building blocks we just offered for warfare are actually building blocks for something bigger than warfare – namely human nature. Our evolutionary story so far has been highly selective. As noted at the outset, we have backgrounded the important role of kinship, as humans evolved more stable reproductive bonds, which obviously played an important role in the attitudes of individuals toward one another in small groups (Chapais 2008). Further in this context, humans also became cooperative breeders, regularly providing child care for offspring who were not their own, and this clearly would have affected emotions and motivations for collaboration and altruism as well (Hrdy 1974). Most likely, both of these processes played a key role in the earliest stages of the story we are telling here, as humans were becoming more tolerant with one another around food. But, as also argued at the outset, these kinds of processes, important as they are, would not help us to explain the more cognitive aspects of coordinating and communicating toward joint goals, nor would they explain humans' tendencies to socially select others with regard to their cooperative behaviors. To explain these, we need not just prosocial tendencies, but also joint intentionality (Tomasello et al. 2012) and motivations for various kinds of collaboration. All of the phenomena highlighted in the preceding sections, the key building blocks, are tied to cooperation.

Anthropologist Agustin Fuentes (2004) has noted that cooperation and competition are not mutually exclusive. Instead, he argues we must recognize that cooperation within groups was, and continues to be, an important aspect of human evolution. Of course, in our society today we often see sensationalized headlines about violent events, with media oftentimes emphasizing the negative aspects of human behavior. As Fuentes (2012) notes, if ten people were murdered in New York City on one day, it would be a front-page headline, but a headline that 8 million people got along in the Big Apple will never show up, even though it would be equally true. How can we understand this compassion and does it help us to understand human variability and emergent warfare?

We also should note that mammalian forms of empathy likely have very deep roots that well precede our hominin lineages, such as that seen in dolphins (Connor and Norris 1982). Moreover, our primate cousins, while often considered to be very aggressive, may not be. Robert Sussman and colleagues (2005), comparing across the primate genus, find that primates only spend about 10% of their activity budgets in social interactions. Moreover, less than 1% of the activity budget is spent on agonistic behavior (which includes both direct conflict and aggressive displays). They suggest that these aggressive behaviors are less important, evolutionarily speaking, than the peaceful, friendly, and cooperative interactions that form the basis of "friendships" and allow for access to resources and alliance formations. Secondly, since social relationships are so important for primates, they have developed many ways to ameliorate aggression (Fuentes 2012). Affiliative bonds can thus lead to prosocial behavior. As Tomasello and colleagues (2012) observe, collective or joint intentionality was an important part of the success and evolution of our species, and there is good reason to see a connection between altruistic behaviors and its benefits.

One might ask, then, how warlike behaviors can be tied to our social and biological developments, at least early on in our evolutionary history and at around the same time that we were evolving to be altruistic, affiliative, and prosocial. After all, warfare is somewhat antithetical to sociality. But, that all depends on perspective and social juxtaposition. Because antagonism, violence, and competition are directed against outsiders, participation in warfare can be highly cooperative, empathetic (Straight 2017), affiliative, and prosocial for members of the same community or group. Consider the social bonds that are made and strengthened during the basic trainings and boot camps of military forces around the world. Our bonds of affiliation can become strengthened when we face certain stresses and threats collectively, whether these are predators, adverse weather conditions, or menacing outsiders. As we have suggested throughout this book, we need to see the emergence of warfare and the emergence of peace as potentially two sides of the same coin. Modern warfare as we can see it today can only occur when masses of people agree to cooperate. Warfare involves groups of people, whether in the thousands or dozens, and so cooperative behaviors are vital.

Asking when cooperation became common in humans is as tricky to answer as the question of the origins of war. In fact, it might even be harder. While violence and warfare can sometimes leave traces in the material and bioarchaeological records, compassion is harder to uncover, though not impossible (Spikins et al. 2010). We will come back to this idea in the next chapter.

Socially Cooperative Violence: Emergent Warfare as Epiphenomenon of Emergent Human Nature

Researchers considering the origins of warfare have used proxy and comparable data from primate communities and extant hunter-gatherer societies in order to formulate hypotheses. Through these efforts, different conceptualizations about incipient forms of warfare have resulted, such as lethal intergroup violence (Kelly 2005) or coalitionary killing (Wrangham 1999). While we see these concepts as very important and useful in addressing this research topic, we would use a somewhat different moniker, namely socially cooperative violence. For us, this is not simply a matter of adding a new phrase to the corpus of descriptions about warfare. Rather, it is one that we feel better conveys the complex ways in which cooperative behaviors can lead to both prosocial and antisocial outcomes, to both peaceable and violent encounters between people. Ultimately, we argue that warfare is only made possible through the existence of complex forms of sociality and cooperation. Peacemaking (or what we propose to call peacefare) and warfare are, then, two ends of a spectrum, as they represent patterns of social interaction that were permitted by evolutionary advances in our species.

As a behavioral pattern, socially cooperative violence would have been a very important foundation for emergent warfare. And in this sense, emergent warfare would be distinct from what researchers would describe as lethal raiding among chimpanzees and potentially among our earliest ancestors, where evolutionary fitness is arguably tied to territoriality in conferring greater access to resources for dominant communities (Wrangham 1999). Chimpanzee lethal raiding, referred to by Pickering (2013: 52) as "primeval warfare," appear to be well rooted among the close ape cousins of chimpanzees and humans, and represent a different kind of organized aggression. That being said, while we see potential problems with using chimpanzee data to infer the likelihood for hominin intergroup aggression, we do recognize the possibility that strategies related to organized violence may have been both present and significant at points in our evolutionary history. As we mention in Chapter One, we hypothesize that the capacity to engage in highly cooperative activities opened the door to what can be considered emergent warfare. Once our ancestors became capable of highly complex forms of sociality and cooperation, we see no reason for them to have been incapable of socially cooperative violence. Moreover, when such forms of socially cooperative violence became directed at members of outside communities, when "others" could be definitively identified, emergent warfare would exist as one outcome for a variety of intergroup cultural dynamics and strategies for interaction.

When we talk about emergent human nature, whatever that might mean, we can think of all kinds of behaviors that mark our species today and contemplate when the earliest signals first appear and what they may have looked like in rudimentary form. As discussed in the preceding section, a key driver in hominins becoming human was whatever physical changes that allowed us to engage in complex cooperation, sociality, and niche construction. That allowed us to thrive in so many new environments. Once this "Pandora's Box" for modern human variability in cognition and social behaviors was opened, it meant we had new ways to look at the world, its contents, and ourselves. These tools were neither inherently good nor evil, however. They were simply tools that we could use as we saw fit depending on circumstances.

But when we think about it, there is a certain irony here. Specifically, it is that the very same cognitive capacities that made emergent or complex cooperation and sociality possible also opened the door for warfare. In other words, as we became "better" at socializing and organizing ourselves in larger, more complex organizations, as we became better at cooperating, we also became better at fighting. We became better at finding reasons to fight, at motivating or compelling others to fight, and at devising ways to outcompete, denigrate, injure, and kill adversaries, enemies, or the proverbial "others." And perhaps this means we should not look at warfare as merely abhorrent, abnormal, or anti-cooperative. In contrast, perhaps we should simply view it as a form of human cooperation designed to effectuate certain outcomes. Those outcomes, the motivations for them, are highly varied when it comes to human intentionality and cultural systems. But the ability to practice war and create institutions related to violence and war, these are part of a distinctly human nature, and perhaps appropriately viewed as epiphenomena of human nature and cultural modernity. It meant that joint cooperation by groups to engage in organized violence directed against others would have been a new and sometimes effective tool added to the repertoire of group, behavioral strategies.

If this is a generally valid way to view warfare, then it brings to mind the very complex interplay between various factors and conditions, some of which were outlined earlier. These would include self-reinforcing and interrelated processes of genotypic and phenotypic changes within our physiologies, operating in conjunction with changing environmental and social conditions around us. And round and round the wheel keeps spinning. We are still evolving, both biologically and culturally.

Does having a capacity for war-making mean that all of the earliest bearers of human culture were warlike, and that they usually resorted to the use of violence in surviving and furthering their interests? Absolutely not. We need only look around our world today to see massive cultural variability in how societies view the legitimate and illegitimate uses of violence and warfare. This clearly demonstrates that the possession of a capacity to engage in certain behaviors does mean that we should expect to see evidence of such behavior universally. So much of our decision-making and cultural preferences are dependent on a host of factors, including environmental, social, and historical circumstances. And these circumstances can change from decade to decade, or from minute to minute.

Tomasello and colleagues note (2012: 681) that at some point in our evolutionary journey, humans gained a whole other level of mechanisms for cooperation, including social conventions, norms (internalized into guilt and shame), and institutions, along with a strong in-group bias. For them, these became necessary because of two important, essentially demographic, factors: population growth within groups, and competition between groups. From that standpoint, competition could have played a significant part in the story of behaviorally modern humans, just as much as collaborative, cooperative, and altruistic behaviors. And it is within this sort of social milieu that notions of group identity would have been very important (Tomasello et al. 2012: 682). These ideas about identity could have affected many aspects of cultural life, including with whom you could associate, trade, marry, or even fight.

Tomasello and colleagues (2012: 682) further write that cultural conventions are distinct from behavioral patterns or traditions, in that with the former, all cultural practitioners know and understand the associated practices as conventional. They argue that conventions require some kind of recursive mindreading or common ground as the basis of the agreement, and that this ability evolved initially "as a skill for forming joint goals and joint attention in collaborative activities." Moreover, they hypothesize that because of this cognitive requirement, other great apes lack human-like conventions or such cultural practices.

Along these lines, even if our earliest ancestors of the genus *Homo* engaged in violence, or even organized violence, it is likely that these behaviors were qualitatively different than later forms of collective violence. So, we might ask ourselves: at what point did our behavioral patterns related to organized aggression and violence transition and develop into cultural practices, institutions, and cultural conventions?

In other words, when did what we call socially cooperative violence or emergent warfare begin?

Ultimately, as we have argued throughout the book, the answer to this question is linked to when we became (or started becoming) human. In a way, then, we might say that a lot depends on how one defines human cooperation and joint intentionality. Just as cooperating to co-exist, hunt, gather food, find resources and shelter, and live in a larger community requires sociality and collective intentionality, so too does organizing to attack or defend. At the time of this writing, there is still plenty of debate about when we became human. However, the data are starting to support a gradual transformation, and it is indisputably clear that we were human far earlier than 12,000 years ago. For us, then, forms of emergent warfare likely existed well before sedentary, complex societies of the Holocene.

Impact and Consequences of Emergent Warfare

To be clear, we are not suggesting that warfare is what made us human. In fact, what makes us human is the shared evolutionary history that we have been discussing throughout this book. The fact that we can be both warlike and peaceful, that some groups subsist mostly on hunting while others gain most of their calories by collecting other types of food, and that some cultures are more "peaceful" than others are all aspects of the immense variation that marks human behavior. It is the multiple variations on key traits such as cooperation, food-sharing, and symbolic thought that allowed our species to be so successful. And in order to be successful, our ancestors surely made use of different strategies of living, socializing, and interacting. These strategies likely ran the gamut from peaceful to violent options, depending on perceived needs dictated by social and environmental conditions and contexts. War-making may have contributed to our ongoing evolution as a species, but we suggest that it was more likely epiphenomenal, a byproduct or secondary phenomenon that occurs alongside, and is a product of, the primary process of becoming human. We were already becoming human, and that meant we were becoming more and more capable of cultural practices related to both emergent warfare and emergent peacefare.

And this is what distinguishes human warfare from organized violence and aggression in other species. *Having human culture would have meant having the ability to communicate reasons for war – to compel others with very complex and fluid ideas about insider and outsider identities, to invoke kin relations (real or imagined) or ideological, supernatural, religious reasons for using or justifying forms of violence.* As highlighted in Chapter Three, ethnographic research has shown us that many societies see the effects of words, spells, sacrifices, and other invocations of magic and the supernatural in bringing about harm or defending against assault. If humans of the contemporary and recent world are capable of such sophisticated belief systems, then we must ask when we began to hold such beliefs. We can see that the beliefs, attitudes, and practices surrounding organized violence are highly variable throughout human history, and many become more elaborate as social organizations become more complex.

Certain actions such as captive-taking or sacrifice become even more prevalent and institutionalized on larger scales in politically centralized societies. They can become tools of leaders of ancient states, for instance, in their political agendas.

For a very long time, researchers have asked if states make war or if war makes states. Much archaeological evidence today would suggest that the answer would be "yes" and "yes." The majority of the world's earliest state-level societies exhibit signs of the importance for violence, whether internally or externally directed. And there is much evidence to indicate that organized violence, coercion, and militarism were vital components in the initial emergence of ancient complex polities world-wide (Carneiro 2012; Feinman 2012; Kim 2015). In that manner, it is hard to deny the heavy connection that Kelly (2000) sees between war and social change, what he calls a coevolution of both war and society. Ultimately, we see no reason to believe that people living in non- or pre-state societies would have been physically, culturally, or biologically incapable of organizing themselves for warlike behaviors, for whatever motivations.

In the end, however, we are not arguing about the pervasiveness of warfare (or even propensities for engaging in organized violence), but are merely acknowledging the emergence of the potential for human communities to engage in such behavioral patterns. This is not dissimilar from the argument made by Azar Gat (2015) when he juxtaposes war and peace as complementary behavioral strategies. For Gat, cooperation, competition, and violent conflict are three forms of social interaction, and all three have always been options for people to choose from.

> Violent conflict as a behavioral strategy did not suddenly emerge sometime in later human history. People are biologically well equipped to pursue any of these social strategies, with conflict being only one tool, albeit a major one – the hammer – in our diverse behavioral toolkit.
>
> *Gat 2015: 123*

Where we might quibble with Gat is how much emphasis to place on the prevalence or frequency of violence in the Pleistocene, but we would generally agree with the larger sentiment of a wide-ranging plasticity of human behavior. Certainly, the scant material data that are discernible at the moment do not demonstrate warfare to be common or omnipresent prior to the Late Pleistocene and Holocene. It is likely that, besides a human potential for warfare, a series of other factors (both environmental and cultural) were necessary for it to become a more commonly selected option for action, strategy, and cultural systems. In that sense, then, one might downplay any biological propensity for violence, emphasizing instead choice, agency, and contingency.

False Dichotomies and Emergent Peacefare

Those of our ancestors that possessed the cognitive capacity to make and bear modern human would have possessed the capability to perform actions related to warfare. But, there is an important point to be added here. Having the capacity to conduct warfare activities does not mean all these populations and societies would have chosen to use such behaviors and tactics. Many of us in the modern world do not engage in warfare, but we are all capable of this sort of behavior if presented with the necessary set of circumstances. An archaeologist of the year 3000 may view the 20th century record of Madison, Wisconsin and conclude that there was little to no warfare occurring. But that does not mean inhabitants were incapable of it. And so, talking about whether we are inherently peaceful or warlike might be setting up a false dichotomy, a question that cannot be answered.

War and peace may be opposites in a very literal and definitional sense, but that does not mean we should look these behaviors or social conditions in purely black-and-white terms. After all, what might qualify as peaceful for one person or group of people may not be the case for others. There can be degrees of peace and war. Take for instance our daily lives here in the United States. Most of the country's inhabitants would say that they were living in a state of peace, since most of us do not engage in violence on a daily basis. But does that mean that our society or the country is in a state of peace? For members of our armed forces serving abroad, the current state of life is not necessarily peaceful. Moreover, there are many people in America who would not describe their lives as peaceful, not when they face certain kinds of injustice or even physical threat on a daily basis, depending on their social surroundings and circumstances. The point is that we cannot very easily describe either peace or war as they can be very subjective, contested, and fluid. Human relationships and interactions can cycle through shades of peace and violence very rapidly, and sometimes these leave clear material traces, but sometimes they leave nothing that an archaeologist would find. The very real and significant implication, then, is that relying predominantly on the archaeological record to argue about the existence or prevalence of a social or behavioral pattern runs the risk of offering an incomplete and fragmentary picture.

Peace is not simply a vacuum that lacks violence. Peace is constructed and maintained, hence the notion of active peacemaking or what we call peacefare to complement the notion of warfare. To be able to live in social groups, people need to build and maintain relationships with one another. As groups become bigger, the relationships become more numerous and more complex. Disagreements between people become inevitable, and all groups need ways to avoid, mitigate, or resolve conflicts. Humans have evolved to be very effective at this, and we have created social mechanisms, practices, and institutions that both directly and indirectly promote stable social interactions. According to anthropologist Christopher Boehm (2012), we might look at certain "peacemaking" behaviors of chimpanzees and bonobos to make inferences about ancestral *Pan*, the common ancestor for their and our lineages, living millions of years ago in Africa. Beyond exploring the roots of warfare, this kind of comparative exercise might yield insights for early and rudimentary forms of peacemaking. In both chimpanzees and bonobos, researchers have observed different ways that they reconcile differences dyadically, and because this is also the case with humans, Boehm proposes that flexible peacemaking abilities are likely ancestral.

This is an interesting argument. While we do not see warfare as a primary factor in promoting human evolution, it is very possible that outbreaks of violence could have promoted changes in cultural patterns. Just as groups could have recognized the potential benefits of engaging in organized violence, they would have been able to judge when such actions would have had deleterious outcomes that far outweighed any potential gains. Arguably, this recognition, combined with the possession of human culture, would have allowed for novel and complex ways to control, regulate, mitigate, avoid, or prevent forms of aggression and uses of violence. For instance, could certain institutions, such as marriage, have been promoted in part to help keep peace within and between communities? Could ideas about the supernatural and the beginnings of religiosity have been devised to help control behavior and prevent inequalities that could lead to violence?

We argue that our ancestors had the capacity to engage in emergent warfare within the last 200,000 years or so. Though it is sobering to think about how far back our warlike behaviors may go, we might take comfort in the idea that the very same abilities allowing us to devise and engage in cultural practices related to warfare, in all of its potential cultural facets, also gave us the abilities to avoid conflict. We were smart enough to know when to use violence, and also how to avoid it. Many species live in large groups and communities and practice forms of sociality. From that standpoint, just living together and cooperating can constitute forms of peacemaking. But, what humans do is qualitatively different, and arguably so because forms of conflict are qualitatively different. Simply put, why and how we fight can have an effect on how we devise ways to avoid fighting. We explore these ideas about peace further in the next chapter.

X-Marks the Spot: Contemplative Speculation on Emergent Warfare

Modern human cognition and capacities allowed for more complex forms of social organization and relationships (both intra-group and inter-group), and for more complex forms of sociality and identity formation. We became better equipped to formulate ideas about our individual and community identities, thus juxtaposing these against identities of others. We were able to better compel others to adhere to certain social rules because of our ideas about community, the world around us (visible and invisible), and ideas about right/wrong, equity, fairness, egalitarianism, and justice. This meant that violence could be tied to ideas, could be made legitimate and sanctioned, or deemed illegitimate or wrong. These ideas, and the ability to communicate them, led to transformations in human intergroup violence. This is when human warfare truly changed in a qualitative sense.

There is enormous diversity and plasticity in behaviors that constitute what it means to be human. At the same time, there are important attributes and capacities separating humans (and hominins) from other members of the natural world.

TABLE 6.1 Behavioral traits that have been associated with the appearance of modern humans

Behavior	Suspected first appearance
Hunting	1.75 million years ago
Controlled use of fire	780,000 years ago
Language	500,000 years ago
Behavioral modernity	200,000 years ago (possibly earlier)
Use of projectile implements	400,000 years ago (possibly earlier)
Emergent warfare/emergent peacemaking	500,000–300,000 years ago

The connection between humanity and practices of collective violence is an important one to investigate, but we conclude that, on an even broader level, warfare, aggression, cannibalism, and other forms of violence importantly reflect human capacities for complex patterns of behavior, communication, symbolic thought, and cognition. The practices of warfare among anatomically modern humans are qualitatively different than forms of organized violence discernible in other species. In the end, we argue that language, which supports the complex relationships that allowed our early ancestors to solve myriad problems, may also be directly linked to the advent of warfare in a way that has not yet been adequately investigated. It is a human set of capacities allowing for complex forms of co-operation, strategizing, and rationalizing that set the stage for a qualitative change in patterns of organized violence among and between groups. Once behavioral modernity appeared in our evolutionary history, it arguably opened the door for forms of socially cooperative violence and emergent warfare to enter our repertoire of diverse cultural practices.

Works Cited

Arensburg, B., A.M. Tillier, B. Vandermeersch, Henri Duday, LA Schepartz, and Yoel Rak. 1989. A Middle Palaeolithic Human Hyoid Bone. *Nature* 338(6218), 758–760.

Armit, Ian. 2010. Violence and Society in the Deep Human Past. *British Journal of Criminology* 51(3), 499–517.

Barnard, Alan. 2012. *Genesis of Symbolic Thought.* Cambridge University Press, Cambridge.

Bednarik, Robert G. 2005. Middle Pleistocene Beads and Symbolism. *Anthropos* 100(2005), 537–552.

Binford, Lewis R. 1981. *Bones: Ancient Men and Modern Myths.* Academic Press, New York.

Blumenschine, Robert J. 1987. Characteristics of an Early Hominid Scavenging Niche. *Current Anthropology* 28(4), 383–407.

Boehm, Christopher. 2012. Ancestral Hierarchy and Conflict. *Science* 336(6083), 844–847.

Bouzouggar, Abdeljalil, Nick Barton, Marian Vanhaeren, et al. 2007. 82,000-year-old Shell Beads from North Africa and Implications for the Origins of Modern Human Behavior. *Proceedings of the National Academy of Sciences* 104(24), 9964–9969.

Bunn, Henry. 2001. Hunting, Power Scavenging, and Butchering by Hadza Foragers and by Plio-Pleistocene Homo. In *Meat-Eating and Human Evolution*, edited by Craig Stanford and Henry Bunn, pp. 199–218. Oxford University Press, Oxford.

Bunn, Henry T., and Alia N. Gurtov. 2014. Prey Mortality Profiles Indicate that Early Pleistocene Homo at Olduvai Was an Ambush Predator. *Quaternary International* 322–323, 44–53.

Capasso, Luigi, Elisabetta Michetti, and Ruggero D'Anastasio. 2008. A Homo Erectus Hyoid Bone: Possible Implications for the Origin of the Human Capability for Speech. *Collegium Antropologicum* 32(4), 1007–1011.

Carneiro, Robert. 2012. The Circumscription Theory: A Clarification, Amplification, and Reformulation. *Social Evolution & History* 11(2), 5–30.

Cavallo, John A., and Robert J. Blumenschine. 1989. Tree-stored Leopard Kills: Expanding the Hominid Scavenging Niche. *Journal of Human Evolution* 18(4), 393–399.

Chagnon, Napoleon. 1988. Life Histories, Blood Revenge, and Warfare in a Tribal Population. *Science* 239(4843), 985–992.

Chapais, Bernard. 2008. *Primeval Kinship: How Pair-Bonding Gave Birth to Human Society*. Harvard University Press, Cambridge, MA.

Chapais, Bernard. 2014. Complex Kinship Patterns as Evolutionary Constructions, and the Origins of Sociocultural Universals. *Current Anthropology* 55(6), 751–783.

Conard, Nicholas J., Jordi Serangeli, Utz Böhner, et al. 2015. Excavations at Schöningen and Paradigm Shifts in Human Evolution. *Journal of Human Evolution* 89, 2015, 1–17.

Connor, R.C., and K.S. Norris. 1982. Are Dolphins Reciprocal Altruists? *American Naturalist* 119(3), 358–374.

Deacon, Terrence W. 2010. *On The Human: Rethinking The Natural Selection Of Human Language*. Available at: https://nationalhumanitiescenter.org/on-the-human/2010/02/on-the-human-rethinking-the-natural-selection-of-human-language/.

Dediu, Dan, and Stephen C. Levinson. 2013. On the Antiquity of Language: The Reinterpretation of Neandertal Linguistic Capacities and Its Consequences. *Frontiers in Psychology* 4(July), 1–17.

d'Errico, Francesco, Christopher Henshilwood, Graeme Lawson, et al. 2003. Archaeological Evidence for the Emergence of Language, Symbolism, and Music – An Alternative Multidisciplinary Perspective. *Journal of World Prehistory* 17(1), 1–70.

Dominguez-Rodrigo, Manuel, J. Serrallonga, J. Juan-Tresserras, L. Aicala, and L. Luque. 2001. Woodworking Activities by Early Humans: A Plant Residue Analysis on Acheulian Stone Tools from Peninj (Tanzania). *Journal of Human Evolution* 40(4), 289–299.

Dominguez-Rodrigo, Manuel, and Travis Rayne Pickering. 2003. Early Hominid Hunting and Scavenging: A Zooarchaeological Review. *Evolutionary Anthropology* 12(6), 275–282.

Dor, Daniel, Chris Knight, and Jerome Lewis. 2014. Introduction: A Social Perspective on How Language Began. In *The Social Origins of Language*, edited by Daniel Dor, Chris Knight, and Jerome Lewis, pp. 1–12. Oxford University Press, Oxford.

Dugatkin, Lee. 1999. Cheating Monkeys and Citizen Bees: The Nature of Cooperation in Animals and Humans. Free Press, New York.

Dunbar, Robin. 1998. *Grooming, Gossip, and the Evolution of Language*. Harvard University Press, Cambridge, MA.

Feinman, Gary. 2012. Circumscription Theory and Political Change: From Determinism to Mechanisms and Parameters. *Social Evolution & History* 11(2), 44–47.

Fitch, W.T. 2000. The Phonetic Potential of Nonhuman Vocal Tracts: Comparative Cineradiographic Observations of Vocalizing Animals. *Phonetica* 57(2–4), 205–218.

Fitch, W.T. 2009. Fossil Cues to the Evolution of Speech. In *The Cradle of Language*, edited by R. Botha and C. Knight, pp. 113–134. Oxford University Press, Oxford.

Fuentes, Agustin. 2004. It's Not All Sex and Violence: Integrated Anthropology and the Role of Cooperation and Social Complexity in Human Evolution. *American Anthropologist* 106(4), 710–718.

Fuentes, Agustin. 2012. *Race, Monogamy, and Other Lies They Told You*. University of California Press, Berkeley.

Fuentes, Agustin. 2014. Human Evolution, Niche Complexity, and the Emergence of a Distinctively Human Imagination. *Time and Mind* 7(3), 241–257.

Fuentes, Agustin. 2015. Integrative Anthropology and the Human Niche: Toward a Contemporary Approach to Human Evolution. *American Anthropologist* 117(2), 302–315.

Fuentes, Agustin. 2017. *The Creative Spark: How Imagination Made Humans Exceptional*. Dutton, New York.

Gat, Azar. 2015. Proving Communal Warfare Among Hunter-Gatherers: The Quasi-Rousseauan Error. *Evolutionary Anthropology* 24(3), 111–126.

Hare, Brian, and Michael Tomasello. 2004. Chimpanzees Are More Skilful in Competitive than in Cooperative Cognitive Tasks. *Animal Behaviour* 68(3), 571–581.

Henshilwood, Christopher, Francesco d'Errico, Marian Vanhaeren, Karen van Niekerk, and Zenobia Jacobs. 2004. Middle Stone Age Shell Beads from South Africa. *Science* 304(5669), 404.

Hrdy, Sarah. 1974. Male-Male Competition and Infanticide among the Langurs (*Presbytis entellus*) of Abu, Rajasthan. *Folia Primatologica* 22(1), 19–58.

Isaac, Glynn. 1978. The Food-Sharing Behavior of Protohuman Hominids. *Scientific American* 238(4), 90–108.

Joordens, Josephine, Francesco D'Errico, Frank P. Wesselingh, et al. 2014. Homo Erectus at Trinil on Java Used Shells for Tool Production and Engraving. *Nature* 518(7538), 228–231.

Jones, Terry, and Mark Allen. 2014. The Prehistory of Violence and Warfare among Hunter-Gatherers. In *Violence and Warfare Among Hunter-Gatherers*, edited by Mark Allen and Terry Jones, pp. 353–371. Left Coast Press, Walnut Creek, CA.

Kelly, Raymond. 2000. *Warless Societies and the Origin of War*. University of Michigan Press, Ann Arbor.

Kelly, Raymond. 2005. The Evolution of Lethal Intergroup Violence. *Proceedings of the National Academy of Sciences* 102(43), 15294–15298.

Keeley, Lawrence, and Nicholas Toth. 1981. Microwear Polishes on Early Stone Tools from Koobi Fora, Kenya. *Nature* 293(5832), 464–465.

Kissel, Marc, and Agustin Fuentes. 2016. From Hominid to Human: The Role of Human Wisdom and Distinctiveness in the Evolution of Modern Humans. *Philosophy, Theology and the Sciences* 3(2), 217–244.

Kissel, Marc, and Agustin Fuentes. 2017. Semiosis in the Pleistocene. *Cambridge Archaeological Journal* 27(3), 397–412.

Kim, Nam. 2015. *The Origins of Ancient Vietnam*. Oxford University Press, Oxford.

Krause, Johannes, Carles Lalueza-Fox, Ludovic Orlando, et al. 2007. The derived FOXP2 Variant of Modern Humans Was Shared With Neandertals. *Current Biology* 17(21), 1908–1912.

Laland, Kevin N., Tobias Uller, Marcus W. Feldman, et al. 2014. Does Evolutionary Theory Need a Rethink? Yes, Urgently. *Nature* 514(7521), 161–164.

Laland, Kevin N., Tobias Uller, Marcus W. Feldman, et al. 2015. The Extended Evolutionary Synthesis: Its Structure, Assumptions and Predictions. *Proceedings of the Royal Society B: Biological Sciences* 282(1813), 1–14.

Lieberman, Philip. 2007. The Evolution of Human Speech: Its Anatomical and Neural Bases. *Current Anthropology* 48(1), 39–66.

Lovejoy, Owen. 2009. Reexamining Human Origins in the Light of *Ardipithecus ramidus*. *Science* 326(5949), 74e1–74e8.

Martínez, I., M. Rosa, R. Quam, et al. 2013. Communicative Capacities in Middle Pleistocene Humans from the Sierra de Atapuerca in Spain. *Quaternary International* 295, 94–101.

Marks, Jonathan. 2002. *What Does It Mean to Be 98% Chimpanzee*. University of California Press, Berkeley.

Marks, Jonathan. 2015. *Tales of the Ex-Apes: How We Think about Human Evolution*. University of California Press, Berkeley.

McBrearty, Sally, and Alison Brooks. 2000. The Revolution that Wasn't: A New Interpretation of the Origin of Modern Human Behavior. *Journal of Human Evolution* 39(5), 453–563.

Noble, William, and Iain Davidson. 1991. The Evolutionary Emergence of Modern Human Behaviour: Language and Its Archaeology. *Man* 26(2), 223–253.

O'Brien, Michael J., and Kevin N. Laland. 2012. Genes, Culture and Agriculture: An Example of Human Niche Construction. *Current Anthropology* 53(4), 434–470.

Odling-Smee, John, Kevin N. Laland, and Marcus W. Feldman. 2003. *Niche Construction: The Neglected Process in Evolution*. Princeton University Press, Princeton, NJ.

Pickering, Travis. 2013. *Rough and Tumble: Aggression, Hunting, and Human Evolution*. University of California Press, Berkeley.

Pruetz, Jill, and Paco Bertolani. 2007. Savanna Chimpanzees, Pan troglodytes verus, Hunt with Tools. *Current Biology* 17(5), 412–417.

Quam, Rolf, and Yoel Rak. 2008. Auditory ossicles from Southwest Asian Mousterian Sites. *Journal of Human Evolution* 54(3), 414–433.

Raffield, Ben, Claire Greenlow, Neil Price, and Mark Collard. 2015. Ingroup Identification, Identity Fusion and the Formation of Viking War Bands. *World Archaeology* 8243(February), 1–16.

Renfrew, Colin. 1996. The Sapient Behaviour Paradox: How to Test for Potential? In *Modelling the Early Human Mind*, edited by Paul Mellars and K. Gibson, pp. 11–15. McDonald Institute, Cambridge.

Seyfarth, Robert, and Dorothy Cheney. 2008. Primate Social Knowledge and the Origins of Language. *Mind & Society* 7(1), 129–142.

Spikins, Penny, Holly Rutherford, and Andy Needham. 2010. From Homininity to Humanity: Compassion from the Earliest Archaics to Modern Humans. *Time and Mind* 3(3), 303–325.

Straight, Bilinda. 2017. *Could Group-Organized Violence Be Rooted in Empathy?*. Available at: https://www.sapiens.org/debate/evolution-empathy-violence/

Sussman, Robert, Paul Garber, and Jim M. Cheverud. 2005. Importance of Cooperation and Affiliation in the Evolution of Primate Sociality. *American Journal of Physical Anthropology* 128(1), 84–97.

Sussman, Robert, and Joshua Marshack. 2010. Are Humans Inherently Killers? Center for Global Nonkilling. *Global Nonkilling Working Papers* 1, 7–50.

Tallerman, Maggie. 2005. Introduction: Language Origins. In *Language Origins*, edited by Maggie Tallerman, pp. 1–10. Oxford University Press, Oxford.

Terrell, John. 2014. *A Talent for Friendship*. Oxford University Press, Oxford.

Tomasello, Michael, Alicia P. Melis, Claudio Tennie, Emily Wyman, and Esther Herrmann. 2012. Two Key Steps in the Evolution of Human Cooperation: The Interdependence Hypothesis. *Current Anthropology* 53(6), 673–692.

Turchin, Peter. 2016. *Ultrasociety: How 10,000 Years of War Made Humans the Greatest Cooperators on Earth*. Beresta Books, Chaplin, CT.

Vanhaeren, Marian, Francesco d'Errico, Chris Stringer, Sarah James, Jonathan Todd, and Henk Mienis. 2006. Middle Paleolithic Shell Beads in Israel and Algeria. *Science* 312(5781), 1785–1788.

Washburn, Sherwood, and C.S. Lancaster. 1968. The Evolution of Hunting. In *Man the Hunter*, edited by Richard Lee and I. Devore, pp. 293–303. Aldine, Chicago, IL.

White, Tim D., Berhane Asfaw, Yonas Beyene, et al. 2009. Ardipithecus Ramidus and the Paleobiology of Early Hominids. *October* 326(5949), 64–86.

Whiten, Andrew, and David Erdal. 2012. The Human Socio-cognitive Niche and Its Evolutionary Origins. *Philosophical Transactions of the Royal Society of London. Series B, Biological Sciences* 367(1599), 2119–2129.

Wrangham, Richard. 1999. Evolution of Coalitionary Killing. *Yearbook of Physical Anthropology* 42(S29), 1–30.

Wrangham, Richard, and Dale Peterson. 1996. *Demonic Males: Apes and the Origins of Human Violence*. Houghton Mifflin, Boston.

7

THE DURABILITY OF PEACE

We must all learn to live together as brothers - or we will all perish together as fools.
Martin Luther King, Jr., Commencement Address for Oberlin College,
June 1965, Oberlin Ohio[1] www.oberlin.edu/external/
EOG/BlackHistoryMonth/MLK/CommAddress.html

In his watershed volume *War Before Civilization* (1996), Lawrence Keeley makes a strong case for researchers to be open to the likelihood that warfare was just as significant for smaller-scale societies of the prehistoric past as it is for people living in a modern world dominated by nation–states. He also discusses the fragile nature of peace. While we would agree with his larger arguments about the universal potential for warfare behaviors and cultural practices among societies of all scales and types, regardless of time and place, we would make the argument that peace should not be viewed as fragile. Indeed, it may be that the opposite is true, that in order to promote peaceful conditions, various moral systems, "crosscutting ties" (Fry 2006), and bonds between groups need to be very strong, robust, and dynamic. Peace may have the appearance of being fragile, but that is only if one starts from the assumption that some form of absolute peace is the norm, and that peace is merely the absence of conflict. There is no such thing as a complete, permanent, and utter absence of conflict, tension, and competition for any society. Indeed, depending on one's definition of peace, there have been vast stretches of relative peace for much of humanity throughout our history. It all depends on what kind of peace you are talking about. At the end of the day, though, peace is a product of social convention and efforts.

Additionally, peace is a relative term, dependent on the kind of peace one is trying to define. Is it the absence of all forms of violence? Is it an easy and carefree state of existence, or stability maintained by threat of law, sanction, reprisal, or retribution (whether by others or by some cosmic force or deity)? Does it involve

FIGURE 7.1   Martin Luther King, Jr. circa 1963. *Source: National Parks Service, USA*

social justice and equality for all people within a society and is it devoid of any kind
of structural violence or discrimination? Just as practices and attitudes related to
warfare are highly variable along cultural dimensions, so too are the notions and
practices of peace.

   Anthropologist Paul Roscoe (2013: 475) notes an oddity in how many anthropologists approach war and peace, often phrasing them in binary terms, "as though
communities are either at war or at peace." For some researchers, peace is defined
as the absence of combat, but for us peace cannot be defined simply as the absence
of war. Peaceful conditions for some may not be for all. A community may be at
peace with outside communities, but within it some members may feel injustices or
threats (e.g., structural or cultural violence). Similarly, a community may be at peace
internally, but maybe because there is solidarity in the face of an outside threat.

Would either of these hypothetical examples show people living in "peace"? The upshot is that violence and the potential for it are not non-existent – violence is merely kept in check, and peace is something that is maintained. There are many ways that peace can be constructed and nurtured, and sometimes it is done so through tacit threats of violence, as paradoxical as that might sound. Arguably, both human warfare and human peace have resulted from cultural invention.

Noted scholar Johan Galtung (1990) argued that cultural or structural peace is the antithesis of cultural violence. And, as we observed in an earlier chapter, cultural violence is viewed by Galtung (1990: 292) as "any aspect of a culture that can be used to legitimize violence in its direct or structural form." Hence, when forms of structural violence are being perpetrated on people, violence that can lead to harmful effects even if they do not involve the direct application of physical force, then cultural practices and institutions can have a hand in either promoting or preventing such injurious effects. As argued by Peter Verbeek (2013: 62), peace is modified by culture in both human and non-human animals, and it involves behavior through which individuals and groups "experience low levels of aggression and engage in mutually harmonious interactions."

In this chapter, we will not go into exhaustive detail about what researchers have written about peace. The larger mission of this book was to explore warfare. But, as we discussed in the last chapter, our journey into the research landscape of warfare in its earliest possible manifestations took us firmly into terrain where the evolution of humanity has to be considered, and in that regard our evolving cooperative behaviors that helped make communities socially stable become an important part of the conversation. And so our journey now takes us on a brief foray into general ideas about peacemaking and its earliest manifestations, what we are proposing to call emergent peacefare. We see the developmental trajectory of cooperation for maintaining stable and peaceable life as inseparable from emergent warfare.

Conflict Mitigation in the Animal World

Although we may be unique in our ways of warfare, we know that other species have the ability to participate in intergroup competition, aggression, and violence. Similarly, other animals have the ability to avoid conflict and promote stability through a variety of behaviors. We may be the most socially capable, but we are not alone in a capacity for conflict avoidance and resolution. From an evolutionary standpoint, conflict of any type is costly. At the extreme it leads to death. But there are other, less obvious costs. Primate studies have shown that individuals who are attacked by an aggressor are more likely to be subjected to renewed attacks, either by the same or a new aggressor (Arnold et al. 2011). The subjects of aggression also spend less time foraging after attacks, since they are busy monitoring the new social environment. This suggests that any species marked by occurrences of aggressive behavior would also develop tools to lessen the ramifications. Reconciliation reduces the costs of conflict for all parties, and according to a review by Kate Arnold and colleagues (2011), reconciliation behaviors occur not just in primates but in domestic goat, hyenas, and between cleaner fish and their clients.

One debate, relevant for us in terms of what these behaviors mean for the "mind" of the individuals, is what reconciliation means about awareness of mental states. Early research into this question suggested that reconciliation requires self-awareness and being able to attribute mental states to others, a high-level cognitive ability referred to as "theory of mind." Later research cast doubt on this (Bshary and Wurth 2001) and most scholars seem to think that this is not necessary. Cleaner fish, which remove parasites from larger fish, have been shown to engage in what may be reconciliation behaviors toward their "clients" (Bshary and Wurth 2001). They are also more willing to reconcile with partners who would be considered more "valuable." Since, as far as we know, no one has suggested that fish have a theory of mind, this could suggest that simple reconciliation does not require such high-level thinking.

However, we must note that many of these studies examine dyads. Real world interactions are a lot more complex. In the end, though, much research currently shows us that social animals cooperate and reduce stress by seeking each other's company, and this is particularly apparent in primates (Hart and Sussman 2011: 33). "Based on the latest research, friendly and cooperative behaviors provide psychological, physiological, and ecological benefits to social primates which are positively reinforced by hormonal and neurological systems" (Hart and Sussman 2011: 33).

Non-Human Primates

Research that would be particularly telling and pertinent for "peace" behaviors in humanity is related to how aggression is mediated and mitigated in non-human primates, providing hints for how humans have become so good at cooperating. Much work has been done to study why primates live in groups and how they ameliorate the stress that can be caused by aggression (Arnold et al. 2011). Long-term studies on primates have shown that conciliatory practices and reconciliation are common after aggression occurs. A meta-analysis of some of these studies shows a wide variety of behaviors. Even within a single species, sometimes it is the victim who initiates the reconciliation and sometimes it is the aggressor, depending on the group. Perhaps not surprisingly, monkeys who are removed from their mother before weaning do not show reconciliation behaviors, suggesting that socialization is a key part of this behavior (Arnold et al. 2011). This work supports what is known as the "social evolution hypothesis," which states that conciliation is necessary in socially living species. A secondary hypothesis suggests that these behaviors will occur most between two individuals when there is a positive fitness benefit (Arnold et al. 2011).

Noted primatologist Frans de Waal (2000) argues that while we can clearly see aggression in many species, it might be productive to view it not as an antisocial instinct and instead as a potential tool of both competition and negotiation. "Humans share with many animals the ability to cooperate despite the ever-present potential of competition over food, mates, and space" (de Waal 1996: 38). As de Waal (2000) points out, chimpanzees will kiss and embrace after fights, while other non-human primates will engage in similar sorts of "reconciliations." When social relationships are important for a species, then "one can expect the full complement of natural checks and balances" that can promote cooperative and peaceful interactions within animal societies (de Waal 2000: 586). Much research suggests that among primates, the cognitive prerequisites for reconciliation are minimal (de Waal 2000: 588). Moreover, as members of these communities recognize the social benefit for avoiding and mitigating the effects of conflict, they have been observed to participate in different behaviors, such as those variably described as "policing," "pacification," and "third-party mediation" (de Waal 2000: 589). For de Waal, these tactics are elaborations on an underlying behavioral mechanism that protects cooperative bonds within social groups. "The evolutionary advantages of reconciliation are obvious for animals that survive through mutual aid: Reconciliation ensures the continuation of cooperation among parties with partially conflicting interests" (de Waal 2000: 589).

As we discussed earlier in the book, many researchers have cited the observations of chimpanzee lethal organized aggression and violence as support for the notion that such forms of violence could have been evolutionarily adaptive for our earliest ancestors. But, there is plenty of intriguing research to suggest that we look at how behaviors can be varied, conditional, and flexible. For instance, based on many years of observation of baboon behavior in Kenya, Robert Sapolsky (2013) notes that forms of prosociality and aggression are not simply hard-wired or biologically ingrained. Indeed, he argues that these behaviors can be heavily influenced by eco-logical circumstances as well as the transmission of "cultural" or social behaviors. By way of example, he cites one troop of baboons being observed to possess a "culture" of low aggression and high affiliation among its members. This involved the transmission of an assemblage of prosocial behaviors. According to Sapolsky (2013: 431), variation in temperament and personality in this group, combined with the deaths of certain males, resulted in a very distinctive social atmosphere, which was then transmitted to new troop members and allowing for these largely coopera-tive behaviors to persist beyond the "founder" generation. The key takeaway here is that "substantial, radical change in social behavior does not require changes in the building blocks of social behavior" (Sapolsky 2013: 435). In the end, Sapolsky rec-ognizes the malleability of baboon social systems, which in turn forces us to consider analogous flexibilities in our own long history of cultural and biological change.

Peacemaking and Human Nature

Social and cooperative behaviors are clearly not unique to humans, especially when one looks toward the non-human primates. Researchers Douglas Fry and Anna Szala (2013) stress that when we consider intraspecific agonism in humans (which loosely refers to behaviors related to aggression, defense, and avoidance) and other mammals, a key principle in evolutionary development is that of restraint. In other words, as competition and conflict are a natural part of life, restraint has fostered the emergence of behaviors that tend to minimize the costs of agonistic interactions, resulting in more restrained forms of competition that do not inevitably lead to highly damaging actions. The researchers refer to these evolved behavioral patterns as part of "restrained, non-lethal aggression."

Though we can see conflict avoidance and minimization throughout the natural world, there is something fairly unique about our abilities to construct social mechanisms to promote "peace." As the prominent paleoanthropologist Ian Tattersall (2011: 11) has observed, *Homo sapiens* is an unusually cooperative species and is social in a very particular manner. We "live to a remarkable extent in environments that we re-create in our heads" (Tattersall 2011: 11). Seeing the world around us, consisting of our physical surroundings, our social landscapes, and the various abstract and unknowable bits, means that we have at our disposal so many more complex ways to envision and effectuate social relationships and outcomes. "So, where all primates have evolved social-cognitive skills for cooperating and competing with group/community members, humans have also evolved skills for establishing distinct cultural groups, with different physical and symbolic markers (social institutions, artifacts, language, etc.)" (MacKinnon and Fuentes 2011: 138).

Indeed, some researchers argue that "altruism" (which can be viewed as behavior that benefits others at one's own expense) is only possible with animals capable of "self-transcendence," meaning that it emerges only with modern human beings that possessed the requisite brain structures for that type of cognition and thinking (Cloninger and Kedia 2011: 97). "Altruism emerges in human beings along with other aspects of the perception of unity, such as science, art, and spirituality" (Cloninger and Kedia 2011: 97).

Many researchers see highly cooperative behaviors as key to the earliest stages of our evolutionary development. For instance, Hart and Sussman (2011: 35) suggest that some of our earliest ancestors were likely targeted as prey by very dangerous predators, and that living and cooperating in groups was necessary for survival. In this view, an urge to cooperate and get along would have been important, and perhaps more crucial than any urge to compete with or fight one another. This perspective thus emphasizes an evolutionary repertoire of sociality, interdependence, and mutual protection.

As we have argued throughout this book, humans have taken many of the behaviors we share at an underlying, basic level with other species, and transformed them into far more complex patterns. Our forms of sociality illustrate this pattern. Humans seem to naturally form bonds with others. In fact, one of the most extreme forms of punishment is banishment or sociality confinement (Montagu 1976). Studies of the effects of solitary confinement indicate it produces significant and severe health effects, with one prisoner noting that confinement can "alter the ontological makeup of a stone" (Smith 2006: 475).

By studying how non-kin associate with each other, perhaps we can see how large-scale partnerships evolved. If friendship is a source of compassion, it can clue us into ideas about the emergence of peace. Interestingly, John Terrell (2014) argues that the ability to form friendships, even with people we have just met, is among the defining traits of our species. For Terrell this ability to form social networks is:

> an evolved human trait marking us apart from most other species on Earth just as surely as the other diagnostic traits that have been singled out as being characteristic of our kind, such as walking upright on two legs, having opposable thumbs and a prominent chin, and possessing the powers of both speech and complex abstract reasoning.
>
> *Terrell 2014:17*

Friendships allow us to transfer information and bring people together.

If human friendships are different from that seen in primates, maybe tracing their origins and characteristics could shed light on the origins of compassion. But what do we know about the origins of friendship? While the word "friend" is used more than either mother or father in spoken and written English (Hruschka 2010) the answer is not much. Some scholars have argued that it may have evolved as a form of kin selection; in early hunter-gatherer societies, everyone you met would have been a relative and thus, so the theory goes, we evolved to treat everyone like kin no matter what. Later, when groups got bigger we retained this ability (Alexander 1979). Primatologist Joan Silk (2002) notes some problems with this hypothesis, such as the fact that people in foraging societies do meet non-kin and strangers often. Others suggest it evolved as a way to provide basis for trade and alliances (Kenrick and Trost 2000). Terrell (2014) suggests it allows for trading of valuable information, to mobilize people into action, and to provide buffers against stress. Dan Hruschka (2010) compared ethnographic descriptions of how different cultures interacted and described friendships. Using these data, he defines a friendship-like relationship as "a social relationship in which partners provide support according to their abilities in times of need, and in which this behavior is motivated in part by positive affect between partners" (Hruschka 2010: 68). Or, as Silk concludes: "All we can say at this point is that human friendships seem to present a puzzle for evolutionary biologists" (2002: 438).

Hruschka notes that humans, unlike other primates, have the capacity for cumulative cultural learning, which allows both tools and activities to be preserved for generations. This allows not only for the exchange of food and other goods, but also mentoring, guard duty against neighboring groups, safe haven, support, and other behaviors, all of which are orders of degrees different from what chimpanzees do. Thinking back to our discussion in the previous chapter on the emergence of the human cultural niche, perhaps we are seeing the increased reliance on these very social networks that seem to be a distinctively human behavior.

> I propose that the psychological systems underlying the ability and propensity to cultivate friendships were selected (or at least not rooted out by selection) because they uniquely addressed common adaptive problems of

cooperation and mutual aid in uncertain contexts. In other words, friendship, as a system regulating altruistic behavior, solves a computational task in uncertain environments that cannot be met by simple reactive exchange strategies, such as tit-for-tat accounting.

Hruschka 2010: 10

The Construction of Peace: Cultural Mechanisms and Practices for Peacefare

As mentioned in Chapter One, the position we take in this book is that a foundation of behaviorally modern cognition and other faculties provided our ancestors with the tools to organize, cooperate, socialize, and see the world around them in ways very similar to us living today. This means that within the past 200,000+ years, humans the world over would have had the requisite abilities to bear all forms of human culture, including forms of emergent warfare and emergent peacefare. Indeed, we suspect that certain social behaviors and cultural practices may have been adopted precisely to help mitigate and control violence.

Peace is not a natural condition for humans, but is socially constructed and maintained. "Peace is not an effortless inertial or 'natural' state to which people and societies revert in the absence of perturbation" (Keeley 1996: 157). As a species, we are capable of suing for peace, as well as creating elaborate institutions to help avoid, mitigate, and resolve conflict, both within and between societies/groups. In some cases, we can even shape conflict in ways that foster ever more complex forms of social configurations and cooperative relationships. Some researchers, like anthropologist Michael Wilson (2013: 380), view peace as more of an "achievement," something that requires work and effort. Others, like Lawrence Keeley (1996: 159), argue that sometimes war happens because peace is too costly.

While other species can employ ways to avoid conflict, these are pale reflections for the ways in which we do. Just as our humanity allowed unprecedented forms of organized violence, it also permitted unprecedented forms of peace construction. Our complex ways of interacting, regardless of social organizational type, have fostered these kinds of practices and institutions. Our humanity continues to allow novel social forms to emerge. War and peace have not reached their evolutionary or developmental climaxes. Just as our species continues to evolve physically, so too do our behaviors, cultures, and institutions. Hence, in the same ways that we are capable of elaborate, complex, and horrific levels of violence, the same permissive capacities can result in sophisticated forms of cooperation, information sharing, and peaceful coexistence.

A nature/nurture dichotomy when it comes to war is thus a spurious and misleading one. As soon as we became "human," however long ago that may have been, however gradually or abruptly it may have occurred, we undoubtedly possessed the cognitive and physiological tools to formulate and possess cultural traditions, which in turn opened the doorway for both emergent peace and emergent warfare. "A capacity to select strategically from this range of potential behaviours may have been more important than any innate capacity for violent aggression, and empathy would have been crucially important for early humans to develop close-knit cooperative communities" (Armit 2010: 2).

Our feeling is that it is misleading to conclude that either war or peace is the "natural" state of humanity. Rather, we acknowledge how both are culturally constructed. Essentially, human culture allows people to make critical decisions when it comes to practices of violence (or the avoidance of it). This, it would seem, is a main difference between humans and all other species. Earlier in the book, we introduced Richard Wrangham's (1999) imbalance-of-power hypothesis, which sees lethal organized aggression among chimpanzees as support for the idea that intergroup coalitional killing was part of an evolutionary adaptation. Implied in this argument is that chimpanzees will almost always participate in lethal raiding and ambush when the right conditions present themselves, when they have overwhelming numerical superiority, and when there is minimal risk of self-injury. But even if this hypothesis were valid for chimpanzees, though, we would point out that humans do not always make the predictable decisions to engage in or refrain from violence. Our cultural preferences and systems are far too complex. Indeed, people make decisions to practice violence and risk injury and death for all sorts of reasons.

In their research, psychologists Jeremy Ginges and Scott Atran (2011) demonstrate that decisions made to use deadly intergroup violence are strikingly insensitive to perceived likelihood of success or efficacy. Instead, judgments about the use of war are heavily influenced by ideas of morality, ethics, and duty. Accordingly, the researchers suggest that their findings support theorized links between the evolution of within-group altruism and intergroup violence.

Because we fight for all kinds of reasons, we find ourselves needing to devise highly sophisticated ways to avoid fighting. Humans have the capacity to envision peace, and we possess the creativity to manufacture social conditions that promote conflict resolution and avoidance of violence. Our mechanisms and systems of peace are not foolproof, but they do allow us to lower the likelihood that organized violence occurs, to minimize the conditions that lead to violence. That again speaks to our unique abilities as a species. Through ethnographic research, many anthropologists have provided important insights into cultural practices related to cooperation, stability, and peaceful interactions. And, of course, ethnographic research on smaller-scale societies and their ways of constructing and maintaining stability and peace are most salient for our notions of emergent peacemaking, as the majority of human history was devoid of larger-scale, highly complex societies. Douglas Fry (2011) cites comparative ethnographic research on nomadic foraging societies worldwide and has identified some commonalities when it comes to cultural practices and mechanisms that promote stability, peace, and justice. These include community sanctioned execution, contest, and third-party mediation.

Through cross-cultural scholarship combined with extensive ethnographic research on the Gebusi people, part of a small-scale, decentralized society of Papua New Guinea, anthropologist Bruce Knauft (2011: 222) argues that human patterns of violence are extremely variable in character and degree, and also in their intensity and absence. In approaching studies of peace, Paul Roscoe (2013) argues that peace can be understood as the outcome of political production, with processes that generate and maintain it. He cites his own ethnographic work with the Yangoru Boiken communities in Papua New Guinea to illustrate how competitive pig-exchange practices can help transform potentially lethal conflicts over land-tenure into non-violent, symbolic conflicts. In this manner, communities are able to maintain peace through a combination of both motives and mechanisms. Such mechanisms are manifested in systems of social signaling wherein sets of competitive displays serve as transparent signals of military strength, allowing potential adversaries the chance to assess probable outcomes before committing to actual physical confrontations.

In her own work in Papua New Guinea, anthropologist Polly Wiessner (2009) illustrates the egalitarian institutions of the Enga and their impact on practices of warfare and exchange. According to Wiessner (2009: 172), "Egalitarian institutions and their accompanying ideologies do much to reduce the transaction costs of exchange." Individual group members are treated as equals, allowing all to defend their rights and be defended by kin, and such equality helps to ensure trust necessary for delayed or long-distance exchange. Institutions, practices, and norms promote predictability, stability, and social justice, even in the absence of an overarching policing or governing structure. The Enga created elaborate systems of exchange that helped regulate outbreaks of violence and warfare, so that even when there were disputes or competition over resources and land, the constructed social mechanisms offered people a way to coexist beyond the violence. "The marriage of warfare and exchange to produce peace was a complex process" (Wiessner 2009: 180). Seen in this fashion, both war and peace are highly organized and cooperative undertakings. Another important argument made by Wiessner is that even relatively egalitarian societies are highly complex, thus complicating our traditional conceptions of "complex societies." Ultimately, her research shows us that smaller-scale societies of our remote past could have been marked by very intricate and sophisticated forms of social organization and cultural institutions – reinforcing our notion that peace is not simply the absence of war or conflict.

Using ethnographic data on smaller-scale societies, foraging societies, Kelly (2000: 60) argues that there is a strong pattern of covariation between kin group member liability and the conceptualization of marriage as a group transaction. The research supports an earlier hypothesis proposed by anthropologist Edward Tylor (1889) that outmarriage can function to blunt violence between local groups (Kelly 2000: 62). Along a similar line of thinking, Ferguson (1990: 36) observes, "Matrilocal post-marital residence weakens or eliminates fraternal interest groups, and creates cross-cutting ties between men in different local groups. This encourages the peaceful resolution of conflict among neighbors, and is commonly associated with localized peace." Interestingly, Ferguson notes that this makes external warfare more logistically feasible, since it makes mobilization of larger forces more viable.

This brings to mind an earlier point we made, that when we define peace we have to keep in mind that it is relative and does not always apply to all relationships (internal and external) for a society and its members. It also suggests that perhaps some of our cultural practices may have arisen in response to other practices. For instance, we might ask if there is any connection between monogamy and conflict mitigation. Monogamy can be arguably viewed as a biological, evolutionarily adaptive behavior to ensure less competition over mating and greater parental investment in care of offspring. Beyond that, it is interesting to consider how culturally varied practices of marriage can be tied to ways to establish social connections not only between individuals but also between larger societies (e.g., alliances). Similarly, choices in trading partners and occupational specialization that can also be shaped due to concerns over conflict or competition. One might even ask if early forms of religious systems and moral codes were developed as a means to promote group cohesion, stability, and minimization of conflict. Did we invent deities in part to help us get along?

Implications for Human (Naturenurtural) Evolution: Emergent Peacefare

Violence, both within and among societies, is statistically abnormal. We must understand normal behaviors before we can understand statistically and behaviorally abnormal ones as well as the cultural contexts in which the latter occur. To focus mainly or only on rare, abnormal behaviors is a "'5 O'Clock News' view of human behavior" (Sussman 2010: 515). While important, aggression and violence are only part of a wider behavioral repertoire of the human cultural niche. Empathy, compassion, friendship, and altruism are equally important aspects of human social life. Tracing the evolution of these behaviors, while perhaps more difficult and less newsworthy, can inform on the emergence of both war and peace. Simon Baron-Cohen and Sally Wheelwright (2004:163) write:

> Empathy is without question an important ability. It allows us to tune into how someone else is feeling, or what they might be thinking. Empathy allows us to understand the intentions of others, predict their behavior, and experience an emotion triggered by their emotion. In short, empathy allows us to interact effectively in the social world. It is also the "glue" of the social world, drawing us to help others and stopping us from hurting others.

As this quote suggests, being able to understand another's perspectives, what is sometimes called having a theory of mind, is important for much of daily life. Humans are not only remarkably compassionate to family members; we also extend this sympathy to strangers, pets, and abstract objects (i.e., love of country) (Spikins et al. 2010). For this topic, we face two related questions: 1) how different is our ability to be compassionate and peaceful compared to other primates; and 2) when did this become a human-like behavior?

In their research on the evolution of human cooperation and reciprocity, economists Samuel Bowles and Herbert Gintiss (2011) argue that humans evolved into a highly cooperative species because cooperation was very beneficial to the members of groups that practiced it. It allowed people to construct social institutions that heightened group-level advantages associated with high levels of cooperation. "These institutions proliferated because the groups that adopted them secured high levels of within-group cooperation, which in turn favored the groups' survival as a biological and cultural entity in the face of environmental, military and other challenges" (Bowles and Gintiss 2011: 4). The authors cite three main reasons why altruistic social preferences supporting cooperation became such an important part of our species. First, groups devised ways to protect their altruistic members from exploitation by the self-interested. These include shunning, ostracism, and even execution of violators of cooperative norms. Second, humans adopted prolonged and elaborate systems of socialization to internalize cooperative norms. Third, between-group competition for resources and survival was crucial in human evolutionary dynamics. For Bowles and Gintiss, the high stakes of intergroup competition and the contribution of altruistic cooperators to success in these contests meant that sacrifice on behalf of others, extending beyond immediate family and even to strangers, could proliferate. "This is part of the reason why humans became extraordinarily group-minded, favoring cooperation with insiders and often expressing hostility toward outsiders" (Bowles and Gintiss 2011: 4). As we noted earlier, the ability to conceptualize and communicate kinship, whether with biologically related people or through fictive bonds, allowed for the formation of bonds that could be harnessed to promote both internal peace and cooperation as well as outwardly directed violence and aggression.

Researchers Robert Boyd and Peter Richardson (2009) also see the connection between cooperation, cultural adaptation, and human evolutionary change. They recognize moral systems with sanctions and rewards as crucial in improving the reproductive success of individuals who lived in "culturally evolved cooperative social environments." For them, such systems led to the evolution of other motives like empathy and social emotions like shame.

In the end, it is very difficult to conclude how exactly cultural and biological changes worked in tandem throughout the long and complicated process of human evolutionary development. But, we can postulate that once our cognitive abilities allowed for it, we began to cooperate in increasingly complex ways, devising social institutions that helped to encode and regulate norms of behavior. As we noted in the preceding section, institutions related to marriage may have been particularly effective in promoting cooperation and minimizing conflicts within and between communities. And there is intriguing research to suggest that kinship and marriage are marked by grammar in ways reminiscent of languages (Barnard 2012: 42), raising the possibility that these sorts of institutions can also be associated with modern human culture and cognition. Along this line of thought, one could argue that language and kinship recognition may have been important building blocks for both emergent warfare and peacemaking. Thus, highly cooperative social behaviors were keys for people to engage in and avoid fighting.

Fuentes (2012: 115) persuasively talks about the myth of human aggression, systematically outlining the core facets and assumptions of a larger perspective that sees humans (particularly males) as the product of evolutionary transformations that made them genetically predisposed to aggression. He points out there is no research to support a genetic basis for aggression, or to suggest that humans are much more likely to "rely on aggression and violence than on cooperation and mutualistic interactions" (Fuentes 2012: 117). The upshot is that rather than being biologically predisposed to aggression, we have learned to use aggressive behaviors (sometimes collectively), when we see it as necessary. Hence, human aggression is not an evolutionary adaptation. But, Fuentes notes that it is important to keep in mind that aggression is still important. "Positive social relationships are so central to primate societies that the possibility of aggression, even rare aggression, can elicit a whole suite of behavioral patterns that have evolved to ameliorate, or fix, the damage done by aggression between members of a group" (Fuentes 2012: 125). This is part of what is referred to as the valuable relationships hypothesis, which suggests that the tendency to reconcile is affected, in part, by the value that relationship confers on the individuals (Watts 2006).

If we take that line of thinking a step further, we can ask how the evolution of cooperative behaviors within a culturally modern or symbolic context would have fostered the emergence of a new set of tools and behaviors aimed at not only fixing the damage done by aggression, but to also regulate and prevent such actions. The ability to communicate complex ideas, beliefs, feelings, and intentions, could have aided in these sorts of emergent peacemaking behaviors. Moreover, rather than being limited to interactions within a group, the human brain and its potential for complex sociality and abstract cognition would have facilitated such peacemaking efforts between groups as well.

In the end, our complexities in thought, communication, and behavior meant that we were better equipped for highly varied, sophisticated, and plastic cultural systems. It meant that we were better able to engage in cooperative violence than our earliest ancestors. Concurrently, it meant that we were also much more creative and capable in creating conditions to promote, guarantee, encourage, or enforce justice, equity, stability, and peace. The evolution of cooperative behaviors not only opened doors for warfare, but also for ways to socialize, to get things done collectively, and to thrive in larger groups. We became very capable in seeing and avoiding potential conflict in a fashion quite unprecedented in nature. Harkening back to Raymond Kelly's important publication (2000: 161) on warfare's origins, he concludes that war and society coevolve, and one "central aspect of this coevolution is that the elaboration of peacemaking goes hand in hand with the origin and development of war." We would agree, and would stress all of the ways in which we have evolved to interact and live in very complex ways with one another as the drivers for emergent warfare and peacemaking. Our abilities to think and communicate in abstract terms, to establish complex systems of cultural practices, institutions, and norms, separated us from other members of the natural world. As bearers of human culture and language, our capacity for highly complex cooperation furnished novel forms of cultural practice.

A Compassionate Species?

In a very interesting article, Penny Spikins and colleagues (2010) examine evidence of compassion in the paleoanthropological record. One of the best-known cases, dating to some 1.7 million years ago, is a find from Dmanisi, Georgia. One of the hominins from this site, usually considered to be *Homo erectus*, had lost all of his or her teeth but survived for several years, suggesting that it had support from others. A second example, dating to 1.5 million years ago, is another *Homo erectus* individual. Suspected to be a woman, this individual suffered from hypervitaminosis A, which would have been debilitating. However, she survived long enough for the disease to affect the bone, which indicates an advanced stage of illness. It also suggests she was cared for by others. In yet another case reported from the Sima de los Huesos site in Spain (discussed in Chapter Four), one of the fossilized skulls recovered from the site shows signs that the individual suffered from lambdoid single suture craniosynostosis, which means that the cranial bones fused earlier than normal. This would have impacted the cognitive ability of the person, yet she or he survived for five years, suggesting that even people who were not yet able to obtain status in a given community were looked after by others.

Similar observations have been made with the Neandertals, with evidence that many of those that were injured show ample signs of healing, thus suggesting that they were cared for while they recovered. Of course, we have very little information about cultural perceptions or attitudes about these individuals, and how they may have been treated. We simply know that they survived various illnesses and injuries, and so care must be taken when interpreting these finds (Dettwyler 1991). But, at the moment we can postulate that cooperation in our earliest ancestors could have been linked to notions of compassion between individuals.

Moving away from the signs of skeletal trauma, other indicators of the human capacity of compassion and peace comes from the dependency infants and children have on their caregivers. Babies, as any parent knows, are cute but mostly helpless and taking care of offspring is a huge investment.[2] There is good reason to believe that evolution has acted to produce a care-giving response to babies. Ashley Montagu (1976: 158) suggests that this tendency to care for others is a derived human trait. A "high premium has been placed on the ability to minister to the dependent needs of the infant."

An "Archaeology of Peace"

Anthropologist Brian Ferguson (2013: 228) points out that significant stretches of time in the archaeological record of many regions are largely devoid of obvious signs of warfare, and that should lead us to hypothesize that elements of local cultures combined in systems to maintain peace and prevent war. As we have pointed out in earlier sections, however, not all forms of collective violence and warfare will leave obvious and durable material signatures in the archaeological record (see Table 3.1), so care must be taken not to overgeneralize. That being said, we do agree with his suggestion (2013: 229) "that as archaeologists search for signs of war, they also consider the possibility that humans are capable of systematically dealing with conflict in peaceful ways." Despite the plethora of studies since the 1990s documenting the existence of warfare in various parts of the world during the Holocene, our understanding of humanity would not be complete without explicitly acknowledging the ways in which prehistoric societies were able to avoid warfare. More archaeological research is needed with an aim for explaining how social practices and systems have promoted stability. To that end, one might say there is a need for the "archaeology of peace" (to complement the "archaeology of warfare" that has burgeoned in recent decades, as detailed in Chapter Three). For us, the clarion call is a bit more nuanced – rather than simply an archaeology of peace, we would emphasize the need for an archaeology of conflict avoidance or active peacemaking, what might be considered peacefare.

An example of how this sort of research starting point can be operationalized can be seen in a recent publication by archaeologists Timothy Kohler and colleagues (2015), wherein they offer a detailed case study of cultural change during the late first and early second millennia AD in the North American Southwest area. Analyzing archaeological data to chart changing patterns of violence, the researchers note that violence in specific areas seemed to correlate with changing levels of maize production per capita. They also observed that such structural tendencies were occasionally overridden by sociohistorical factors, such as the expansion and demise of local polities. Very interestingly, the research suggests that violence generally declined through time in specific areas due to a combination of factors, such as the increased social span of polities, the nature of religious practice, and increased adherence to a set of nonviolent norms.

Climbing Out of the Abyss

Political scientist John Vasquez (1995: 211) describes peace as something learned – where people get together and figure out how to get along, to develop a variety of ways to settle disputes and resolve conflicts without the use of collective violence. This can be applicable at various levels, whether the interpersonal, the intergroup, or the international. As he notes, peace does not just happen – it is subject to structural influences and conscious actions of groups.

Throughout this book, we have attempted to show you that emergent warfare is tied to emergent ways of being human. But, that does not mean we are naturally and biologically predisposed to being warlike or violent. When we talk about emergent warfare, we are referring to the onset of a capacity for humans to have organized themselves in sophisticated ways in order to recognize and effectuate strategies that use violence. To be emphasized here are the abilities to cooperate and organize, not to be violent. By that logic, the same cognitive and communicative abilities that permit these organized behaviors also permit humans to recognize new and complex ways to build relationships that can both resolve and avoid conflict. Besides simply moving and running away from competitors, rivals, and threats, people can take the long view when it comes to building complex webs of sociality and cooperation. Essentially, then, when we refer to the time of emergent warfare, we are thus also talking about a time of emergent peacemaking. We suspect and propose that systematic ways of fighting are thus coincident and have likely co-evolved with complex peacemaking. Margaret Mead (1940) argued that warfare is a cultural invention, and we would agree with this sentiment, while also adding two caveats to this general perspective. First, its "invention" is likely much older than she may have believed, and did not involve some specific and pivotal moment. Warlike behaviors emerged in sort of piecemeal fashion, with groups learning to use socially cooperative violence for achieving shared and collective goals. Second, we ought to view peace in a similar light – not as some primordial and idyllic state of nature for humans, but as a cultural invention as well, replete with socially variable ways of promoting stability, resolving differences, and minimizing the potential for competing interests to result in the use of violence.

Brian Ferguson (2011) rightly argues that there is insufficient evidence to support the notion that humans are predisposed to war. We generally agree with this assertion, despite our belief that humans were likely capable of violent sociocultural patterns early on in the emergence of modern humans. His views are not all that divergent from ours when he writes (2011: 249) that humans possess an extremely flexible nature. "Our orientation toward war, for it or against it, and our practice, depends on situations, inclusively defined as running from basic environmental circumstances, through social structures, to values and beliefs" (Ferguson 2011: 249).

At the crux of our argument is the highly plastic range of choices and strategies for living associated with humans. In her survey across primates, anthropologist Karen Strier (2011) recognizes a high degree of social plasticity and demographic variation. She makes two key observations that we can apply to our questions about the complex relationships between cooperation, competition, violence, and human evolution. First, she notes that social behavior is especially sensitive to local conditions and circumstances (2011: 179). Selection pressures can fluctuate on shorter and more micro-level timescales, even within the lifetimes of a primate individual. This means that a great deal of primate behavioral patterns may not be the adaptive result of longer-term, genetically determined evolutionary development but may be much more expedient responses to pressures, stimuli, and situations. Related to this observation, Strier (2011: 189) writes that local conditions can thus favor cooperation or competition at different times in an individual's lifespan. In the opportunism of phenotypic plasticity, Strier sees selectively neutral or even deleterious social outcomes just as likely as adaptive ones. "The ability to move between cooperative and competitive modes, and social plasticity in general, may be the underlying adaptation of primate evolution" (Strier 2011: 189).

The larger implication of these two observations is that any presence within the Pleistocene of socially cooperative violence or emergent warfare, as we have conceived of them in this book, does not necessarily mean that violence and warfare were evolutionary adaptations. As argued in the previous chapter, we see propensities toward cooperative behaviors as a vital prerequisite for emergent human nature, with the latter resulting in a highly plastic range of possible behavioral and social patterns. Warfare, in this light, can be viewed as an epiphenomenon of sorts for emergent modern human culture, added to an increasingly complex and sophisticated range of behavioral patterns. Taken a step further, then, the uses of socially cooperative violence, whether at 100,000 years ago or today, do not necessarily result in evolutionary change in our species. It simply reflects the complexity in choices and options that our brains and cultures confer upon us.

Early members of our evolutionary lineage undoubtedly evolved certain traits that enabled them to excel at socializing. As we have seen, while many argue that competition and aggression were important in our evolutionary toolkit, as reflected by the similarities in human and chimpanzee uses of coalitionary violence, others would point to our abilities to cooperate as being a chief driver of evolution. Indeed, it is interesting that recent experiments with chimpanzees suggest their possession of a theory of mind but only in competitive situations with each other, and not in cooperative ones. This says something about how the most crucial aspect of cultural evolutionary success in humanity is our ability to cooperate. One might also wonder if our success as a species is at all tied to our abilities to control and mitigate the effects of conflict when necessary. This does not necessarily mean we are "peaceful" or non-violent as a species. It simply means that we can devise

FIGURE 7.2 Knotted Gun sculpture by Carl Fredrick Reutersward at the United Nations building in New York City. © *Zheng Zhou. Licensed under Creative Commons 3.0*

complex ways to be peaceful because living in peace usually confers the most optimal outcomes for us, even if that sometimes means we get along with each other by "othering" or "demonizing" people outside of our communities or groups. In that case, peace is a relative term, of course. But, if we accept that there is no such thing as total peace (just as there is no, nor has there ever been, a total state of perpetual human warfare for any society), we can start to appreciate the intricacies and complexity of peace.

Notes

1 Available at: www.oberlin.edu/external/EOG/BlackHistoryMonth/MLK/Comm Address.html
2 Both of us have kids, and we are sure this book would have been finished much earlier if we did not spend most of our day trying to find where the kid left her shoes. . . .

Works Cited

Alexander, R.D. 1979. Natural Selection and Social Exchange. In *Social Exchange in Developing Relationships*, edited by R.L. Burgess and T.L. Huston, pp. 197–221. Academic Press, New York.

Armit, Ian. 2010. Violence and Society in the Deep Human Past. *British Journal of Criminology* 51(3), 499–517.

Arnold, Kate, Orlaith Fraser, and Filippo Auriel. 2011. Postconflict Reconciliation. In *Primates in Perspective*, edited by Christina Campbell, Agustín Fuentes, Katherine C. MacKinnon, Simon Bearder, and Rebecca Stumpf, pp. 608–625. 2nd edition. Oxford University Press, New York.

Barnard, Alan. 2012. *Genesis of Symbolic Thought*. Cambridge University Press, Cambridge.

Baron-Cohen, Simon, and Sally Wheelwright. 2004. The Empathy Quotient: An Investigation of Adults with Asperger Syndrome or High Functioning Autism, and Normal Sex Differences. *Journal of Autism and Developmental Disorders* 34(2), 163–175.

Bowles, Samuel, and Herbert Gintiss. 2011. *A Cooperative Species*. Princeton University Press, Princeton, NJ.

Boyd, Robert, and Peter Richardson. 2009. Culture and the Evolution of Human Cooperation. *Philosophical Transactions of the Royal Society B* 364(1533), 3281–3288.

Bshary, Redouan, and Manuela Wurth. 2001. Cleaner Fish Labroides Dimidiatus Manipulate Client Reef Fish by Providing Tactile Stimulation. *Proceedings. Biological Sciences / The Royal Society* 268(1475), 1495–1501.

Cloninger, C. Robert, and Sita Kedia. 2011. The Phylogenesis of Human Personality: Identifying the Precursors of Cooperation, Altruism, and Well-Being. In *Origins of Altruism and Cooperation*, edited by Robert Sussman and C. Robert Cloninger, pp. 63–107. Springer, New York.

Dettwyler, Katherine. 1991. Can Paleopathology Provide Evidence for "Compassion"? *American Journal of Physical Anthropology* 84(4), 375–384.

de Waal, Frans. 1996. The Biological Basis of Peaceful Coexistence: A Review of Reconciliation Research on Monkeys and Apes. In *A Natural History of Peace*, edited by T. Gregor, pp. 37–69. Vanderbilt University Press, Nashville, TN.

de Waal, Frans. 2000. Primates – A Natural Heritage of Conflict Resolution. *Nature* 289(5479), 586–590.

Ferguson, R. Brian. 1990. Explaining War. In *The Anthropology of War*, edited by Jonathan Haas, pp. 26–55. Cambridge University Press, Cambridge.

Ferguson, R. Brian. 2011. Born to Live: Challenging Killer Myths. In *Origins of Altruism and Cooperation*, edited by Robert Sussman and C. Robert Cloninger, pp. 249–270. Springer, New York.

Ferguson, R. Brian. 2013. The Prehistory of War and Peace in Europe and the Near East. In *War, Peace, and Human Nature: The Convergence of Evolutionary and Cultural Views*, edited by Douglas P. Fry, pp. 191–240. Oxford University Press, New York.

Fry, Douglas. 2006. *The Human Potential for Peace: An Anthropological Challenge to Assumptions about War and Violence*. Oxford University Press, Oxford.

Fry, Douglas. 2011. Human Nature: The Nomadic Forager Model. In *Origins of Altruism and Cooperation*, edited by Robert Sussman and C. Robert Cloninger, pp. 227–247. Springer, New York.

Fry, Douglas and Anna Szala. 2013. The Evolution of Agonism: The Triumph of Restraint in Nonhuman and Human Primates. In *War, Peace, and Human Nature: The Convergence of Evolutionary and Cultural Views*, edited by Douglas P. Fry, pp. 451–474. Oxford University Press, New York.

Fuentes, Agustin. 2012. *Race, Monogamy, and Other Lies They Told You*. University of California Press, Berkeley.

Galtung, Johan. 1990. Cultural Violence. *Journal of Peace Research* 27(3), 291–305.

Ginges, Jeremy, and Scott Atran. 2011. War as a Moral Imperative (Not Just Practical Politics by Other Means). *Proceedings of the Royal Society B* 207(1720), 2930–2938.

Hart, Donna, and Robert Sussman. 2011. The Influence of Predation on Primate and Early Human Evolution: Impetus for Cooperation. In *Origins of Altruism and Cooperation*, edited by Robert Sussman and C. Robert Cloninger, pp. 19–40. Springer, New York.

Hruschka, Daniel. 2010. *Friendship: Development, Ecology, and Evolution of a Relationship*. University of California Press, Berkeley.

Keeley, Lawrence. 1996. *War Before Civilization*. Oxford University Press, Oxford.

Kelly, Raymond. 2000. *Warless Societies and the Origin of War*. University of Michigan Press, Ann Arbor.

Kenrick, D.T., and M.R. Trost. 2000. An Evolutionary Perspective on Human Relationships. In *The Social Psychology of Personal Relationships*, edited by W. Ickes and S. Duck, pp. 9–35. John Wiley & Sons, New York.

Kohler, Timothy, Scott Ortman, Katie Grundtisch, Carly Fitzpatrick, and Sarah Cole. 2015. The Better Angels of their Nature: Declining Violence Through Time Among Prehispanic Farmers of the Pueblo Southwest. *American Antiquity* 79(3), 444–464.

Knauft, Bruce. 2011. Violence Reduction Among the Gebusi of Papua New Guinea – And Across Humanity. In *Origins of Altruism and Cooperation*, edited by Robert Sussman and C. Robert Cloninger, pp. 203–225. Springer, New York.

MacKinnon, Katherine, and Agustin Fuentes. 2011. Primates, Niche Construction, and Social Complexity: The Roles of Social Cooperation and Altruism. In *Origins of Altruism and Cooperation*, edited by Robert Sussman and C. Robert Cloninger, pp. 121–143. Springer, New York.

Mead, Margaret. 1940. Warfare Is Only an Invention, Not a Biological Necessity. *Asia* 15(8), 402–405.

Montagu, Ashley. 1976. *The Nature of Human Agression*. Oxford University Press, New York.

Roscoe, Paul. 2013. Social Signaling, Conflict Management, and the Construction of Peace. In *War, Peace, and Human Nature: The Convergence of Evolutionary and Cultural Views*, edited by Douglas P. Fry, pp. 475–494. Oxford University Press, New York.

Sapolsky, Robert. 2013. Rousseau with a Tail: Maintaining a Tradition of Peace Among Baboons. In *War, Peace, and Human Nature: The Convergence of Evolutionary and Cultural Views*, edited by Douglas P. Fry, pp. 421–438. Oxford University Press, New York.

Silk, Joanna. 2002. Using the 'F'-word in Primatology. *Behaviour* 139(2–3), 421–446.

Smith, Peter Scharff. 2006. The Effects of Solitary Confinement on Prison Inmates: A Brief History and Review of the Literature. *Crime and Justice* 34(1), 441–528.

Spikins, Penny, Holly Rutherford, and Andy Needham. 2010. From Homininity to Humanity: Compassion from the Earliest Archaics to Modern Humans. *Time and Mind* 3(3), 303–325.

Strier, Karen. 2011. Social Plasticity and Demographic Variation in Primates. In *Origins of Altruism and Cooperation*, edited by Robert Sussman and C. Robert Cloninger, pp. 179–192. Springer, New York.

Sussman, Robert. 2010. Human Nature and Human Culture. *American Anthropologist* 112(4), 514–515.

Tattersall, Ian. 2011. Cooperation, Altruism, and Human Evolution: Introduction Part I. In *Origins of Altruism and Cooperation*, edited by Robert Sussman and C. Robert Cloninger, pp. 11–18. Springer, New York.

Terrell, John. 2014. *A Talent for Friendship*. Oxford University Press, Oxford.

Tylor, Edward. 1889. On a Method of Investigating the Development of Institutions; Applied to Laws of Marriage and Descent. *Journal of the Anthropological Institute* 18, 245–269.

Vasquez, John. 1995. The Learning of Peace: Lessons from a Multidisciplinary Inquiry. In *Beyond Confrontation*, edited by John Vasquez, James Turner Johnson, Sanford Jaffe, and Linda Stamato, pp. 211–228. University of Michigan Press, Ann Arbor.

Verbeek, Peter. 2013. An Ethological Perspective on War and Peace. In *War, Peace, and Human Nature: The Convergence of Evolutionary and Cultural Views*, edited by Douglas P. Fry, pp. 54–77. Oxford University Press, New York.

Watts, David P. 2006. Conflict Resolution in Chimpanzees and the Valuable-Relationships Hypothesis. *International Journal of Primatology* 27(5), 1337–1364.

Wiessner, Polly. 2009. Warfare and Political Complexity in an Egalitarian Society. In *Warfare in Cultural Practice*, edited by A. Nielsen and W. Walker, pp. 165–189. University of Arizona Press, Tucson.

Wilson, Michael. 2013. Chimpanzees, Warfare, and the Invention of Peace. In *War, Peace, and Human Nature: The Convergence of Evolutionary and Cultural Views*, edited by Douglas P. Fry, pp. 361–388. Oxford University Press, New York.

Wrangham, Richard. 1999. Evolution of Coalitionary Killing. *Yearbook of Physical Anthropology* 42(S29), 1–30.

8

THERE AND BACK AGAIN

Beloved by many readers worldwide, J.R.R. Tolkien's *The Hobbit* was full of adventure, romantic notions of heroism, and, yes, warfare. Although published in 1937 as a children's fantasy book, the story is not without its share of politics, machinations for domination, villains, enemies, war, and attempts to build peace. Interestingly, its main protagonist, Bilbo Baggins, is plucked from an idyllic, calm, and peaceful environment for a foray into the wider world of Middle Earth, and his eyes are opened to how people (and other creatures) behave when they have competing agendas and visions for how the world should look. Exposure to this reality is what leads to Bilbo's maturation. In a way, Bilbo's journey from a quiet pocket of the world to the chaos of a bigger one mirrored the experience of young soldiers sent off to theaters of conflict during World War I. Against the backdrop of both World Wars, marked by horrific destruction and unimaginable loss of life, it is perhaps not surprising that many scholars of the 20th century hypothesized that perhaps our earliest social worlds were not as violent as our modern one, thus giving us hope that we were not doomed to war-making. Visions of a premodern or prehistoric past largely devoid of the miseries associated with war surely drove a lot of research, speculation, and public imagination about the recent invention or origins of human warfare. This led many researchers to equate seemingly warless (or seldom warlike), small-scale societies observed ethnographically with our ancestral communities in prehistory, to make the argument that war is largely a product of the ambitions of leaders presiding over vast populations within highly complex societies (see Chapter Three).

But a surge in archaeological research on ancient and prehistoric warfare around the world in recent decades has complicated and muddied this view, showing us that our prehistoric, nonstate ancestors were not always peaceful. And so, to venture "there and back again," we must return to the very first questions that framed this book. Why do we make war? Have we always been fighting one another? As we have tried to demonstrate in this book, these are questions with far too many possible answers. It would be difficult to settle on any one answer and be satisfied with it. Nevertheless, we would address those questions with another pertinent question, specifically of when we became human. Answering that question tells us when we first had the ability (and thus the option) to fight in organized ways.

The present evidence suggests that warfare, in various cultural forms, has fairly deep roots, deeper than a general shift in subsistence patterns from more mobile, foraging lifeways to more sedentary and agricultural ones. After all, warfare encompasses a very wide range of cultural behaviors, views, values, and practices, and is not restricted to categories of societies. It is a human phenomenon, and one need not live in a settled, agricultural society to be capable of organizing with fellow community members to perform violence. But, recognizing a deeper antiquity for the "invention" of warfare, or of its various bits, does not mean we are biologically hardwired to fight, that we are forever doomed to live in a world where war will always be of constant significance. As sobering as the reality might be when considering deeper origins of warfare, the narrative tells but one small part of the story of becoming human.

The other, equally pertinent, part of the story is that becoming human also meant becoming capable of seeing the social and physical worlds around us in very different ways. It meant becoming capable of relating to one another in increasingly complex fashion. And, pertinent to our questions in this book, it meant recognizing the potential benefits and pitfalls of competitive and aggressive behavior, of organized violence – meaning that we needed novel ways to avoid and resolve conflicts. To deny the existence of both warfare and peacefare in our ancestors living in nonstate, smaller-scale societies is to deny them the ability to perceive and understand the environmental and cultural topographies around them in ways that we are capable of today, and to deny them the agency to make decisions that made cultural sense to them. Surely our ancestors faced many of the same harsh choices and realities that many of us do today. And surely they were just as creative and inventive in imagining solutions to various problems.

In this chapter, we discuss some of the implications for the research we have outlined in the preceding sections. How does our trip down the rabbit hole inform us about human nature and the processes by which we became human? Furthermore, can we use these data to better understand the causes and consequences of modern warfare?

Warfare and Its Implications for the Evolution of Human Nature

In his acceptance speech for the Nobel Peace Prize, President Barrack Obama suggested that:

> War, in one form or another, appeared with the first man. At the dawn of history, its morality was not questioned; it was simply a fact, like drought or

disease – the manner in which tribes and then civilizations sought power and settled their differences.

Is this view accurate? It depends on how one interprets "the first man." If the President is referring to behaviorally modern people, then we would tend to agree. But, if he is referring to our earliest ancestors, then he would be expressing a belief commonly held by many that we are, by our very nature, prone to war. This perception about humanity and violence is not just held by many in the general public, but also by many researchers who link aggression and organized violence directly to our evolution as a species. For some, we are the current developmental outcome of millions of years of evolutionary change wherein violence and competition have shaped our adaptations. If this is the case, does it mean that the potential for peace runs contra to our innate desires? That would suggest that pacifists, while not destined to fail, have their work cut out for them. Of course, just because something is biologically innate does not mean that we have to follow

FIGURE 8.1   President Barack Obama receiving the 2009 Nobel Peace Prize.
Source: The White House, USA

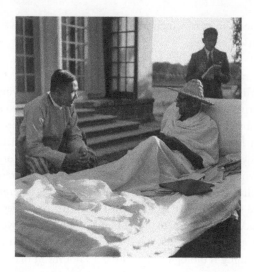

FIGURE 8.2   Mohandas "Mahatma" Gandhi, circa 1947. *Source: Ministry of Information & Broadcasting, India*

that desire. Our genes affect us, but they do not control us. But we would be hard pressed to discover a Paleolithic Gandhi.

In the absence of a written record it would be difficult to know how our ancestors viewed war. For the ones that were biologically and behaviorally like us, perhaps they counted both pacifists and warmongers among them. And perhaps one's identity as either would have been fluid and subject to changing social conditions. Some scholars have suggested that the periods of peace in the past were rare and fleeting, which would imply that peace is something we must constantly work toward (see Chapter Seven). For us, while we do not necessarily see periods of either peace or war as fleeting and rare, we do recognize the need for people to construct peace through institutions, ideological systems, morals, and other cultural practices. Likewise, we do not agree with the notion that we have evolved to be naturally aggressive and violent.

Yet, Obama's implicit warning resonates. The son of an anthropologist, Obama is expressing a deep-seated belief that humans are predestined to be warlike. Yet, it is often unclear just what is meant by "the dawn of history." And, as we have strived to make clear, the situation is far from certain. Even if early forms of war, what we would subsume under a label of emergent warfare, are as old as humanity, it does not mean that we are predestined for war, or that we are innately warlike. As noted at the beginning of this book, the anthropological perspective writ large allows for a more inclusive view of what humanity means, fully acknowledging variability as a major characteristic of human behavior. The fact populations can at times be warlike, and at times more peaceful, should not come as a surprise. Rather, it shows how culture, along with many other exogenous factors, influences behavior – how our behaviors and cultural norms are exceedingly plastic. "To say that humans have a propensity for violence says nothing. We also have a propensity for nonviolence" (Sussman 2010: 515).

We have both the capacity to be incredibly violent and the potential to be very peaceful. *The flexibility of human nature is the key to understanding both our success as a species and our evolutionary history*. To ignore the role culture played in human evolution is ahistorical. We have evolved to be "naturenurtural" beings (Fuentes 2012) with more than one way to express human existence.

[handwritten margin note: Violence = root in evol]

[handwritten margin note: Warfare needs culture]

The Origins, Prevalence and Significance of "Violence" and "Warfare"

As cogently argued by archaeologists Terry Jones and Mark Allen (2014: 354), because a hunting and gathering adaptation and its lifeways characterized the vast majority of humanity's past, how we answer the question about the origins of warfare boils down to whether we can trace an unbroken chain of violence and warfare from the earliest hominins, through a long prehistory of hunting and gathering, up to the appearance of communities marked by more sedentary and agricultural ways of life. As they observe, the presently available ethnographic and archaeological evidence derived from Holocene Epoch communities supports a "long chronology" of warfare, indicating that its roots are to be found well before the rise of civilizations, cities, writing, intensive farming, and other cultural developments of the mid-Holocene. But, just how far back do these roots go? Secondly, what is meant by "long"?

At the moment, we favor a perspective that does not see some revolutionary moment for the start of warfare – rather, we see elements of "warfare" gradually emerging piecemeal, in lockstep with other developmental milestones of humanity. Indeed, this is the reason we have chosen to talk about warfare in emergent form. As we have seen along our journey through the copious research that exists, there is no question that violence is a natural part of the world, just as much as cooperative, prosocial, and nonviolent behaviors. The question is when the uses of violence transition into something very complex, organized, culturally nuanced, and even institutionalized. For that question, we would say look to the emergence of our symbolic culture, and all signs currently point to a time frame of about 300,000 years ago, and potentially even earlier. This was, of course, part of a larger set of gradual shifts in human developments, both in physical composition and behavioral expressions. But that would be our best guess at the moment. To be sure, there is no unequivocal material evidence for warfare in the archaeological record of the world predating the Late Pleistocene. In fact, a study of the worldwide sample of fossils of *H. sapiens* shows that only about ~2% of the sites show any evidence of violence before 10,000 years ago (Kissel and Piscitelli 2014). Nevertheless, because we view all humans as being capable of choosing to cooperate with one another to both formulate group identities and to engage in violence against members of other groups, we make the assumption that warfare, however rare and infrequent, did happen in some fashion before the Late Pleistocene.

This does not mean that we view our Ice Age past as a Hobbesian world rife with chaos and violence, where peace and nonviolent cooperation were rare. Far from it. It simply means we recognize an enormous range of plasticity in human behavior, especially once we develop certain cognitive faculties that allow our cultural practices, our perceptions of the world around us, and our ways of living, to really take off. Indeed, we argue that the potential for humans to organize themselves in complex ways to engage in violence meant that the stakes were raised to find new ways to construct peace and prevent competing interests and conflicts from resulting in violent choices. Recall that what makes anthropology distinct from other sciences is its adherence to the notion of variation. Just as there is not one way to raise a family, to make a living, to marry, or to worship, we must remember that violence is socially mediated in many very different ways.

War: What Is It Good For?

Taking an evolutionary approach to the question of warfare leads to the question of *why* it exists. The hypothesis of emergent warfare, as offered earlier in the book (see Chapters One and Six), allows us to see its evolution as gradual rather than punctuated. Most animals engage in fights that are non-lethal in nature (Smith and Price 1973), leaving us wondering why humans would evolve lethal conflict. Humans, as hyper-cooperators (Fuentes 2012: 212), would have evolved methods of restraints against violence, rather than evolved toward more violence (Miklikowska and Fry 2012). As noted by Lawrence Keeley (1996: 158), "Warfare is ultimately not a denial of the human capacity for social cooperation, but merely the most destructive expression of it."

Though destructive, warfare represents groups cooperating for certain mutual objectives. If killing is not the goal, perhaps there are other benefits to warfare. In some societies, access to land or material goods is the driving force for war (Meggitt 1977). Reasons for war can also be revenge (to avenge insults or earlier raids), or to display strength to your neighbors (Chagnon 1968). Access to sacred land is another important precursor to war. Among the Enga of Papua New Guinea, warfare is seen as the last resort as a way to reestablish balance of power or to avenge a wrong, but rarely over access to land itself (Wiessner 2006). But beyond tangible and economic sorts of benefits and gains, we know that humans sometimes also engage in violence and killing because of beliefs and ideas, oftentimes as a result of shared systems of such ideas. And sometimes, conflict, competition, and warfare with outsiders can function to promote bonds and cohesion within a group itself.

When asking "why war?" we need to think about what is called the level of selection. For example, we could ask the question at the level of the group (does a city prosper by engaging in warfare by adding to its coffers?) or at the individual level (does a single warrior gain an evolutionary advantage by joining a warring party?). Some scholars have argued that evolution happens only at the gene-level (Dawkins 1976) while others argue for what has been called multilevel selection, where selection happens both at the gene and group level[1] (Wilson and

Wilson 2007). Recent research into evolutionary theory has shown that there are types of inheritance, such as behavioral and symbolic ones, that can be passed down non-genetically, which further complicates these issues (Jablonka and Lamb 2005; see also Turchin 2016).

Depending upon how you answer the question about our innate tendencies you may choose to invoke different types of data. If it is true that people are naturally aggressive toward others, then it should be possible for the ruling class to convince others to fight strangers, rather than engage in conflict over personal matters. In other words, if we are by nature aggressive, it should not take too much convincing to get soldiers to kill enemies. However, if this were not the case then armies would have to find ways to train soldiers to kill despite what might be a tendency toward non-violence. We would need to socialize ourselves to fight, given the right conditions, just as much as we might need to socialize ourselves to refrain from fighting, again under the right circumstances. In other words, culture plays a tremendous role in mediating attitudes and behaviors related to both violence and nonviolence, and we probably should not assume a default natural state.

Some scholars have suggested that soldiers have to be trained to kill, rather than innately shooting at the enemy (see Grossman 2009), and that emotional training is just as important as other aspects of military training activities (Hughbank and Grossman 2013). In a highly controversial study, researcher S.L.A. Marshall (1968) concluded that the majority of soldiers (~75%) in World War II never fired on the enemy. Furthermore, data from aerial dogfights suggests that less than 1% of pilots accounted for more than 30% of the aircraft shot down, with most fighter pilots not shooting down a single plane (Grossman 2009). Author Lt. Col. Dave Grossman argues that there is an innate resistance to killing fellow humans, and that only modern training can condition soldiers to kill. Changes in training tactics significantly decreased the number of soldiers who misfired on purpose, suggesting that it is conditioning, rather than innate tendencies, that make someone a good soldier. Switching from using bull's-eye targets at a firing range to targets shaped like a person allowed armies to train soldiers to fire without thinking. As an example, he cites how highly trained modern armies fight against guerilla forces. For Grossman, it is the training that allows invasion forces to have such a disparity in kill ratios, while the non-trained armies rely on posturing more than actual firing of weapons. Richard Hughbank and Dave Grossman suggest that "One major, modern revelation in the field of military psychology is the observation that this resistance to killing one's own species is also a key factor in human combat" (Hughbank and Grossman 2013: 497).

While this kind of research has not gone without its critics, it suggests that we need to be careful when assuming a natural state of human behavior. Another, equally controversial way to examine the roots of aggression is to study members of society whom are often perceived to be more violent and aggressive than others and ask why this is the case. For example, the occurrence of violence in youth gangs may not be because they comprise inherently violent members, but more likely because gang violence is affected by social ecology (Wrangham and Wilson 2006).

Older gang members tend to be the ones who goad the other, younger members into fighting. However, the violence perpetrated by younger members was also less lethal, with the average age being 19 for youth gang members committing murder (Wrangham and Wilson 2006). This may suggest that it takes time for a member of the group to have the drive or willingness to actually commit murder.

Some, like Samuel Bowles (2009) suggest that rather than asking whether ancestral humans of the Late Pleistocene were largely "peaceful" or "warlike," we might ask a different question. If more cooperative groups were more likely to prevail in conflicts with other groups, was there sufficient intergroup violence to influence the evolution of human social behavior? Bowles believes the answer is yes, that there could have been a proliferation of "group-beneficial behaviors" that resulted in altruistic behaviors within groups that could have been quite costly to the individual. In that way, the decisions made by people to sacrifice or risk their well-being for the sake of their larger community (i.e., warfare) could potentially be tied to both culture and genetic predispositions related to altruism.

Interestingly, Matthew Zefferman and Sarah Mathew (2015) discuss how many participants of war willingly fight and risk their health and lives, fighting alongside and in support of people that are not relatives or kin. In that regard, human warfare presents an evolutionary conundrum, as there is no parallel in the natural world for other species to exhibit this kind of behavior. Recognizing this, Zefferman and Mathew (2015) suggest that this may be because humans were subject to group-structured cultural selection to overcome this collective action hurdle, a perspective somewhat related to that offered by Bowles. Going back to our discussion in Chapter Six of the building blocks for socially cooperative violence and emergent warfare, we would emphasize the notions of kinship, group identity, and social substitution.

Some scholars have suggested that there is an evolutionary advantage to warfare for the individuals themselves (Glowacki and Wrangham 2014; Macfarlan et al. 2014). The best-known example comes from work among the Yanomami of Brazil, discussed in Chapter Two of this book. Napoleon Chagnon (1988) argued that Unokais, men who have killed someone else and have undergone a purification ritual, have more children (almost three times as many) than those who are non-Unokais. To him and others, this suggests that violence is adaptive in this society as it leads to greater reproductive success. To be clear, Chagnon himself does not draw wide-reaching conclusions from his work, and suggests that the ultimate explanation for this pattern is unknown. Others, however, have used these data to endorse a hypothesis that warfare leads to greater inclusive fitness for warriors (Ghiglieri 1999; Pinker 2002), which could explain why warfare evolved when it seems to be detrimental to the population as a whole.

As noted by Ferguson (1989) there are some problems with this interpretation of the Yanomami data. For one, a man is more likely to become Unokai as he gets older. Older men will have more children than younger men, skewing the results. Ferguson also notes that headmen are almost all Unokai and that headmen tend to have more children. Finally, becoming Unokai comes with it a high risk of being a victim of revenge killing, and that the victims of these killings are not factored into Chagnon's data, since it does not include Unokai who have been killed. While Chagnon has answered some of these criticisms (Chagnon 1989), the issue of the age of the men in the sample is still debated (Miklikowska and Fry 2012).

Among the Waorani of Ecuador, a population that has a reputation for being even more warlike then the Yanomamo, the opposite connection was found: warriors had lower reproductive success. Stephen Beckerman and colleagues (2009) tried to answer the critiques of Chagnon's study by including both living and dead warriors, and they provided data to examine the correlation between age and reproductive fitness. What they found was that more aggressive men have fewer children who survive to reproductive age. Likewise, for the Cheyenne, a Plains tribe also recorded as being warlike and aggressive, being a war chief leads to death at a younger age and a lower fitness value (Moore 1990).

It is perhaps not surprising that we see such varied results. The small sample of cases presented above should make it clear that the picture is not as simple as is often suggested. One may ask why warfare among the Waorani persisted when it had a negative fitness value attached. A possible explanation is that they may have recognized the dangers of war, but felt the need to earn a reputation for ferocity to discourage others from attacking them. While plausible, the data show that reputation for ferocity did not really discourage violence against the individual (Beckerman et al. 2009).

We emphasize what the authors of the Waorani paper write: "Our findings indicate that the Yanomamo situation, in which the more aggressive men had elevated indicators of individual fitness, does not apply to warlike tribal societies in general. The culture-specific particulars of the situation are important" (Beckerman et al. 2009: 8139). The anthropological insight here is that we need to pay attention to the culturally specific aspects of populations rather than assume something broad about human behavior from a single dataset.

Hawkish Doves or Dovish Hawks: Interpreting the Archaeological Record

As discussed in Chapters Three and Four, the archaeological record is one of the key datasets for understanding the origins of war. While the process of making silent bones and artifacts speak is far from easy, it is also the only direct evidence we have for the behavior of humans for the majority of our evolutionary time. While archaeologists several decades ago may have underplayed the role of violence in prehistory, other scientists have long believed that war and aggression are embedded in our nature. The idea that the state of nature is a state of war is not a new one. While best associated with Thomas Hobbes, it was, for instance, a view held by many classical Greek writers (Dawson 1996). Yet, Hobbes himself did not necessarily think that his ideas applied to an actual past rather than an ahistorical one (Dawson 1996).

One theme we have addressed is the difference between scholars who see warfare as a practice that has always been a part of our behavior (the so-called "hawks") and those who argue it is a recent invention, characterizing human history only since the origins of complex, sedentary societies (the so-called "doves") (see Allen 2014). What we have tried to do is to provide a more realistic, and thus more complicated, view, using the concepts of socially cooperative violence and emergent warfare to provide a lens through which the early data can be viewed. Anthropology itself is often about taking ideas everyone assumes to be true and breaking these concepts down to test their validity. While we agree with Keeley (1996) that archaeologists were overly pacifying the past, at the same time the majority of students we encountered in classrooms seem to think this way as well, which may be a reflection of what they see in the news and read in their history books.

If both the so-called doves and hawks are accessing the same data, how is there such a divide in views? Are we being influenced by preconceived views? Or, is it that each camp is providing overly simplified views and that people are perhaps talking past each other. Academics are known for having strong opinions, and those involved in research on warfare seem to be particularly argumentative.

To us, there are some major reasons why the examination of the same material evidence has resulted in such a large theoretical divide separating scholarly opinion. First, debates have hinged on the definition of warfare itself. For some scholars, certain acts of violence do not qualify as warlike, and so evidence of interpersonal violence or feuding would not be considered unless accompanied by unequivocal evidence that they were part of a wider set of cultural practices or beliefs. Second, because the totality of evidence from the Pleistocene is on balance sparser than archaeological data from more recent temporal contexts, there is far more room for ambiguity. This has resulted in a wide range of interpretative variation. Some researchers see the number of cases indicating trauma as evidence for the significance of violent behaviors, whereas other researchers see the same evidence as supporting the insignificance of violent behaviors. It is a "glass half-full or half-empty" situation. However, it is important to use these data correctly, as the interpretation of the archaeological information can be used by different people to support specific agendas.

Political leaders, science writers, and scholars alike rely on the archaeological record to support assertions that warfare is ancient, as old as our genus (Pinker 2011; Shermer 2016). For some, such as science writer Michael Shermer (2016), warfare existed when our earliest ancestors emerged, and those who critique this view are "aggressive anthropologists" who think that our ancestors lived in "peace and harmony." We would note, however, that archaeological evidence of warfare from the Late Pleistocene cannot be readily extrapolated to represent hundreds of thousands of years, if not millions, of human evolutionary history. In that sense, we can see problems in certain perspectives that tend to compress the timeline of human evolution. To illustrate, in making the argument that our earliest ancestors were far more violent than we are today, Pinker (2011) presents data generated by anthropologists and archaeologists. The data in Pinker's (2011) list of prehistoric war victims come from a temporal slice dating from ~14,000 to ~700 years ago, with three sites from Africa, nine from North America, eight from Europe and one from Asia (see Ferguson 2013a and Kim 2012 for critiques). The sites in the dataset would indeed be considered old from a historic perspective. But, human history did not start in the Late Pleistocene, and such a view misses much of the evolutionary pressures that affected our ancestors.

This view also extrapolates the existence of certain instances of warfare to represent the majority of interactions between communities of modern humans and hominins throughout millions of years of evolutionary and cultural change. As one example, the famous case of Crow Creek (see Chapter Three) is listed by Pinker. As mentioned before, the population of maize horticulturalists from this site was generally malnourished, and a mixture of overpopulation, food stress, climatic instability, and process of land use may have fostered a climate in which the massacre occurred (Zimmerman and Bradley 1993). The cultural context of this site suggests sedentism and the creation of village-life. Overall, these features are not truly representative of the kinds of societies that likely existed throughout much of human history prior to the Holocene (see Kelly 2000).

In terms of human evolutionary history, these are relatively recent events. Hominin history extends to at least 6 million years ago. The earliest stone tools date to potentially over 3 million years ago and we have archaeological evidence of hunting that is 2 million years old. The examples given in Chapter Four show that interpersonal conflict was far from rare. Yet, the best archaeological examples that so-called "hawks" often give center around the time of increased sedentism, which is close to the time period that so-called "doves" view as associated with the origins of war. In other words, *perhaps the issue is not so much a debate about warfare but about when the history of humanity begins*. If you take a long view of human origins, looking at the human evolutionary record from our split with the apes, then the archaeological evidence of warfare is rather late (i.e., millions of years after our split from *Pan*). If, however you take a more historical perspective, mostly from written records and pictorial images, then warfare may be as old, or older than, civilization (predating "civilizations" by hundreds of thousands of years). Viewed in this way, we can better understand where this general disagreement lies. The larger issue at stake is: who counts as human? We return to this question below, as well as to the question of why an anthropological voice is vital for such conversations and debates.

When it comes to hawkish and dovish views, we would note that most researchers probably fall into shades of both categories, with differences of degree separating their perspectives. Indeed, this is how we would characterize ourselves – as having a foot in both hypothetical camps as we continue to soak in the data. We end this section by reiterating that, when it comes to interpreting the archaeological record, a host of factors can affect the archaeological visibility of any actions that we might consider related to emergent warfare, obscuring them from scientific discovery and study. While larger-scale, sedentary societies engaging in violent interactions may leave far more material traces for us to see, violent encounters between smaller groups, especially if they are infrequent, can result in virtually no material traces. Antagonism or conflict between communities need not be permanent, and can manifest themselves violently on very rare occasions, with few people being severely affected. This might result in one victim in a given encounter, which we might conservatively interpret as homicide, even though a scenario of intergroup violence is also possible.

To be sure, ethnographic research for many smaller-scale societies of the contemporary world can lead to very different conclusions about the prevalence and significance of warfare versus homicide or feuding among mobile, foraging communities (see Fry and Soderberg 2013 and Gat 2015). Whether or not a homicide qualifies as a warfare activity ultimately depends on two things: the context of that event and how one defines warfare. We would also need to note that not all violence, whether lethal or non-lethal, will leave clear signatures in bones (see Chapter Three). For many Pleistocene human remains, we do not always have access to the entire body. Hence, it can be difficult to determine if they were ever subject to intra-species violence. And this is before we even consider the use of perishable materials and other preservation issues. When one considers all of the variables, it is remarkable to see any evidence of violence in the deeper past. That being said, the fact that we have indicators for Pleistocene violence means that we should be open to the possibility of organized violence in the Pleistocene, and that we should continue to seek out new ways to address hypotheses about emergent warfare.

Why an Anthropological Voice Is Necessary

Anthropologist Walter Goldschmidt (2011: 272) writes: "It is time for anthropologists to take back the understanding of human nature as our responsibility to social theory." In this spirit, we would say the same for theories about warfare's origins. As highlighted above, the material evidence can be used, juxtaposed, and represented in very different ways to support any number of general views on the nature of violence and its prevalence in the human past. Much of this enterprise depends on tweaks of definitions, how much weight one assigns to certain classes of data, and how data from outside of anthropology are brought to bear in the discussions. There are benefits and challenges inherent in the use of anthropological data, and many people will extrapolate what they need in order to support their arguments. Sometimes this is done conservatively, and sometimes the final arguments stretch beyond the bounds of the data. We all have a stake in the final evaluations of these datasets, as they have implications for how we should view our prospects for peace in various social settings. For us, these observations mean that there is a greater need for anthropological voices to speak to non-specialists and the wider public.

In 1986, a meeting of international scientists was convened by the Spanish National Commission for UNESCO, in Seville, Spain. These scientists, who came from a diverse array of disciplinary backgrounds such as psychology, neuropathology, anthropology, psychobiology, animal behavior, sociology, and many others, issued a general statement about violence, essentially refuting the idea that organized human violence is biologically determined. "The emergence of modern warfare has been a journey from the primacy of emotional and motivational factors, sometimes called 'instincts,' to the primacy of cognitive factors" (Seville Statement). They conclude that "the same species who invented war is capable of inventing peace. The responsibility lies with each of us."

The Seville Statement has not gone without its critics. Steven Pinker argues that it is an example of trying to legislate morality. He also accuses signers of the statement of creating a strawman, saying it is clear that humans do not have a violent brain any more than they have a peaceful brain. "No one needs the bromides of the Seville Statement or its disinformation that war is unknown among animals" (Pinker 1997: 5). At one level, we must agree with Pinker that some of the tenets offered in the Seville Statement may be a bit simplistic. However, we also must remember that just because chimpanzees commit coalitionary killings, we cannot necessarily equate it with "warfare" behaviors we see in our species. Analogy and metaphor are incredibly powerful, but we cannot mistake them for being absolute likenesses.

Ultimately, Pinker and the signers of the Seville Statement are drawing from the same data and coming to opposite conclusions. What can this mean for our attempts to understand the nature and evolutionary arc of warfare? As we have tried to point out in this book, the data on these topics are quite diverse. No one can be an expert on all of them, which means we often have to rely on other scientists to help us understand not just the scientific studies, but the underlying assumptions and methodologies used in these studies.

The data on war are used and discussed by scholars, journalists, politicians, and lay people. As anthropologists, we firmly believe that furnishing anthropological data alone is not enough. What is also needed for these ongoing areas of research and debate is accurate and balanced presentation of such anthropological data by anthropologists. Accordingly, anthropologists ought to be aware of the responsibility their research efforts entail. As noted by Jon Marks, narratives about human origins are reflexive: "They are narratives specifically about who we are and where we came from, they are simultaneously narratives of kinship and ancestry, which are universally culturally important" (2015: xii). As social scientists, we need to be aware that the data we produce, and how we talk about these data, can affect how these ideas, concepts, and theories are perceived by the community at large. And it is not enough to simply compile our research for academic and scholarly consumption. We have an obligation to bring our voices into more public arenas of inquiry and debate. And we have an obligation to do so in balanced ways that allow all of us to be critical consumers.

To illustrate, let us revisit the remarkable case of Nataruk, the ~10,000-year-old site in Kenya discussed in Chapter Four. While relatively new as a case study, it is likely that this site will join Jebel Sahaba as the best evidence of violence and possible warfare in the Upper Paleolithic or Late Pleistocene. In the paper announcing this discovery, Lahr and colleagues (2016) suggest two interpretations for why this event occurred. Their first is that it was raided for resources (be it territory, food, people, or something else). If this is the case, they suggest it demonstrates that the underlying socioeconomic conditions that characterize warfare in the more recent past can be extended to 10,000 years ago. Secondly, they note it could simply be the result of two rival groups meeting and violence breaking out. "In either case, the deaths at Nataruk are testimony to the antiquity of inter-group violence and war" (Lahr et al. 2016: 397).

While we are open to the idea that underlying socioeconomic conditions may have precipitated the violence, and that we are seeing evidence indicating warfare at 10,000 years ago, we would hesitate to hastily conclude that we know the motivations of the violence. To be sure, motivations rooted in competition over resources could have been significant. But, such a view assumes something about the economic reasons for warfare and violence. By privileging a certain class of data, this perspective then ignores or downplays the possibility (and reality) that people engage in violence for all kinds of reasons. It is certainly true that war often has an economic basis. We can point to modern wars that are fought over access to oil and other natural resources. However, wars can and have been fought for myriad other reasons. For instance, it is equally plausible that the Nataruk area was seen as a sacred space, and that fighting occurred in response to the desecration of the sacred. If we accept that humans 10,000 years ago were like us then we also have to accept that they could have had reasons for fighting and aggression just as culturally nuanced and complicated as our own.[2] This would not negate the evidence at the site, but paints a broader image of the variability inherent in human behavior, of highly flexible cultural logics behind decisions to use violence. We cannot simply assume that people will always fight (or avoid fighting) for the same exact reasons.

Returning to an earlier point about how far-reaching, influential, and impactful anthropological data on warfare can be, one need only consider the public attention generated in the mere weeks after the Nataruk findings were made public. For example, the venerable *New York Times* felt the need to editorialize on the case.

> If warfare is indeed common from the dawn of human history, does that suggest that we will never cease fighting? Not necessarily. A propensity for violence, even if it is innate, has been more than matched throughout our existence by a preference for peace—a fact the bones of the victims of the battle of Nataruk cannot show.
>
> New York Times *Editorial board, 2016*

You may not be surprised to learn that this discovery received much attention from a variety of scholars (one of us had an advanced copy of the paper, and had a bet with a colleague about how many news stories would appear talking about the "origins of war"). They all have strong views about human nature and see the same evidence as supporting their conception of our past and present. Douglas Fry, a skeptic of claims for very early warfare, argued that while it looked like a massacre of one group by another, it did not necessarily show war occurring (Gorman 2016).

For our part, we see organized violence as having deep roots. But this does not necessarily contradict the overall hypothesis that war is a cultural invention

(Mead 1940). After all, specific languages are cultural inventions, but they are predicated on specific biological predispositions. Anthropologist Brian Ferguson has produced numerous, insightful publications on warfare, with some important conclusions about the phenomenon and its relationship to human nature. We would generally agree with Ferguson's (2013: 192) position that human beings have not evolved a predisposition to inflict deadly violence on people outside their own social group, that our behavior "is plastic, open equally to both altruistic cooperation and deadly conflict." We also believe he is right when he argues that wars happen as a matter of cultural and historically specific practicalities. In other words, warfare is part of social life, and people choose to use violence when they feel it is necessary. It is not inevitable. Beyond that, our opinions diverge a bit from his positions. While we agree that warfare is a cultural activity, we take the stance that this acknowledgment warrants a recognition that all people who are potential bearers of human culture (like us living today) would have had the same agency in choosing whether and when to fight or not. Faced with that recognition, then, we do not think that it is possible to easily conclude that war is a late development or invention in human evolutionary history, as Ferguson (2013: 229) implies when he writes: "War sprang out of a warless world." We could say that writing sprang out of a "writing-less" world, or that farming emerged out of a world without farming. But, even if humans do not have a predisposition to inflict deadly violence, using physical force is as much a part of our biological make-up as it is for much of the natural world. And when presented with certain situations, humans will choose to use their physical and mental faculties to make decisions to achieve desired outcomes. This may involve violence (whether of the inter-species or intra-species variety), or it may involve cooperation (usually intra-species, at least until we began domesticating animals). In that respect, while war may have sprung out of a warless world, we argue it did so at around the same time that being humans sprang out of a "humanless" world.

Could language have been the key? In comparing organized violence among chimpanzee groups versus that of Yanomamo communities, Wrangham and Peterson note that language among the latter allows for distinctions in human warfare, such as "planning, formality, ritual, and treaties." They also correctly note that language "is not needed for the violence itself, the carrying out of a lethal raid" (Wrangham and Peterson 1996: 72). We generally agree with these notions, but there is one issue with this perspective. While the researchers do point out the significance of both language for humanity and a commonality between chimpanzees and humans when it comes to behaviors related to violent raiding, they do not sufficiently emphasize the ramifications of language. Yes, language makes certain actions and behaviors possible for human groups. But the ability to speak requires a base of faculties that further distinguishes humans from the natural world. Our behavioral patterns and sociality are marked by complexities in symbolic thought and cognition that are unmatched in other species. Language is but one tool in our toolkit, allowing us to create and bear forms of culture much more varied and complex than any we might see within chimpanzee communities. By that token, then, our practices related to lethal and organized violence are different as well, and fall within a larger rubric we would call socially cooperative violence. Though there may be something to their argument that humans and chimpanzees are the only two species known to share a unique combination of social characteristics, namely male-bonded communities and male-driven lethal intergroup raiding (Wrangham and Peterson 1996: 47), we would argue that our cultural practices related to intergroup violence have changed so dramatically through time that there is a very significant qualitative difference in how such forms of violence are not only perpetrated by humans, but also perceived.

This issue of contention gets at the crux of the matter. Where do we draw the lines to distinguish between being human and being non-human? Should there be more or less boxes to categorize different kinds of "culture"? Much of this depends on whether one is a "lumper" or "splitter." When viewed on its surface, forms of intra-species, organized violence such as raiding may be lumped together with raiding performed by Yanomamo warrior parties. However, one could also point out the many differences, just as some might argue that Yanomamo raiding is very different from a 20th century German blitzkrieg offensive. While we would argue that raiding and ambushes perpetrated by humans qualify as forms of human warfare, we hesitate to lump lethal raiding conducted by other species into the very same category. It is a matter of perspective. We espouse a more inclusive definition of warfare as it relates to human culture. This means that the difference between a blitzkrieg and a Yanomamo intervillage raid lies predominantly in the kinds of technologies being used. However, the abilities to create these technologies, to fathom their utility, and to understand the long-term and wider consequences of these actions, lie within the domain of humanity. When it comes to modern warfare versus emergent warfare, though there may be some differences between technologies, scale, and tactics, they are both marked by actors that possess the same capacities for culture and symbolic thinking. Wrangham and Peterson (1996: 69) do acknowledge that when chimpanzee raiding is compared to Yanomamo raiding,

> the gulf that divides our two species is unmistakable. Because language makes discussion and meaning possible, the cultural dimensions to human war will always make it richer, more complicated, more exciting, as well as more self-deceiving and confused, than chimpanzee intercommunity violence.

Although we acknowledge the potential common threads between humans and chimpanzees in intergroup violence, we would take their observation much further. The gulf that divides us does not simply make the cultural dimensions of human war richer and more complicated – it makes human war qualitatively different.

With the onset of certain physical and cognitive capacities in our species, we had new and different choices and strategies available when conflicts of interest arose, sometimes making warfare a more appealing option than others. The wide and complex range of choices stems from the enormous plasticity in both our cognitive abilities and in our cultural values. We likely fought for, and avoided fighting, for many cultural reasons, and not just as organisms adapted to behave and react in specific ways to changing environmental conditions. Indeed, several leading researchers have recently noted that there is mounting evidence for very different trajectories of cultural evolution in different parts of the world when it comes to parallel cultural evolutionary pathways, such as among modern *Homo sapiens* in Africa and Neandertals in Europe (Kuhn and Hovers 2013). Given these potential variabilities, it would be difficult to say much at all about adaptiveness of warlike behaviors. It is more likely that adaptations promoting forms of cooperative and social behavior were most critical, making warfare one of a suite of possible behaviors involving cooperation and organization. In that regard, *emergent warfare was an outcome of human evolution, as opposed to being a primary driver of it.*

The Significance of Emergent Warfare and (for) Emergent Peacefare

> With every day, and from both sides of my intelligence, the moral and the intellectual, I thus drew steadily nearer to that truth, by whose partial discovery I have been doomed to such a dreadful shipwreck: that man is not truly one, but truly two.
>
> *Excerpt from* The Strange Case of Dr Jekyll and Mr Hyde
> *by Robert Louis Stevenson, 1886: 106*

> Indeed, it may be that we should see violence not in isolation, but at one end of a spectrum that extends from empathy and friendship to antipathy and hate.
>
> *Ian Armit 2010: 2*

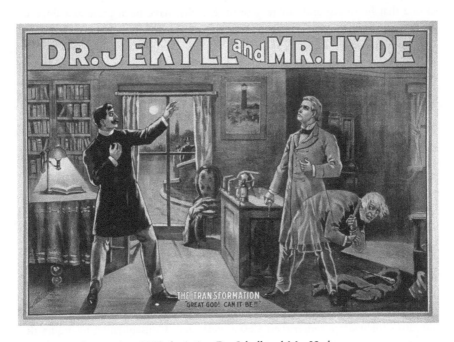

FIGURE 8.3 Poster circa 1870 depicting Dr. Jekyll and Mr. Hyde

As discussed in Chapter Two, Paul Roscoe's (2007) research suggests that we may have a hardwired aversion to killing members of our own species. It is only as our ancestors evolved heightened intelligence that afforded "envisioning of the future" that allowed humans to disable their aversions. This is in contrast with the idea that male chimps and humans share an innate disposition to kill, one deeply rooted in the distant evolutionary past. If Roscoe is correct that this intelligence is a pre-requisite for human warfare, this fits well with other lines of evidence discussed here. Along with "heightened intelligence," people can be compelled, coerced, or convinced to engage in organized killing through appeals to morals, values, and other cultural constructs. In the end, this underscores the importance of culture as much as biology.

Our hypothesis about the onset of socially cooperative violence and emergent warfare is based on a comprehensive survey of evidence from across various anthropological subfields, and suggests that the origins of modern human behavior are tied not only to human culture, but also to the capacity for both violence and for peace. As outlined in Chapter Six, Raymond Kelly's idea about social substitutability is a very important one when considering the emergence of a permissive condition for war – namely, the human ability to see all members of a group as interchangeable parts of a culturally identifiable whole. Kelly (2000: 161) further argues that war and society also coevolve with peace. "One central aspect of this coevolution is that the elaboration of peacemaking goes hand in hand with the origin and development of war" (2000: 161). The upshot here is that cultural practices play a major role in the origins of both war- and peacemaking. In that regard, our argument is similar to one that he offers, and our review of data that have been presented since his 2000 publication provides further support.

So when did we become bearers of human thought, behavior, and culture? As highlighted throughout the book. the archaeological record for hallmarks of modern human behavior, such as symbolic thought, is highly controversial, but faint signs from the data indicate that humans were able to create objects with embedded meanings by some 200,000 to 300,000 years ago and maybe earlier. Perhaps the capacity for social intelligence and language are at the root of all of these behaviors. After all, using beads, ochre, and other forms of ornamentation allow an individual to announce who she is and where she comes from. As this book was being finished, new dates for *H. sapiens* at 300,000 years ago were announced from the site of Jebel Irhoud, Morocco (Hublin et al. 2017). If this interpretation holds up, it suggests a more complex picture for the origin of our species, but still fits within the general narrative of the humanization of hominins being a slow process rather than a singular event.

In discussing aggression and human nature, Agustin Fuentes (2012) makes the argument that war is a relatively recent phenomenon in the timeline of human history. While acknowledging fossil evidence of the occurrence of violence among our earlier ancestors, Fuentes notes a general absence of unequivocal archaeological indicators for warfare earlier than 12,000 years ago. Consequently, he argues that we are not biologically predisposed to violence. "War is not a part of our evolutionary history, but it is obviously a major part of our current potential" (Fuentes 2012: 132). We agree with elements of this overall position, but would suggest that there is sufficient circumstantial evidence available indicating that intergroup conflict and uses of violence, namely emergent warfare, were present during the Pleistocene. In providing an alternative perspective, we would point to issues over archaeological visibility and perceptions of warfare, which bring us to a different conclusion about its antiquity and its significance.

Based on our interpretations of the corpus of evidence, from a variety of disciplinary perspectives, we would argue that warfare, at least in incipient forms, was present well before the Holocene. It did not simply appear once we started to become sedentary. Behavioral or cultural patterns typically do not emerge overnight, and are usually marked by longer sequences of development, learning, innovation, and experimentation. As we established in this book, warfare is not simply the product of a biological predisposition to aggression and violence. It required many key ingredients, both cultural and biological.

And this brings us to a final point about warfare and its relationship to human evolution. To a certain degree, we agree with the statement made by Fuentes about warfare being a part of our current potential, and not of our evolutionary history. In concert with his view, we do not see humans as the ultimate products of evolutionary adaptations that promoted physical or behavioral systems associated with aggression and violence. Like Fuentes (2012: 136), we see in both humans and primates degrees of social complexity, history, and context that help to explain "why a certain form or pattern of aggression occurs." Where we diverge from his position, however, is in the idea of how war is "a major part of our current potential." Because we see no qualitative differences between the cognitive and cultural potential that humans possess today, as compared to those at 12,000 years ago, 50,000 years ago, or perhaps even 200,000 to 300,000 years ago, we propose that warfare, or at least nascent forms of warfare, would have been just as much a major part of our potential along a temporal continuum wherein our ancestors were bearers of behavioral and cultural modernity. In other words, as soon as we became fully "human" in the ways that we are today, there would have been no biological barriers to use violence when the right conditions, be they environmental or social, called for it. This says nothing about propensities, frequencies, or inevitabilities. It simply means that we should not assume a Holocene starting point for warfare as a default position.

In that sense, then, warfare or emergent warfare could have been potentially significant for human evolution, insofar as we see intimate links between biological and cultural evolutionary change. If aggression is a part of the suite of behavioral patterns for many species of life in the world, then it stands to reason that once we began to think and communicate in highly symbolic ways, then observations, interpretations of meaning and intention, all related to aggression, could have shaped our perceptions of threats, intergroup identities, social interactions, and worldviews. Moreover, and quite importantly, right around the same time people would have begun to fully appreciate all of the potential beneficial and deleterious aspects of violence, especially if organized and competitive. That could have had profound effects on efforts to avoid conflict, perceived inequalities, antagonistic competition, and other such situations. Ideas and actions geared toward peacemaking, stability, equity, and so forth (i.e., emergent peacefare) could have become very important. In that way, consequently, we argue that emergent warfare could have been an important facet of our evolutionary past, even if it was not a key driver of human evolution. So, like Fuentes, we recognize war as a major part of human potential, but we see that potential existing far earlier than the Holocene Epoch. We see emergent war as a part of our potential for as long as we have been "human."

Fuentes (2012: 30) writes that humans have all-encompassing worldviews, or "schemata," that are shaped by the society they are raised in, a process that might be viewed as enculturation or "enskillment" wherein humans learn to be humans by imitation and cultural transmission. We would agree with this general perspective, and would apply it to our questions about emergent warfare and emergent peacefare. In our view, humans are essentially biologically wired to absorb perceptual data and assign highly complex meaning to actions, and this would include all manner of cultural and social cues. With all of the evidence we now have at hand about the gradualness of developmental processes leading to modern humanity, we would speculate that various strategies, practices, beliefs, and decision-making related to hunting, survival, group identity, and many other aspects of rich social life could have made use of violence from time to time, and that violent practices, once introduced and found to have situational efficacy, could have become a part of human schemata and enculturation. Humans today are cultural sponges, and we would speculate that all humans living in the Pleistocene would have been as well.

Carolyn Nordstrom, in her book on modern warfare in Mozambique, refers to the "factx" of war, a term she uses

> to underscore the observation that, at least in the context of war, something is always wrong with the facts that one is given. The facts of war emerge as essentially contested figures and representations everyone agrees are important, and no one agrees on. People generally *assume* that statistical facts concerning war are less biased than political declarations and tools of propaganda, but we seldom ask how basic information like internationally accepted figures concerning casualties, traumatization, and refugees come into being.
>
> *Nordstrom 1997: 43*

In similar spirit, we have to remember that despite claims to the contrary, all scholars (ourselves included) have biases.[3] While some may have more of a political axe to grind than others, separating the facts from the "factx" is difficult when discussing something as deeply controversial as warfare. However repugnant and cruel it is, it is hard to escape the conclusion that it is part of our world today and has clearly been so for much of recorded history, if not longer. Moreover, just because many of us find it repugnant and cruel does not mean that all societies of the world's past did as well. If anthropology teaches us anything, it teaches us that cultural systems are extremely variable in attitudes and worldviews.

It should be clear by now that our position is neither with the hawks nor the doves (nor do we think that these terms accurately reflect the majority of scholars). The anthropological lesson is clear: violence, while having biological roots, is mediated by culture. Interpersonal conflict was a part of the evolutionary history of our species, just as it is for all primates that live in groups. Humans, with our distinctive cultural niche, have created complex forms of socially cooperative and organized violence that do not exist in other species. Yet we have also created ways to promote peace. This is not to say that other primates do not engage in analogous behaviors. But they have different evolutionary paths and, while useful in a comparative approach, such comparisons can only go so far in telling us about the origins of human warfare and peacefare.

Where does this leave us in our study of the evolutionary origins of warfare? Violence seems endemic in our society, both in the news and in popular culture. Studying how our ancestors, both recent and distant, responded to pressures can clue us in to how we can deal with similar pressures today. While warfare as most present-day people conceive of it was not in place 200,000 years ago, humans at that time still had to cope with interpersonal violence and other external pressures. Our ancestors found successful solutions to these problems (we know they were successful, otherwise they would not be our ancestors!). Today, as we face news of violence in multiple forms almost daily, can we extract any useful information from the anthropological record?

While skeptics would say no, we are more optimistic. As our colleague Agustin Fuentes (2012) notes, if we accept the hypothesis that we are naturally violent, then we will more readily accept violent acts as part of our nature. "This is a danger-ous state of mind that traps us in a vicious cycle of inaction and futility when it comes to moving forward as societies invested in understanding and managing violence" (Fuentes 2012: 154). But human nature is more complex than this. Since warfare is so variable between and within populations, we know that it must be more than just a genetic or evolutionary disposition to be aggressive that makes war in the 21st century so pervasive. War was not a constant fact of human life. Instead, its frequency and intensity likely grew out of biocultural factors as humans increased their social networks. As discussed in Chapter Five, we know that there are genetic predispositions to act aggressively under certain environmental conditions. Rather than argue this has ramifications for understanding hominin history (for which we simply do not know enough about the social and ecological environment to determine how these genes would have functioned), we can use our knowledge of anthropology to help mitigate the effects of these genes.

If our hypothesis of emergent warfare is correct, then we expect more examples like the remarkable finds at Nataruk to eventually be identified, thus suggesting show how cultural and biological processes created situations where raiding and warfare were sometimes endemic and at other times unknown. But we also expect to see signs of hyper-cooperation, something related to our hypothesis about emergent peacefare. Contemporary evidence of this may be seen in recent studies showing how people of the same religious group will cooperate with each other even if they do not know each other (Purzycki et al. 2016). As discussed in our chapter on peace, while non-human animals are capable of cooperation, humans have evolved this capacity to its fullest extent. We are able to keep track of past events for a long time (to both reward those who have helped us and punish those who have cause harm) and, importantly, we are able to transfer this social information to others, through multiple means of communication (Melis and Semmann 2010).

Although we cannot, based on the available evidence, conclude that forms of organized violence were responsible for adaptions in the early stages of the emergence of our genus, we do acknowledge that violence did occur and that, given the right conditions, our ancestors would have participated in intergroup violence. This advent of emergent aspects of warfare would have coincided with when our ancestors started thinking and behaving the way that we do today. Given this assumption, we would not be surprised to see evidence of organized and socially cooperative violence that could be considered emergent warfare as early as 200,000 years ago. This is where we situate ourselves in the current debates about warfare's origins, and we look forward to seeing future evidence that will support, refute, and complicate our ideas.

To be clear, we suggest that divorcing violence from its larger cultural context misconstrues its relevance to broader questions of interest to evolutionary anthropology. It is not that we are more violent than our ancestors or that we are less violent, since the cultural aspects of violence, such as how it is constructed, mitigated, and performed, cannot be removed from other aspects of being human. As a biocultural species, it is difficult, if not impossible, to reconstruct the evolution of warfare without also understanding the larger picture of human evolution. As we have tried to demonstrate, becoming and being human was a long process that has its roots well before the rise of civilizations and professional armies. Thus, emergent warfare cannot be seen as a recent phenomenon or invention. The same is true for emergent peacefare. After all, even a modern-day peaceful society can be violent if necessary and so-called violent places have times of peace. We would argue the same is the case for the past. Communities could be peaceful and violent, depending on the specific internal and external pressures, whether we are talking about social conditions or environmental factors. To argue that the past is devoid of the same possibilities of the more recent world is to deny the humanity of the past.

In the end, the rabbit hole that the study of emergent warfare entails is a deep one, with enough tunnels that it is more like the complex network of warrens created by naked mole rats. We have only scratched the surface in our dealings with these questions. What makes us human is the power to transcend our genes, our evolutionary history, and our recent past. Not only can we transcend them, but we are capable of fathoming the ability to even do so. Tracing the origins of these distinctive human abilities is at the heart of anthropological research and will prove to be an infinitely fascinating field of study for many years to come. We did not become human because of war, and we did not evolve to make war. Through human evolution, we became capable of conceiving of and engaging in both warmaking and peacemaking.

Notes

1 Interested readers can look at the paper by Nowack and colleagues (2010) and the debate that ensued.
2 Indeed, one can look at the interesting site of Gobekli Tepe in present-day Turkey for signs of highly complex ritual practices. There is good evidence that the site was a sacred area over 11,000 years ago for hunter-gatherer communities to come together and participate in monumental constructions and ritual activities.
3 Some research suggests that it is extremely difficult to correct our most deeply-held beliefs. When confronted with facts and corrections, many people tend to increase their misperceptions. In other words, our (mis)beliefs get stronger when confronted with contradictory data (Nyhan and Reifler 2010).

Works Cited

Allen, Mark. 2014. Hunter-Gatherer Conflict: The Last Bastion of the Pacified Past? In *Violence and Warfare Among Hunter-Gatherers*, edited by Mark Allen and Terry Jones, pp. 15–25. Left Coast Press, Walnut Creek, CA.

Armit, Ian. 2010. Violence and Society in the Deep Human Past. *British Journal of Criminology* 51(3), 499–517.

Beckerman, Stephen, Pamela I. Erickson, James Yost, et al. 2009. Life Histories, Blood Revenge, and Reproductive Success among the Waorani of Ecuador. *Proceedings of the National Academy of Sciences of the United States of America* 106(20), 8134–8139.

Bowles, Samuel. 2009. Did Warfare Among Ancestral Hunter-Gatherers Affect the Evolution of Human Social Behaviors? *Science* 324(5932), 1293–1298.

Chagnon, Napoleon. 1968. *Yanomamö: The Fierce People*. Case Studies in Cultural Anthropology. Holt, Rinehart and Winston, New York.

Chagnon, Napoleon A. 1988. Life Histories, Blood Revenge, and Warfare in a Tribal Population. *Science* 239(4843), 985–992.

Chagnon, N.A. 1989. Response to Ferguson. *American Ethnologist* 16(3), 565–570.

Dawkins, Richard. 1976. *The Selfish Gene*. Oxford University Press, Oxford.

Dawson, Doyne. 1996. The Origins of War: Biological and Anthropological Theories. *History and Theory* 34(2), 1–28.

Ferguson, Brian. 1989. Do Yanomamo Killers Have More Kids? *American Ethnologist* 16(3), 564–565.

Ferguson, R. Brian. 2013. The Prehistory of War and Peace in Europe and the Near East. In *War, Peace, and Human Nature: The Convergence of Evolutionary and Cultural Views*, edited by Douglas P. Fry, pp. 191–240. Oxford University Press, New York.

Fry, Douglas and Patrik Soderberg. 2013. Lethal Aggression in Mobile Forager Bands and Implications for the Origins of War. *Science* 341(6143), 270–273.

Fuentes, Agustin. 2012. *Race, Monogamy, and Other Lies They Told You*. University of California Press, Berkeley.

Gat, Azar. 2015. Proving Communal Warfare Among Hunter-Gatherers: The Quasi-Rousseauan Error. *Evolutionary Anthropology* 24(3), 111–126.

Ghiglieri, Michael P. 1999. *The Dark Side of Man: Tracing The Origins of Male Violence*. Perseus, Reading, MA.

Glowacki, Luke, and Richard Wrangham. 2014. Warfare and Reproductive Success in a Tribal Population. *Proceedings of the National Academy of Sciences* 112(2), 348–353.

Goldschmidt, Walter. 2011. Notes Toward a Human Nature for the Third Millennium. In *Origins of Altruism and Cooperation*, edited by Robert Sussman and C. Robert Cloninger, pp. 271–281. Springer, New York.

Gorman, James. 2016. Prehistoric Mass Killing in Africa Offers Clues on the Origin of War. *New York Times*, January 21.

Grossman, Dave. 2009. *On Killing: The Psychological Cost of Learning to Kill in War and Society.* Back Bay Books, Boston.

Hublin, Jean-Jacques, Abdelouahed Ben-Ncer, Shara E. Bailey, et al. 2017. New Fossils from Jebel Irhoud, Morocco and the Pan-African Origin of Homo Sapiens. *Nature* 546(7657), 289–292.

Hughbank, Richard and Dave Grossman. 2013. The Challenge of Getting Men to Kill. In *War, Peace, and Human Nature: The Convergence of Evolutionary and Cultural Views*, edited by Douglas P. Fry, pp. 495–513. Oxford University Press, New York.

Jablonka, Eva, and Marion Lamb. 2005. *Evolution in Four Dimensions: Genetic, Epigenetic, Behavioral, and Symbolic Variation in the History of Life.* MIT Press, Cambridge, MA.

Jones, Terry, and Mark Allen. 2014. The Prehistory of Violence and Warfare among Hunter-Gatherers. In *Violence and Warfare Among Hunter-Gatherers*, edited by Mark Allen and Terry Jones, pp. 353–371. Left Coast Press, Walnut Creek, CA.

Kelly, Raymond. 2000. *Warless Societies and the Origin of War.* University of Michigan Press, Ann Arbor.

Keeley, Lawrence. 1996. *War Before Civilization.* Oxford University Press, Oxford.

Kim, Nam. 2012. Angels, Illusions, Hydras and Chimeras: Violence and Humanity. *Reviews in Anthropology* 41(4), 239–272.

Kissel, Marc and Matthew Piscitelli. 2014. *Evidence of Interpersonal Violence in Pleistocene Populations: Introducing a New Skeletal Database of Modern Humans to Test Theories on the Origins of Warfare.* Poster presented at the 79th Annual Meeting of the Society for American Archaeology. Austin, Texas, April 26.

Kuhn, Steven and Erella Hovers. 2013. Alternative Pathways to Complexity: Evolutionary Trajectories in the Middle Paleolithic and Middle Stone Age. An Introduction to Supplement 8. *Current Anthropology* 54(S8), S176–S182.

Lahr, M. Mirazón, F. Rivera, R.K. Power, et al. 2016. Inter-group Violence among Early Holocene Hunter-gatherers of West Turkana, Kenya. *Nature* 529(7586), 394–398.

Macfarlan, Shane J., Robert S. Walker, Mark V. Flinn, and Napoleon Chagnon. 2014. Lethal Coalitionary Aggression and Long-term Alliance Formation among Yanomamö Men. *Proceedings of the National Academy of Sciences of the United States of America* 111(47), 16662–16669.

Marks, Jonathan. 2015. *Tales of the Ex-Apes: How We Think about Human Evolution.* University of California Press, Berkeley.

Marshall, S.L.A. 1968. *Men Against Fire: The Problem of Battle Command.* William Morrow, New York.

Mead, Margaret. 1940. Warfare Is Only an Invention, Not a Biological Necessity. *Asia* 15(8), 402–405.

Meggitt, Mervyn J. 1977. *Blood is Their Argument: Warfare Among the Mae Enga Tribesmen of the New Guinea Highlands.* Mayfield Publishing Company, Palo Alto, CA.

Melis, Alicia P., and Dirk Semmann. 2010 How Is Human Cooperation Different? *Philosophical Transactions of the Royal Society B: Biological Sciences* 365(1553), 2663–2674.

Miklikowska, Marta, and Douglas P. Fry. 2012. Natural Born Nonkillers. In *Nonkilling Psychology*, edited by Daniel Christie and Joam Evans Pim, pp. 43–70. Center for Global Nonkilling, Honolulu, HI.

Moore, John H. 1990. The Reproductive Success of Cheyenne War Chiefs: A Contrary Case to Chagnon's Yanomamo. *Current Anthropology* 31(3), 322.

New York Times Editorial board. 2016. Is Warfare in Our Bones? *New York Times*, January 23, p. SR12.

Nordstrom, Carolyn. 1997. *A Different Kind of War Story*. University of Pennsylvania Press, Philadelphia.

Nowak, Martin, Corina E. Tarnita, and Edward O. Wilson. 2010. The Evolution of Eusociality. *Nature* 466(7310), 1057–1062.

Nyhan, Brendan, and Jason Reifler. 2010. When Corrections Fail: The Persistence of Political Misperceptions. *Political Behavior* 32(2), 303–330.

Pinker, Steven. 1997. *How the Mind Works*. Norton, New York.

Pinker, Steven. 2002. *The Blank Slate: The Modern Denial of Human Nature*. Viking, New York.

Pinker, Steven. 2011. *The Better Angels of Our Nature: Why Violence Has Declined*. Viking, New York.

Purzycki, Benjamin Grant, Coren Apicella, Quentin D. Atkinson, et al. 2016. Moralistic Gods, Supernatural Punishment and the Expansion of Human Sociality. *Nature* 530(7590), 327–330.

Roscoe, Paul. 2007. Intelligence, Coalitional Killing, and the Antecedents of War. *American Anthropologist* 109(3), 485–495.

Shermer, Michael. 2016. *On Slates and Tweets: A Reply to David Sloan Wilson on Ancient Warfare and the Blank Slate*. Available at: https://evolution-institute.org/blog/on-slates-and-tweets-a-reply-to-david-sloan-wilson-on-ancient-warfare-and-the-blank-slate/.

Smith, John Maynard, and George Price. 1973. The Logic of Animal Conflict. *Nature* 246(5427), 15–18.

Stevenson, Robert Louis. 1903 [1886]. *Strange Case of Dr. Jekyll and Mr. Hyde*. C. Scribner's Sons, New York.

Sussman, Robert. 2010. Human Nature and Human Culture. *American Anthropologist* 112(4), 514–515.

Turchin, Peter. 2016. *Ultrasociety: How 10,000 Years of War Made Humans the Greatest Cooperators on Earth*. Beresta Books, Chaplin, CT.

Wiessner, Polly. 2006. From Spears to M-16s: Testing the Imbalance of Power Hypothesis among the Enga. *Journal of Anthropological Research* 62(2), 165–191.

Wilson, David Sloan, and Edward O. Wilson. 2007. Rethinking the Theoretical Foundation of Sociobiology. *The Quarterly Review of Biology* 82(4), 324–348.

Wrangham, Richard and Dale Peterson. 1996. *Demonic Males: Apes and the Origins of Human Violence*. Houghton Mifflin, Boston.

Wrangham, Richard, and Michael L. Wilson. 2006. Collective Violence: Comparisons between Youths and Chimpanzees. *Annals of the New York Academy of Sciences* 1036(1), 233–256.

Zefferman, Matthew and Sarah Mathew. 2015. An Evolutionary Theory of Large-Scale Human Warfare: Group-Structured Cultural Selection. *Evolutionary Anthropology* 24(2), 50–61.

Zimmerman, L.J., and L.E. Bradley. 1993. The Crow Creek Massacre: Initial Coalescent Warfare and Speculations About the Genesis of Extended Coalescent. *Plains Anthropologist* 38(145), 215–226.

INDEX